The Black Romantic Revolution

Matt Sandler is director of the MA program in American Studies at Columbia University's Center for the Study of Ethnicity and Race. He was previously an adjunct professor at Louisiana State University, Gettysburg College, and the University of Oregon. His writing has appeared in a number of journals, anthologies, and online publications. He is from Miami, Florida.

The Black Romantic Revolution

Abolitionist Poets at the End of Slavery

Matt Sandler

VERSO
London • New York

First published by Verso 2020
© Matt Sandler 2020

1 3 5 7 9 10 8 6 4 2

Verso
UK: 6 Meard Street, London W1F 0EG
US: 20 Jay Street, Suite 1010, Brooklyn, NY 11201
versobooks.com

Verso is the imprint of New Left Books

ISBN-13: 978-1-78873-544-5
ISBN-13: 978-1-78873-543-8 (LIBRARY)
ISBN-13: 978-1-78873-546-9 (US EBK)
ISBN-13: 978-1-78873-545-2 (UK EBK)

British Library Cataloguing in Publication Data
A catalogue record for this book is available from the British Library

Library of Congress Cataloging-in-Publication Data

Names: Sandler, Matt, author.
Title: The black romantic revolution : abolitionist poets at the end of
    slavery / Matt Sandler.
Description: First edition. | London ; New York : Verso Books, 2020. |
    Includes bibliographical references and index. | Summary: "During the
    pitched battle over slavery in the United States, Black writers-enslaved
    and free-allied themselves with the cause of abolition and used their
    art to advocate for emancipation and to envision the end of slavery as a
    world-historical moment of possibility. They borrowed from the European
    tradition of Romanticism-its lyric poetry, prophetic visions-to write,
    speak, and sing their hopes for what freedom might mean. Authors like
    Frances Ellen Watkins Harper, George Moses Horton, Albery Allson
    Whitman, and Joshua McCarter Simpson conceived the Civil War as a
    revolutionary upheaval on par with Europe's stormy Age of Revolutions" —
    Provided by publisher.
Identifiers: LCCN 2020015400 (print) | LCCN 2020015401 (ebook) | ISBN
    9781788735445 (paperback) | ISBN 9781788735438 (library binding) | ISBN
    9781788735469 (ebk)
Subjects: LCSH: American poetry —African American authors —History and
    criticism. | American poetry —19th century —History and criticism. |
    Romanticism —United States —History —19th century. | Liberty in
    literature. | Slavery in literature. | African Americans in literature.
Classification: LCC PS153.N5 S255 2020 (print) | LCC PS153.N5 (ebook) |
    DDC 811/.309896073 —dc23
LC record available at https://lccn.loc.gov/2020015400
LC ebook record available at https://lccn.loc.gov/2020015401

Typeset in Sabon by MJ & N Gavan, Truro, Cornwall
Printed in the UK by CPI Group (UK) Lrd, Croydon CR0 4YY

*Dedicated to the memory of
Marcellus Blount,
teacher, friend, and fellow romantic,
without whom this book would not exist.*

Is it possible to believe that the slaves who were whipped into building the pyramids saw their work in a lyrical light?
—Antonio Gramsci, 1930

Naturally and necessarily the enemy of literature, it has become the prolific theme of much that is profound in argument, sublime in poetry, and thrilling in narrative. From the soil of slavery itself have sprang forth some of the most brilliant productions, whose logical levers will ultimately upheave and overthrow the system. Gushing fountains of poetic thought, have started from beneath the rod of violence, that will long continue to slake the feverish thirst of humanity outraged, until swelling to a flood it shall rush with wasting violence over the ill-gotten heritage of the oppressor.
—Lucius Matlack, 1849

Power from my tongue flows like a river
—George Moses Horton, 1845

Thus we have found how yearns the poorest slave
For freedom—how at patriotism's shrine,
The ardor of exile is divine

—Albery Allson Whitman, 1884

Oh, life is fading away, and we have but an hour of time! Should we not, therefore, endeavor to let its history gladden the earth?
—Frances Ellen Watkins [Harper], 1859[?]

Contents

Introduction

The Fugitive Romance

In early 1861, the abolitionist lecturer, organizer, and poet Frances Ellen Watkins Harper took an interest in the case of Sara Lucy Bagby, who had escaped from slavery in western Virginia to Cleveland, Ohio. Bagby's arrest under the Fugitive Slave Law attracted significant attention; four Southern states had already seceded, and it was widely considered a test of Northern allegiance to the Compromise of 1850, which had provisionally settled conflict about the reach of slavery in the West. Harper had married the previous fall, taking her husband's poetic surname, and she intended to settle in Ohio, which by then had been traversed by fugitives from the Southwest for decades. As she had since the start of her career as an abolitionist a decade and a half earlier, Harper responded to the news about Bagby's case with a poem, entitled "To the Union Savers of Cleveland: An Appeal from One of the Fugitive's Own Race." Announcing herself as a Black woman, she addressed the white Ohioans who hoped to avoid the outbreak of sectional conflict by sending Bagby back to slavery. She took their politically expedient moral weakness as the occasion for a prophecy:

> Men of Cleveland, had a vulture
> Sought a timid dove for prey
> Would you not, with human pity,
> Drive the gory bird away?

Had you seen a feeble lambkin,
　　Shrinking from a wolf so bold,
Would ye not to shield the trembler,
　　In your arms have made its fold?

But when she, a hunted sister,
　　Stretched her hands that ye might save,
Colder far than Zembla's regions,
　　Was the answer that ye gave.

On the Union's bloody altar,
　　Was your hapless victim laid;
Mercy, truth, and justice shuddered,
　　But your hands would give no aid.

And ye sent her back to the torture,
　　Robbed of freedom and of fright.
Thrust the wretched, captive stranger.
　　Back to slavery's gloomy night.

Back where brutal men may trample,
　　On her honor and her fame;
And unto her lips so dusky,
　　Press the cup of woe and shame.

There is blood upon our city,
　　Dark and dismal is the stain;
And your hands would fail to cleanse it,
　　Though Lake Erie ye should drain.

There's a curse upon your Union!
　　Fearful sounds are in the air;
As if thunderbolts were forging
　　Answers to the bondman's prayer.

Ye may bind your trembling victims,
　　Like the heathen priests of old;
And may barter manly honor
　　For the Union and for gold;–

But ye cannot stay the whirlwind,
  When the storm begins to break;
And our God doth rise in judgment
  For the poor and needy's sake.

And your guilty, sin-cursed Union
  Shall be shaken to its base,
Till ye learn that simple justice
  Is the right of every race.

"To the Union Savers of Cleveland" was broadcast throughout the abolitionist press. First published in the Ohio-based abolition newspaper *The Anti-Slavery Bugle* on February 23, 1861, it was then reprinted in William Lloyd Garrison's *Liberator* on March 8. Bagby's "fame" came to include the fact that she was the last person in the United States returned to bondage under the Fugitive Slave Law. She was finally freed from slavery a few months later, when Union forces took West Virginia in the summer. Harper's poem is what one of her contemporaries, James Monroe Whitfield, called "a song of fiercest passion": it orchestrates love, rage, and sadness at once. It begins with a depth of feeling for its subject so intense as to seem inhuman; Bagby is a "timid dove" and "feeble lambkin"; her captor a "gory bird" and a "wolf." With these simply fabled figures, Harper implicates her Northern, white contemporaries in the systemic, national, and epochal crime of slavery, now overdue for a reprisal.[1]

The poem's combination of deep feeling and prophetic vision is characteristic of Romanticism: the movement in art and thought which coalesced in Europe at the end of the eighteenth century, and ultimately spread throughout the colonized world. This book suggests that, in the middle decades of the nineteenth century, an independent and distinct form of Romanticism took shape among the Black writers of the US abolition movement and radical Reconstruction. Harper and her contemporaries borrowed and transformed the techniques and theories of Romanticism in an effort to bring about the end of slavery and the self-conscious regeneration of Black community. They understood the Civil War era as a belated iteration of Romantic revolution, and imagined their liberation as a part of an ongoing, total cultural and political transformation.

Harper's poem is an example of Black Romanticism in its most acutely engaged form, framing the day's events in terms of vast historical and geopolitical struggle. Notice the way that she warns her audience of the coming storm. The figure of the "whirlwind" recalls Ezekiel's vision of the destruction of Jerusalem in the Old Testament; a story retold in the African-American spiritual song "Ezekiel and the Wheel." Romantic aesthetics often mixed sacred and secular in this way; it was conventional to associate revolution and God's judgment. Reports of her reading suggest Harper had likely read in Jules Michelet's *History of the French Revolution* (1847): "Believe, hope! Right, though postponed, shall have its advent; it will come to sit in judgment, on the dogma and on the world. And that day of Judgment will be called the Revolution."[2]

In returning to and taking seriously Black Romantic prophecies like Harper's, this book dwells on the question of revolution in nineteenth-century America. Was the Civil War really the "whirlwind" Harper forecast? Or was it merely a squall line in a longer struggle? Did the war really purge the "curse" she perceived on the Union? Or is the nation's "base" still quaking? Are the "thunderbolts" crashing in response to the "bondman's prayer" instances of divinely ordained progress, or some more cyclical, or less shapely, model of history? In the 1790s, the British Romantic radical William Blake had insisted that prophecy does not predict the future, but instead speaks the spiritual truth of a moment in time: "the voice of honest indignation is the voice of God." In its juxtaposition of ordinariness and apocalyptic vision, Harper's demand for "simple justice" resists paraphrase, assimilation, even reparation. The seemingly absolute present of her poem should draw twenty-first-century American readers into perilous self-doubt. She and her contemporaries did not seek the meager citizenship rights they were ultimately afforded; their visions of freedom remain unfulfilled today.[3]

Harper was born free in Baltimore, Maryland, and took the cause of the enslaved as her calling for the first half of her life. The subtitle of "To the Union Savers of Cleveland" makes a gesture of racial solidarity across the legal division of freedom and slavery; it is "An Appeal from One of the Fugitive's Own Race." Taking racial identification as her starting point, Harper recounts the economic and gendered consequences of slavery, noting how even white Northerners, by their submission to Southern planters, "barter manly honor / For the Union and for gold." In the expansiveness of the poem's vision, as it takes into its sweep slavery, capitalism, and sexual violence, Harper made an important early contribution to the political culture of Black women's sisterhood and what came to be known as Black feminism. Harper articulates the threat of rape in metaphorical but unmistakable terms, carefully disclosing the "the torture ... where brutal men may trample, / On [Bagby's] honor and her fame." This formulation does not so much dissemble about rape as totalize and intensify its systemic implications. Later in 1861, Harriet Jacobs's *Incidents in the Life of a Slave Girl* explored the psychosexual suffering of Black women in slavery at greater length and in more meticulous detail. In its condensed prophetic vision, Harper's poem imagines the consequences of slavery's sexual violence beyond the limits of the individual to national, historical, and cosmological dimensions.[4]

The failure to defend Bagby indicts the entire project of American democracy, and Harper leaves it to her audience to imagine a form of freedom from such violence. Black Romantic writers often rearticulated in negative terms what Euro-American Romantic thinkers thought of as the "spirit of the age"; they saw themselves participating in the ongoing realization of a universal freedom as yet unrealized. The spirit of the age was widely understood to find expression in the work of poets, and poetry became, in the Romantic period, an object of intense ideological dispute and speculation. The Black Romantics, as the self-appointed literary and musical phalanx of a revolution, took on the role Percy Shelley had claimed for poets as "unacknowledged legislators of the World." They wrote, spoke, and sang inspiring judgment on the crime of slavery, the apocalypse of its end, and the passions of Black life both within and beyond its clutches. That their freedom is as yet unattained is not so much a consequence of the failures of Black Romanticism as it is of efforts to suppress it—to return to work like Harper's cannot restore its possibility entire, but its vantages, ambitions, and techniques may still prove useful against the surviving forces it first took on.[5]

"What fugitives and their friends have to tell"

In an extraordinary act of historical revision, W.E.B. Du Bois's *Black Reconstruction* (1935) returned to the middle decades of the nineteenth century, and discovered there what had been willfully forgotten: the revolutionary dreams of Harper and her contemporaries, as well as their shattering. Du Bois finds evidence of revolutionary ideals among both literate Northern Black intellectuals and what he calls the "Black proletariat" or "the mass of slaves." He cites Frederick Douglass describing the Emancipation Proclamation: "The revolution is tremendous." He also finds the same idea animating Black enlistment: " 'We have come to set you free!,' cried the black cavalrymen who rode at the head of the Union Army as it entered Richmond in 1864. ... Here indeed was revolution." These declarations were unified, but not at all necessarily equivalent—each instantiation of revolutionary vision from the abolition movement, to the Civil War, and onward to Reconstruction, had its defining difference. The meaning of the key terms, "revolution" and "freedom," was necessarily multiple and contested.[6]

In theorizing this problem, Du Bois points to distinction between "two theories of the future of America" that came into focus in the aftermath of the war. The first of these he associated with capitalism, industrialism, and what he calls "the American assumption" of "compensated democracy," which conceived citizenship as defined by white men's ability to work for wealth. Du Bois found this limited, and ultimately false, vision of citizenship underpinning the postwar reconciliation of Northern industrialists and Southern landowners. In opposition to this ideological boondoggle, Du Bois found what he called "abolition-democracy," which was forged in the long fight against slavery, and which approached nineteenth-century political theory and political economy from self-consciously universal and idealist perspectives. "Abolition-democracy" imagined that freedom, which had been limited in scope to white men, could be expanded to include Black people, women, and more. The narrative of *Black Reconstruction* follows the fate of this second vision, its provisional political victories and later defeats, as well as its lasting contributions, especially in the system of public education. The culture of "abolition-democracy" does not much occupy the focus of Du Bois's attentions, however.

Black Reconstruction is primarily a work of political and economic history. Its achievement lies in its account of how the "Black proletariat" transformed themselves into historical actors, how enslaved people left plantations, joined the Union Army, and advocated for their own emancipation—indeed entered history, conceived in political and economic terms, for the first time. In the nineteenth century, culture was supposed to take place outside of, but adjacent to, politics and economics; it expressed grievances, hopes, and possibilities unaccounted for but sometimes produced by political economy. The dominant theoretical framework for understanding culture was Romanticism. In 1830, Victor Hugo proposed a formula for the contiguity of culture and politics by declaring that Romanticism was "liberalism in literature."

This straightforward equivalence conceals the contested significance of liberalism and the ambivalent politics of Romanticism; Romantics across the Atlantic world were as likely to be reactionaries as radicals. Even for the radicals, the terms of Hugo's equation were more oppositional than he suggests; later Romantic aesthetics especially tallied the psychological, spiritual, and embodied consequences of legal, political, and economic liberalism. Romanticism was a European-originating, cosmopolitan ideology which sometimes emphasized the local, Indigenous, and rooted, so diasporic Black artists and intellectuals had to make significant revisions to its basic components. Moreover, Romanticism was hardly confined to literature, in Europe or elsewhere. Black thinkers of the nineteenth century understood that to include the illiterate "masses," their "literature" must include oral performance and song. Following all these qualifications, this book departs from Hugo's prescription, and takes as its starting point that Black Romanticism is abolition-democracy in literature.

Harper and her contemporaries took special interest in the figure of the fugitive; narratives of escape from slavery appealed to liberal antebellum audiences. The fugitive represented the will to freedom; his or her impulse to escape was taken not only as proof against Southern claims about the paternalist comforts of plantation life, but also as an indication of Black humanism. The fugitive embodied the contradictions that interested Romantic liberals: a troubled consciousness, burdened with sublime feeling, at once representative of a people and alienated from them—a special, individual case of the universal appeal of freedom, exceptional in his or her will to independence. White artists and intellectuals began to take notice of the dramatic potential of the escape from slavery in the 1830s; the rise of the abolition press in this decade was in no small part fueled by the sensational narratives of fugitives. The British social reformer Harriet Martineau wrote of visiting Ohio, a hotbed of Underground Railroad activity, in her *Retrospect of Western Travel* (1838):

> The finest harvest field of romance perhaps in the world is the frontier between the United States and Canada. The vowed student of human nature could not do better than take up his abode there, and hear what fugitives and their friends have to tell. There have been no exhibitions of the forces of human character in any political revolution or religious reformation more wonderful and more interesting than may almost daily be seen there.

Martineau makes a case for hearing the voices of Black people, on the basis of an ostensibly universal idealism. She finds in their stories a revelation of the spirit of the age. Her framing of their perspective, however, as "wonderful" and "interesting" belies a historical contradiction and a problem of recognition. The fugitives wanted freedom, and white liberals often took this to mean what Du Bois called the "American assumption": freedom as property ownership and a stake in representative government. The fugitives themselves, however, could not have understood the freedom they sought in such strictly material or limited terms. They would necessarily have comprehended liberation primarily as a negation of slavery; its positive form would have had to remain to some degree unknown and imaginary.[7]

Martineau's encouragement to "hear what fugitives and their friends have to tell" leaves room for this prospect, for Black people's conception of freedom as distinct from actually existing liberalism. Although white activists saw abolition and liberalism as continuous, the Black Romantics tended to wonder about the relation between the two political and philosophical modes. They took an urgent interest in defining freedom, but many of them were born into the impoverished freedoms of the antebellum North, and so their relation to the idea was as ambivalent, improvised, and suspicious, as it was idealizing and future-oriented. In listening for these discrepancies, Martineau echoes an earlier, more trenchant argument by the radical Black abolitionist David Walker, who, in his 1829 *Appeal to the Coloured Citizens of the World*, called for racism to be "refuted by blacks *themselves.*" Walker's principal target was Thomas Jefferson, who had claimed in *Notes on the State of Virginia* (1785) that Black people lacked the faculty of imagination and thus the capacity for abstract thought necessary for citizenship.

In the 1830s and 40s, the American abolition movement and Black community newspapers across the country sought to answer Walker's call and to demonstrate, through print culture, Black thought as a counter to racisms like Jefferson's. Poetry and print lyrics played a crucial role in this strategy, serving as texts of both public performance and readerly contemplation, and thus connecting the literate and illiterate audiences coming together in protest against slavery. In an 1841 essay, the white abolitionist Nathaniel Peabody Rogers complained about the prosaic limitations of abolition discourse: "Anti-Slavery is young and rude, and as yet unfertile in bards ... The cause will breed poets, though, by and by. Meantime we must be patient."[8]

Rogers, like Martineau, sensed historical change in the air. His genealogical metaphor strikes a more embodied note than her more abstracted "romance." The fugitives' romance was constitutively interrupted: women like Bagby escaped from slavery to avoid sexual exploitation, while fugitives of both genders often left families and lovers behind. With historically unprecedented brutality, slavery determined the centuries-old predicament of romantic love and lyric poetry, the absence of the beloved. So the romance of the fugitives was defined by negation, both the negation of slavery itself, but also of the bonds of love. Because of this beginning in rupture and estrangement, the fugitive romance, whether it conformed to liberal fantasy or represented a more radically liberatory Black imaginary, could only provide incomplete visions of enslavement and Black life therein. The individuality of fugitivity presented a theoretical problem, neatly formulated in an 1847 lecture by the fugitive from slavery, novelist, playwright, lyricist and abolitionist William Wells Brown: "Slavery has never been represented; Slavery never can be represented." Here the sublimity of slavery lies not just in its representation of freedom by negation, or love under extreme duress, but in the inexpressibility of its terrible violence and the vastness of its experiential multiplicity. The project of abolition as a media strategy thus began from an opposition, posed most trenchantly by Walker and Brown but felt by white collaborators like Martineau and Rogers: the need for Black self-representation and the impossibility of representing slavery. Into this breach, the Black Romantics cast their projective vision.[9]

"The medium of the conspiracy"

In "To the Union Savers of Cleveland," Harper makes Sara Lucy Bagby an ephemeral object of sympathy for white liberals, and at the same time warns them of the epochal consequences of failing to protect her. As it traveled through the abolition press, the poem spoke past these small-minded Clevelanders, to audiences struggling with race, class, legal status, literacy, and political orientation. Poetry and song helped to cement the ties and illuminate the conflicts of interracial abolitionist friendship. It also played an important role in Black community-building and affirmative racial identification, across the divide of freedom and slavery. Black

Romantic lyrics appeared in a variety of print and performance contexts: they were read in scenes of individual contemplation and more collective forms of study; they were sung in formal and informal settings. The market circulation of Black Romantic lyrics was extraordinarily various: James Monroe Whitfield sold his book out of his barbershop, Harper hers on speaking tours of the South during Reconstruction, and Albery Allson Whitman brought his along while preaching in African Methodist Episcopal churches; their lyrics were printed as broadsides, in abolitionist and Black newspapers, and quoted in works of fiction, as well as, crucially, the autobiographical narratives of fugitives from slavery.

Like their white contemporaries in the abolition movement, the Black Romantics approached the antebellum media environment with strategic sophistication. In representing specifically Black voices, experiences, and practices, they also relied on older modes of African diasporic, antislavery, and anticolonial organizing. In his classic history *The Black Jacobins* (1938), C.L.R. James describes the role of ritual in bringing together the participants in the Haitian Revolution, claiming, "voodoo was the medium of the conspiracy." By this formulation, James suggests that African diasporic religious practice, both as a means of communication and an incitement to faith, drew people to the movement. Voodoo provided physical rituals invested with belief in liberated futures; it also provided modes for interpreting historical events with prophetic and cosmological significance.

James focuses in particular to the Bois Caïman ceremony of 1791, conducted by Dutty Boukman (so-named for his literacy, as in Book-man), which sealed the collaboration of a disparate group of enslaved people, maroons, fugitives, and *gens du couleur libre*. This ceremony reportedly involved an oath, which one of the earliest sources, Hérard Dumesle's *Voyage dans la nord d'Haïti* (1824), represented in verse:

> God who makes the sun that lights us from above,
> Who raises up the seas, who makes the storm rage,
> God is there, do you hear? hidden in a cloud,
> And there he watches us, he sees everything the whites are doing!

The God of the whites orders crime, and wants nothing good for
us,
But the god there who is so good orders our vengeance;
He will guide our arms, he gives us assistance;
Throw down the portrait of the god of the whites who is thirsty
for our tears,
Listen to liberty, it speaks in all our hearts.

The storm Harper saw approaching Ohio in 1861 was apparently
not the first storm to figure God's vengeance on slave owners in
the New World. Reports of the Bois Caïman ceremony are con-
flicting and riddled with apocrypha, and the origins of its syncretic
components impossibly various. What matters here is that lyrics
would go on to play similar roles in the US abolition movement,
which had its own uneven network of social groups to organize,
religious authorities to parse, and militancies to direct. This book
thus assumes that, in the secularizing and revolutionary culture of
the antebellum United States, the lyric acted as the medium of the
conspiracy.[10]

The best single example of a Black Romantic lyric function-
ing in this way is Joshua McCarter Simpson's "Away to Canada,"
which ripped across the middle decades of the nineteenth century
like a tornado. Simpson was born free in Ohio sometime in the
early 1820s, and lived through his teens as an indentured laborer
before pursuing his education at Oberlin College. Sometime in the
1840s he began composing songs set to popular minstrel tunes,
which in 1852 he collected in a volume ironically entitled *Original
Anti-Slavery Songs*. In the preface, Simpson claims: "My object in
my selection of tunes is to kill the degrading influence of those
comic Negro Songs, which are too common among our people,
and change the flow of those sweet melodies into more appro-
priate and useful channels." This statement of intention hardly
captures the razor's-edge irony of Simpson's project. "Away to
Canada" was by far his most popular work, not least because
he sets the tale of a fugitive from slavery in the lyric rhythm of
Stephen Foster's enormously popular ballad, "Oh! Susanna"
(1848). As an act of nineteenth-century remixing, Simpson's song

plays on period media dynamics between print lyric, memorization, and performance, but it also renovates dominant sentimental notions of fugitivity with deft ideological ingenuity.[11]

Like Harper's poem, after its initial publication in Ohio, "Away to Canada" was reprinted in the December 10, 1852 issue of William Lloyd Garrison's *Liberator,* as a "fair specimen" of the volume's contents. The poem then began to appear without credit to Simpson in a variety of contexts across the Atlantic. It was printed as a broadside under several different titles, like "Song of the Free" or "Song of a Fugitive Slave." It was collected in an anthology entitled *Poems: Original and Selected by James Watkins, a Fugitive Slave*, published in London in 1859, as "Slave's Escape to Canada." A number of important works of abolitionist prose quoted the poem through this same period. It appears in the portions of Martin Delany's novel *Blake, or the Huts of America* serialized in *The Anglo-African Magazine* from late 1861 to 1862, where it is sung by a group of fugitives as they pass through northern Indiana. A year later, Harriet Beecher Stowe quoted Sojourner Truth singing portions of "Away to Canada" in an April 1863 profile in the *Atlantic*, entitled "The Libyan Sybil." After the war, the poem continued to circulate in print memorials of the abolition struggle. In Sarah H. Bradford's *Scenes in the Life of Harriet Tubman* (1869), a group of fugitives from Maryland to Canada on Tubman's "seventh or eighth" trip sing the tune on the way past Niagara Falls. Simpson republished the lyric in his volume, *The Emancipation Car* (1874), where he makes clear his works' origin in the urgently improvised and convivial social contexts of the Underground Railroad.[12]

"Away to Canada" traveled so widely because it stuck in people's heads, and its stickiness has everything to do with its play on Foster's original minstrel song, which also centered on the perspective of a Black male singer's address to a lost and distant beloved. Blackface minstrel music often focused, in demeaning and absurd ways, on Black love; Foster's song is paradigmatic of this tendency, especially in naturalizing Black people's flight and avoiding slavery as a historical fact. Simpson's revision is to make slavery's systemic function a key element in the romantic narrative. The original subtitle of "Away to Canada" cites "the case of Mr. S" as its basis, thus turning the again centuries-old tradition of the ballad as reportorial news to the news of fugitivity. The anonymity of "Mr. S" was likely required by his circumstances, but it also permits readers and listeners to find in his story a set of generalizations about slavery. The enslaved male singer enumerates to his beloved the reasons for his needing to escape, and through this device "Away to Canada" becomes a panorama of the slave system, *Uncle Tom's Cabin* in the form of a tortured love song. The tempo of Foster's original is allegretto, briskly suggesting a lover's eagerness to return, and what plays for comedy in the original amplifies the fragmentation of fugitive separation in Simpson's rewrite. The temporal and spatial coordinates of the lyric are scrambled, as the speaker addresses his lover intimately and directly long after he has left her behind in the South. With emotional immediacy and ephemeral detachment at counterpoint, the song follows the fugitive's longing from inside the slave system across the northern border.

In this movement between love and its rupture by the slave system, the lyric takes the measure of the fugitive's political awakening. Moments of eavesdropping on white agents of the plantocracy prompt his escape:

> I heard the old-soul driver say,
>   As he was passing by,
> That darkey's bound to run away,
>   I see it in his eye.
> My heart responded to the charge,
>   And thought it was no crime;
> And something seemed my mind to urge,
>   That now's the very time [...]
>
> I heard old master pray last night—
>   I heard him pray for me;
> That God would come, and in his might
>   From Satan set me free;

> So I from Satan would escape,
> And flee the wrath to come—
> If there's a fiend in human shape,
> Old master must be one.

Here Simpson provides a dialectical, vernacular representation of an enslaved consciousness becoming free; a lived experience of the Hegelian dynamic of lordship and bondage. The slave driver's recognition of a desire for freedom in the enslaved ("I see it in his eye") sparks a fugitive self-realization ("My heart responded to the charge"). The master's prayers ("That God would … / From Satan set me free") become the fugitive's ethics ironically transposed ("So I from Satan would escape"). The speaker inverts the conventional racist associations of Blackness with Satan and slavery with sin, in an early Black nationalist interpretation of whiteness as deviltry ("If there's a fiend in human shape, / Old master must be one."). The speaker seems to have intuited the abolitionist interpretation of the slave system as diabolical. All this makes the speaker's address to his enslaved lover an extraordinary mixture of intimacy with religious and political education. These transformative moments, in which the enslaved person feels fundamentally redefined, take on melancholic density in the context of what is essentially a breakup song.[13]

Black women's performances of Simpson's work compounded its ironies, as they negotiated its masculine perspective on fugitive romance. The song appears in a key scene of interracial collaboration between abolitionist women, Stowe's profile of Sojourner Truth in *The Atlantic*, where it is subject to careful revision by two of the most important activists of the period. The profile itself was integral to establishing Truth's reputation among white liberals, not least as a kind of abolitionist oracle, the "Libyan Sibyl." Stowe recalls Truth visiting her Connecticut mansion, and breaking into song, much as she did during her public lectures:

Sojourner was fond of singing an extraordinary lyric, commencing,

> I'm on my way to Canada,
> That cold, but happy land;
> The dire effects of Slavery
> I can no longer stand.
> O righteous Father,
> Do look down on me,
> And help me on to Canada,
> Where colored folks are free!

The lyric ran on to state, that, when the fugitive crosses the Canada line,

> The Queen comes down unto the shore,
> With arms extended wide,
> To welcome the poor fugitive
> Safe onto Freedom's side.

In the truth thus set forth she seemed to have the most simple faith.

The passages from Simpson that Truth sings and Stowe quotes involve the challenge the fugitive romance posed to period domestic ideology. First, the speaker calls for the approval of patriarchal religion that might otherwise judge his fugitive abandonment of couplehood unfairly ("O righteous Father, / Do look down on me"). Later, he identifies freedom and safety in Canada with the maternal embrace of Victorian England ("The Queen comes down … To welcome the poor fugitive"). Stowe expresses a condescending skepticism about the song's "simple faith" in the Commonwealth. Truth may well have emphasized Simpson's Anglophilic stanzas to provoke Stowe's own qualified belief in Liberian colonization, as controversially set down in the late pages of *Uncle Tom's Cabin*. Stowe insists throughout on what she calls Truth's "solemn twinkle of humor … a gloomy sort of drollery which impressed one strangely." These seemingly paradoxical characterizations reflect the unsettling presence of racism in their encounter, and through the song, the women sound their uncertainty about the shared political purpose of abolitionism and women's rights.[14]

It is impossible to tell from the context of the profile whose editorializing had determined which bits of Simpson's lyric made it in to this crucial document. The first quotation from Simpson in the passage above leaves out the following from between its two quatrains:

> My soul is vexed within me so
>   To think that I'm a slave;
> I've now resolved to strike the blow
>   For freedom or the grave.

Stowe and Truth thus elide Simpson's declaration of commitment to fugitivity as a form of masculine violence, born of alienation (in a line borrowed from Lord Byron, about which more later). They leave out other moments in which the speaker's escape seems wrapped up in cavalier self-involvement, most important the lyric's conclusion, when the jubilance of arrival in Canada is cut with the imagined death in slavery of the beloved:

> I've landed safe upon the shore,
>   Both soul and body free;
> My blood and brain, and tears no more
>   Will drench old Tennessee.
> But I behold the scalding tear,
>   Now stealing from my eye,
> To think my wife—my only dear,
>   A slave must live and die.
>
> O, Susannah!
>   Don't grieve after me—
> For ever at a throne of grace,
>   I will remember thee.

One can only guess that the speaker's memories would be small consolation for Susannah, here finally revealed to share the name of the beloved in Foster's original. "Don't you cry for me," indeed! Moments of longing form the core of the romance of fugitivity— they also contradict the notion of the fugitive as an avatar of liberal individualism. Truth's defiant performance of the song expresses both enthusiastic encouragement and forgiving care for those men who escaped, in a generous act of abolitionist cultural-political practice, which, like Harper's poetry, anticipates the emergence of Black feminist thought.[15]

Despite widespread circulation of his lyrics, Simpson himself never made a national reputation. He straddled the anonymity of the folk ballad tradition and the cult of personality that had gathered around the figure of the poet in Romantic ideology. His works' unsigned circulation represents as much the tradecraft of an Underground Railroad conductor as it does some kind of pre-modern bardic indigeneity. Its multiple functions as the medium of abolitionist conspiracy start with its memorable echo of popular song, which helped it travel among such a range of scenes of abolitionist hospitality. The strange pleasures it activated in those scenes were not superficially aesthetic, however, for "Away to Canada" clearly also did ideological work, helping its singers and listeners get over the doctrinal, cultural, and political claims of slavery.

Though Simpson's story is in many respects entirely unique in the history of nineteenth-century culture, his ambitions, in the song, are recognizably fluent in the conceptual vocabulary of transatlantic Romanticism. "Away to Canada" is no doubt a "song of experience" in William Blake's formulation; in it, what Blake called the "cries" of London seem to echo across the Mississippi Valley. Its pleasures derive from the quality of "difficulty overcome" that William Wordsworth finds in the meeting of form and content: the trick of matching its lyric scheme to Foster's parallels the trickeration of the speaker's fugitivity; the song feels like getting away with something. Simpson's play on minstrel music anticipates late Romantic attempts to de-emphasize artistic originality, for instance by Charles Baudelaire, who sought to "make a commonplace," or Comte de Lautréamont, who felt "plagiarism is necessary" to creative work. Simpson does not lay bare the technique of his fugitive persona in the way that Walt Whitman did in *Leaves of Grass* ("I am the hounded slave … Agonies are one of my changes of garments"). He does, however, find in the subjective and choral effects of lyrics on liberal individualism and racial nationalism an effective medium for communicating the conspiracy to end slavery.[16]

"A powerful miracle"

Black poets reconceived Romanticism to break the aesthetic and ideological bonds of slavery, racism, and capitalism in the decades leading up to the Civil War. The straitened conditions of both free and enslaved Black communities, however, militated against their wholesale importation of Romantic convention. To borrow from Wordsworth, "the growth of the [Black] poet's mind" took place in the context of systemic exploitation. Looking back on this period in 1895, Victoria Earle Matthews lamented the "unnaturally suppressed inner lives" of African-American writers, who nonetheless turned to Romanticism to depict psychic interiority under extreme duress. Harper, for instance, described the hopes of fugitives in a letter from Ohio from the 1850s: "Notwithstanding all the darkness in which they keep the slaves, it seems somehow that light is dawning in their minds." This conventional Romantic metaphor mixes sacred and secular—their safe arrival was both everyday illumination and political messianism. Beginning in the antebellum period, the fugitives became a part of the symbolic vocabulary of American freedom, icons of its unfulfilled promise. Rather than auguring the completion of a progressive historical process, the fugitive became a perennial figure of Black life, returning again and again up to the present to remind Americans of the distance between their stated ideals and lived experience.[17]

The fugitive romance, with its flickering appeal to white liberals, was hardly the only preoccupation of Black Romantic thinking. The Black Romantics thought through what they often ironically called the "gloominess" of racism across the history of both slavery and freedom. Early African American poets manipulated the rhetorical and psychodynamic details of racial ideology to liberatory political purposes, in explicitly Black enactments of what Toni Morrison called "playing in the dark." They reconceived the entanglement of ideas about race and the Biblical "blackness of darkness"; like Hawthorne in *The House of the Seven Gables* (1851), they sought to "enrich the shadows" as a mode of political-aesthetic intervention. This book consistently refers to its subjects as "Black," capitalized to distinguish this revisionist relation to racist aesthetics. To make this case, the chapters that follow also focus especially on the parallels between Black Romanticism and the post-Gothic tradition of "Dark Romanticism" in the work of Lord Byron, Edgar Allan Poe, and Charles Baudelaire. These figures tended to take a redemptive view of darkness and a cynical view of actually existing freedoms. The choice of "Black" as a modifier rather than "African-American" also follows this second point: the Black Romantic suspicion of white liberalism and second-class citizenship. They tended to look on claims of white American civilizational superiority with what Stowe found in Sojourner Truth, a kind of "gloomy drollery."[18]

Hegel had acknowledged that assessments of "the spirit of the age" would be subject to the "ruse" or "cunning of reason," and that intellectuals would periodically misrecognize the rational direction of the historical process. Slavery was, and white supremacy still is, a ruse of reason on the grandest scale. Even after the war, the Black Romantics only occasionally conceived their work as an adjunct to the assimilation of Black people to the Union. Most of the poets covered in this book participated in the period's rich efflorescence of Black nationalisms. Mixed in with their appropriation of Romantic ideology, their thinking was fulsomely diasporic, in their emigrationist ambitions, in their critiques of American hypocrisy, and in their reference to identifiably Black cultural practices and cosmologies. Martin Delany compared Black nationalism to the internal colonies of European empires: "We are a nation within a nation;—as the Poles in Russia, the Hungarians in Austria, the Welsh, Irish, and Scotch in the British dominions." Anticipating Amiri Baraka's claim that, "In America, black *is* a country" by more than a century, Delany's comparison draws what would come to be known as African-American life into parallel with ethnic groups that had been the objects of intense poetic imagining during the Romantic period. Just as for the culture heroes of these other peoples, life as representatives of a stateless nation could be overwhelming. At moments in the pages that follow, the Black Romantics' rich and strange array of racial identifications fades into myopic racialism or colorism. In some instances, the main characters of this book indulge Victorian or even eugenic fantasies of sexual hygiene; elsewhere, the crush of American racism and individualism leaves them estranged even from Black communities, floating through lonely and sometimes alcoholic wanderings.[19]

The ideological possibilities of Black nationalism and the prospects for Black citizenship in the United States came into sharp conflict across the middle decades of the nineteenth century. Advocating for Black emigration to western Canada in 1852, Mary Ann Shadd argued that the end of slavery in the United States would only occur as the result of a "powerful miracle." Black Romantic writers' contemplations of that "powerful miracle" produced fractious and critical perspectives on the actual historical unfolding of emancipation. After the end of slavery, they continued to petition for a vision of freedom that far exceeded the attenuated rights of citizenship granted in the hard-won political battles of Reconstruction. They wondered about the history of their moment and its willful forgetting. As new forms of racist social policy replaced chattel slavery, Black abolitionist thought wondered at its own anachronism. Could abolitionism meet the challenge of debt peonage, the convict lease system, lynch law, and segregation? Was abolitionism rendered obsolete by the end of chattel slavery or was it necessary to combat the inevitable excesses of racial liberalism? Had abolitionism conspired with capital, or might its tools help realize American freedoms which had been held out in the dismantling of Reconstruction? In questions like these, the aesthetic and ideological shape of Black Romanticism, by the prophetic design of its authors, projects far beyond the historical bounds of its moment. In so doing, their aesthetic gives measure, scale, and depth to the "profound miracle" which Shadd had assumed to be impossible, and which historians and commentators have understood as an "unfinished revolution," to borrow historian Eric Foner's phrase for Reconstruction. The Black Romantics offer some perspective on what it might look like to finish that revolution.[20]

This book proceeds from here on both conceptual and chronological fronts; it does not posit that Black Romanticism advanced in a linear fashion through the nineteenth century. In this respect, it responds to Hortense Spillers's call for reading the African-American tradition as "a matrix of literary *discontinuities*." The first chapter covers the entire historical period that forms its main focus, from roughly the 1820s to the last decades of the century and beyond. Chapters 2 and 3 cover the antebellum decades and the war. Then Chapters 4 and 5 focus on the postbellum period. The first chapter follows the way Black writers used the British Romantic poet Lord Byron to complicate the notions of Blackness and masculinity that defined abolition and racial uplift. The second chapter focuses on how George Moses Horton conceived his poetic project as a foil to Euro-American narratives of progress and Enlightenment. The third focuses on the free Black poets of the 1850s and '60s, as they wrote lyric poetry about the impending crisis against racist notions of Black sentimentality and insanity. Each of these chapters finds its main characters working in extraordinary circumstances; the narrative focuses on their activist aesthetics, and sets their work in the context of transatlantic Romanticism more broadly.[21]

Some of the most substantial achievements by abolitionist poets appeared in the period after the war. Black Romantics formulated post-slavery visions of African-American identity and community and worked through liberalism's entanglement with capitalism, racism, and sexism. The fourth chapter returns to Harper, and draws focus on her sense of the role of women's work in the political economy of Reconstruction. The last chapter, "A Poetical Revolution," finds Albery Allson Whitman writing epic poems about Black life on the frontier as the hopes of Reconstruction faded. The conclusion turns to later incarnations of Black Romanticism, which ran through the twentieth century to the present on what Ralph Ellison called "the lower frequencies": cultural, historical, and political registers that might seem at first obscure. Finally, a brief bibliographic essay provides suggestions for further reading, and maps the historiographical and theoretical debates that frame the book's arguments.[22]

In taking seriously the prophetic claims of Black Romanticism, this book depicts scenes like fugitives singing Simpson's "Away to Canada," or Harper performing her poetry before an audience of recently freed people, as emanations of the nineteenth-century "spirit of the age." Black Romanticism aspired to the kind of total revolution that interested transatlantic radicals since the 1790s. It reinvented the available models of human character; it imagined new forms of love in new forms of song; it sought to repair the alienations of subjectivity and objectification; finally, it charted new theories of space and time to accompany emergent nationalisms and internationalisms. These goals make sense as those of the cultural column of any modern revolution, but Black Romanticism's particularity, in representing the perspective of an enslaved people as they become nominally free, and a racially stigmatized people navigating pride and solidarity, ramifies into the present, as liberalism still fails to live up to the promise of freedom made in that moment.

The ordnance of the conflict over slavery still dots the American landscape. What follows, then, is a map of old bombs and blast zones, some still unexploded and combustible, awaiting detonation well over a century after their improvisation. Consider the discussions below instructions for the handling of such sensitive material. But these songs of fiercest passion are neither always military nor always aimed at wreaking violence. Consequently, what follows should also read as a collection of messages in bottles, washed ashore by a seemingly unending storm. The dead letters contained therein are the sort that begin in love but scratch their way to hate and sadness and back, so that a world opens up around the blurred and frayed words. A warning, then, in the form of a mixed metaphor: carry this book like a box of rusty little bombs, nestled in bottles by notes whose authors' love was harried by violence.

1

Hereditary Bondsmen, Strike the Blow!

In which Black abolitionists take Lord Byron as a model of freedom and then later his legacy returns to haunt them

O n Wednesday, August 16, 1843, during the afternoon session of the second day of the National Convention of Colored Citizens in Buffalo, New York, Henry Highland Garnet delivered one of the most radical and provocative speeches of the abolition movement. Garnet's "Address to the Slaves of the United States of America" made strange and counterintuitive use of the occasion. In front of an audience of free people, Garnet nonetheless spoke directly to the enslaved, and argued that only they could free themselves from slavery. Despite Garnet's ardor, the delegates to the convention voted to exclude his remarks from the published minutes of the convention, which would only contain a description of the debate about it. Garnet's defense of his address is itself said to be "a masterly effort, and the whole Convention, full as it was, was literally infused with tears." A young Frederick Douglass led the opposition:

> Mr. Douglass remarked, that there was too much physical force, both in the address and the remarks of the speaker last up. He was for trying the moral means a little longer; that the address, could it reach the slaves, and the advice, either of the address or the gentleman, be followed, while it might not lead the slaves to rise in insurrection for liberty, would, nevertheless, and necessarily be

the occasion of an insurrection; and that was what he wished in no way to have any agency in bringing about, and what we were called upon to avoid;... He wanted emancipation in a better way, as he expected to have it.

Douglass's casuistry here represents an early moment of hesitation in what would become a life of carefully studied political decision-making. Garnet's speech stayed with Douglass, however, and he would come around to its perspective over the next decade and a half of organizing.[1]

Garnet's "Address" represented an abandonment of the strategy of moral suasion, which Douglass, following Garrison and the American Anti-Slavery Society, had developed over the preceding decade to plead with white Northerners about the evils of slavery. Moral suasion involved impassioned appeals to the consciences of Northerners in hopes they might exercise political influence over Southern slave owners. Garnet, seeking a more immediate abolition, argues directly to the enslaved: "Brethren, the time has come when you must act for yourselves. It is an old and true saying that, 'if hereditary bondmen would be free, they must themselves strike the blow.' You can plead your own cause, and do the work of emancipation better than others." Garnet's call for violence expands the tradition of revolutionary liberalism and possessive individualism to include Black subjects. He sought to unify the organizing work of the free, literate Black North and the violent revolts of the enslaved South. As support for this performative gesture, he turns to a surprising precedent—the British Romantic poet Lord Byron, specifically Byron's widely read epic poem *Childe Harold's Pilgrimage* (1812–20). The original text, addressing Greeks suffering under the Ottoman empire, reads: "Hereditary bondsmen! know ye not / Who would be free, themselves must strike the blow?"[2]

Despite the initial suppression of Garnet's "Address," an extraordinary array of African-American writers would cite these lines in the coming decades. Martin Delany made them the epigraph to his Pittsburgh newspaper *The Mystery* in the late 1840s. Garnet finally managed to get the "Address" itself into print in 1848, bundled with David Walker's comparably incendiary *Appeal*. Frederick Douglass, revisiting his caution of a decade earlier, quoted the passage in his short story "The Heroic Slave" (1853) and then again later as context for the famous fight with Covey in *My Bondage and My Freedom* (1855). Douglass retained the citation in the later versions of his narrative, *The Life and Times of Frederick Douglass* (1881, 1892). Later, W.E.B. Du Bois used it as the epigraph to a chapter of *The Souls of Black Folk* (1903). This little bit of British Romantic poetry thus appears in most of the major early texts of the Black radical tradition, a kind of shibboleth for the movement. The citation became a refrain of Black radical intellection, and in its rhythmic repetition through the nineteenth century, Black writers signaled their belonging within a world-historical struggle for emancipation. It also acted as ritualized act of cultural appropriation, through which Black abolitionists framed their most vociferous arguments for retributive violence in the voice of a widely admired white European culture hero. Finally, the citation from Byron was a commandment, an authoritative inversion of "Thou shalt not kill," fit to the warped ethical requirements of a slave society.

Variations on the phrase "hereditary bondsmen" were widely used in English to describe the condition of subalterns around the world, especially in areas of colonial interest like Ireland and South Asia. Byron borrowed it from Edward Gibbon, whose *History of the Decline and Fall of the Roman Empire* (1776–89) took the question of slavery's deleterious effect on civic virtue as a consistent theme. Garnet's "Address" to enslaved Black men takes measure of how far beyond the pale New World chattel slavery had taken Euro-American morality, with frequent references to Black families torn apart and the sexual exploitation of Black women in slavery. His case for revolutionary violence develops from an impossible choice between hereditary bondage and death: "You had far better all die—*die immediately*, than live slaves, and entail your wretchedness upon your posterity. ... However much you and all of us may desire it, there is not much hope of redemption without the shedding of blood." In moments like this, Garnet works at the imaginative limits of the abolition movement of the early 1840s. Though the conceit of the speech is its address to the enslaved, of course Garnet was speaking first to his colleagues, the free people of the convention movement, warning them about what their goal of abolition would require, and what would befall their people if it was not achieved.[3]

Byron's call for violence had political and aesthetic dimensions, but its fundamental impacts were epistemological: "Hereditary bondsmen! *know ye not* / Who would be free, themselves must strike the blow?" His advice made practical sense in the context of the uneven demography of New World slave societies, where planter hegemony was maintained even though the enslaved far outnumbered their enslavers. In its ideal form, the "blow" that could upset this dynamic would contain the force of both an immediate, embodied liberation and a change in collective consciousness. With each citation, abolitionists reflected on the conditional dimensions of Byron's point: the enslaved may or may not know that violence would set them free; violence may or may not in fact set them free; and they may or may not commit violent acts in prospective service to their freedom. But they also hoped that the knowing of its truth could be more than individual, that it could have symbolic and thus systemic ramifications.

Over the decade between Garnet's address and his own citations from Byron, Douglass came to reconsider his equivocation between gradual and immediate calls for abolition. Westward expansion and the Fugitive Slave Law had expanded the territorial reach of slavery, but Douglass had also traveled to England and began to consider himself a man of letters in the manner of Rousseau, Goethe, and Byron. Douglass had read Thomas Carlyle's depiction of the man of letters as a "hero" of world literature, who "make[s] manifest to us" the "Divine Idea" unfolding across human history. Increasingly, Douglass represented abolition in the United States as the next iteration of the universal development of human freedom, an idea which for him encompassed the history of revolution and nation-formation in Europe as well as the intercontinental struggle against slavery in the Americas. He was not alone in taking this view, and in a number of instances, the abolitionist interpretation of Byron connected the figurative "blow" for freedom to prophetic visions of world history.[4]

The lines from *Childe Harold* were not the only passages from Byron that would appear across the archive of early African-American literature; practically every well-known Black writer of the nineteenth century quoted the poet and worked through his influence. The point of tracking Byron through early African-American letters is not to prove its derivativeness or give a canonical white author his due, but to make the case that Byron's model suited the cultural and political ends of Black liberation. Nineteenth-century Black radicals took up Byron as a way of processing their relation to the tradition of Romantic revolution. They found he embodied Romantic ideals in a renegade, exiled form of masculinity, grappling with deep psychosexual pain and alienation, identifying that struggle with the revolutionary spirit of the age. They wrote through Byron to imagine a freedom first from slavery's bodily repression, but then also from its psychic consequences and its larger-scale political and ideological entrenchments. The blow, limited in its singularity and its physicality, nonetheless strikes out beyond the thousands of square miles of the antebellum South and the generations of enslaved people. It could liberate a whole people and a whole world.

Black abolitionists' use of Byron extended beyond the justification of physical revolt to mount critiques of slavery as a regime of rape, to displace the moral coordinates of conventional representations of Blackness, to avoid the pitfalls of the market for narratives of slavery, and to deviate within the tradition of revolutionary liberalism. His influence became more controversial in the years after the Civil War, when Black sexuality came under renewed surveillance and when Byron's reputation was increasingly marred by scandal. Byron's radical masculinity, which had been so liberatory, now began to dangerously skirt the stereotypical hypersexualized Black criminal of the Jim Crow era. Byron's emphasis on revolt fit uneasily into ideas about racial uplift and notions of culture as elevating. His articulation of embodied freedom made him less an aspirational exemplar and more a cautionary tale for African-American cultural and political leaders. His reputation as "mad—bad—and dangerous to know" mirrored the conundrum of Black leadership caught between the impulse to revolt, the strictures of racial uplift, and racist stereotypes of Black criminality.[5]

Nineteenth-century African-American culture's intimacy with Byron might well be thought of in contemporary activist terms: he is a problematic ally, mobilizing and authorizing at times, but also inclined to risks and compromises that make collective action more difficult. In one of the few direct comments on New World chattel slavery in his poetry, Byron observed that the end of the transatlantic trade had only served to raise the price of enslaved people. In a journal entry lamenting the effect of slavery on the Americas, he wrote, "I sometimes wish that I was the owner of Africa, to do at once, what Wilberforce will do in time, viz.— sweep Slavery from her desarts and look upon the first dance of their Freedom." These are hardly the thoughts of an ideal white fellow traveler for Black abolitionists—Byron had always been glib and darkly negative, and in the postbellum era this became more of a hindrance than a help to Black radicals.[6]

This chapter traces the cultural politics of Black Byronism, expanding from the incidental but insistent citation of his lines on bondage to a range of antislavery and Black radical ideological possibilities. It finds Byron at the threshold of Romanticism, greeting Black artists and intellectuals as they arrive. It begins by elaborating Byron's attraction for abolitionists, especially around the question of sexual violence in slavery. It then follows a series of poetic projects, by George Moses Horton, George Boyer Vashon, Frances Ellen Watkins Harper, and Albery Allson Whitman, as they put Byron's work to political and aesthetic purposes in different contexts across the nineteenth century. So this chapter moves both chronologically and conceptually, from hereditary bondage and the blow for freedom to Black interiority and world-historical process. Byron by no means encompassed the ideological complexity of Black Romanticism, but he makes an excellent introduction to its possibilities, and shows how Black writers worked through Romantic tradition to envision self-emancipation and imagine Black collectivity.

"Why does the slave ever love?"

Byron was infamous across the political spectrum of nineteenth-century America, as he was throughout the European and Atlantic world. His "oriental tales" about swashbuckling, morally compromised, and archly perceptive heroes were wildly popular, and the way his poems seemed to disclose the details of his lurid personal life further excited his readership. His exile from England after the end of his marriage and his commitment to Greek independence seemed, to audiences around the world, a realization of a radical liberalism that exceeded the political results of the age of revolutions. In an 1832 essay, Henry Wadsworth Longfellow noted the local effects of the Byron craze in the United States: "Every city, town, and village had its little Byron, its self-tormenting scoffer at morality, its gloomy misanthropist in song." Longfellow points to the ironies in Byron's popularity—how a writer so scornful of convention could appeal so widely, how a putatively tortured poetics could take and make such pleasures, and how Byron's provincial imitators could identify with his dramatically cosmopolitan life.

Beyond his obvious links to ideals of freedom, Byron's appeal to Black abolitionists derived from his ethics and his representation of alienated interiority. The Byronic hero consistently reversed the moral coordinates and color symbolism of early nineteenth-century Atlantic culture. In *The Corsair* (1814), for example, Byron's description of his hero Conrad collapses the darkness of Conrad's interiority and the swarthiness of his complexion, pointing to the prospect of his redemption through darkness: "In Conrad's form seems little to admire, / Though his dark eyebrow shades a glance of fire." Through these tricks of light and shade, Byron encoded fragments of autobiography into fictional proxies, drawing the audience in with gossip about his own lurid life, and playing on the dynamics of their sympathies and principles. In these moments, Byron provided Black thinkers with a template for working through the interplay between racist projection and lived experience. If a darkly Byronic character could attract the understanding and identification of contemporary audiences, then perhaps racially Black characters could do the same. In the context of centuries-old associations between skin color and cultural difference, Byron's play with color symbolism and character had important effects for Black Romantic writers.[7]

Byron's preoccupation with slavery in the eastern Mediterranean also interested abolitionists grappling with the more modernized slavery of the so-called "American Mediterranean." In *Don Juan* (1819–24), Byron depicts the luxuriant pleasures of the master class in slave societies with lustful but ironic distance. Shipwrecked on a Greek isle, his protagonist Juan falls in love with the beautiful Haidée. In the course of their courtship, they listen to a local poet whose song reminds the couple of their proximity to "hereditary" slavery:

> Fill high the bowl with Samian wine!
> Our virgins dance beneath the shade—
> I see their glorious black eyes shine;
> But gazing on each glowing maid,
> My own the burning tear-drop laves,
> To think such breasts must suckle slaves.

The visual pleasure of "hereditary" bondswomen's bodies elicits in the poet a kind of political rage. At the moment of pleasure's seeming liberation, it is surrounded by enforced labor. The plot of *Don Juan* finds this problem again and again along its hero's picaresque journey. Haidée's father, the "Moorish" pirate Lambro, returns to find Juan in congress with his daughter, and angrily sends him to be sold into slavery in Constantinople. At the slave market, the sultana Gulbeyaz purchases Juan as a concubine. She dresses him as a woman and deposits him in her husband's harem, hoping to conduct an affair in secret. Juan resists her advances, declaring against all the evidence of his recent experience, that "Love is for the free!" The irony here is a lived ideal: as Byron imagines slavery intervening between lovers, he makes its dialectical opposition to freedom a mode of emplotment.[8]

The Black abolitionists took much from Byron's articulation of freedom as defined by the exercise of romantic love. They used Byronic models to mark the psychosexual consequences of slavery and to highlight the centrality of rape to the slave system. Moreover, Byron's mixture of sincerity and disguise became an important rhetorical and aesthetic strategy for Black writers seeking to speak the truth of sexual violence in slavery. Traveling through Virginia, white Northerner and noted landscape architect Frederick Law Olmsted noted the way Southerners repressed talk about the economic role of enslaved people's sexual reproduction:

> Most gentlemen of character seem to have a special disinclina-tion to converse on the subject; and it is denied, with feeling, that slaves are often reared, as is supposed by the Abolitionists, with the intention of selling them to the traders. It appears to me evident, however, from the manner in which I hear the traffic spoken of incidentally, that the cash value of a slave for sale ... is generally considered among the surest elements of a planter's wealth. ... That a slave woman is commonly esteemed least for her laboring qualities, most for those qualities which give value to a brood-mare is, also, constantly made apparent.

African-American writers of what was after all the Victorian period, with limited access to print and public culture, had to approach this subject carefully. Olmsted describes a discursive situation amongst slaveowners that Byron would call "cant"; despite his propensity to fictional masks, Byron had no patience for ideological dishonesty. No early Black intellectuals or activists could declare allegiance to Byron's libertinage, but they all found inspiration and political utility in his work when they looked for ways of talking about the ruination of Black love by the slave system.[9]

As slavery made territorial gains in the West and the Fugitive Slave Act made Northerners complicit in the policing of the insti-tution, abolitionists sought to amplify the moral crisis by making explicit the sexual violence at the heart of the slave economy. In by far the most expansive period account of this aspect of the system, *Incidents in the Life of a Slave Girl* (1861), Harriet Jacobs turns to Byron at a moment of intense deliberation, having realized that her master, Dr. Flint, has sexual designs on her, just as she falls into what she calls a "love-dream" with another man:

> Why does the slave ever love? Why allow the tendrils of the heart to twine around objects which may at any moment be wrenched away by the hand of violence? When separations come by the hand of death, the pious soul can bow in resignation, and say, "Not my will, but thine be done, O Lord!" But when the ruthless hand of man strikes the blow, regardless of the misery he causes, it is hard to be submissive. I did not reason thus when I was a young girl. Youth will be youth. I loved and I indulged the hope that the dark clouds around me would turn out a bright lining. I forgot that in the land of my birth the shadows are too dense for light to penetrate. A land
>
> > Where laughter is not mirth; nor thought the mind;
> > Nor words a language; nor e'en men mankind.
> > Where cries reply to curses, shrieks to blows,
> > And each is tortured in his separate hell.
>
> There was in the neighborhood a young colored carpenter; a free born man. We had been well acquainted in childhood, and frequently met together afterwards. We became mutually attached, and he proposed to marry me. I loved him with the ardor of a young girl's first love.

In several places here, Byron's language substitutes for truths Jacobs cannot herself utter. Insistently associating the striking of "blows" with the violence of enslavement, Jacobs offers a feminist reinterpretation on the hypermasculine violence of the lines from *Childe Harold's Pilgrimage*. In so doing, she pointedly emphasizes the specific and terrorizing burden Black women bear under slavery.[10]

Later in the passage, Byron reappears in a quotation from *The Lament of Tasso*, which Jacobs uses to characterize the dejection of enslaved lovers. While traveling in Italy from 1816–17, Byron had found in the Renaissance poet Torquato Tasso a mirror for the early years of his exile from England after the breakup of his marriage. Jacobs (a pseudonym for Linda Brent), projects her misery through Byron, himself writing through Tasso. These masks made layers of protection for a fugitive woman revealing the sexual violence of everyday life in slavery, but they also generalized the condition of enslavement. The Byronic notion of slavery as a "separate hell" argues the particularity of the experience of enslaved women, but it also emphasizes the multiplicity of slavery's isolations—the hopelessly imprisoning punishment of its individuations.[11]

Here the consequences of slavery for Black love form the obverse of every antebellum argument for liberalism. The constrained desires of the enslaved and the overpowering desires of the masters challenged transcendental notions of free will and inalienable rights over and over. Black abolitionists emphasized that love, erotic and familial, was the best reason to strike the blow for freedom. Jacobs, on the eve of the Civil War, elaborated this premise in rich and harrowing detail, and made it a central axis for discussions of Black women's freedom. This theme, from Garnet in the 1840s to Jacobs on the eve of the Civil War, made a crucial riposte to the premise of master class paternalism, long thought, following historian Eugene Genovese, to be the most important of the planter class's claims to legitimacy. Black feminist historians have recently illuminated the myriad ways sexual violence was an open secret of Southern paternalism. Black Romantic writing took particular interest in this ideological vulnerability. The fiction of slavery's benevolence could hardly be maintained in the context of such violent, sexual expressions of its power. Invocations of Byron by Black writers, beyond the recommendation of physical revolt, centered on amplifying slavery's perversion of romantic love.

"If thou art bound to leave me ..."

George Moses Horton was among what Longfellow called the "little Byrons" of the antebellum period. He spent the majority of his life enslaved in the vicinity of the University of North Carolina at Chapel Hill. Having arrived at an extraordinary arrangement with his owner, Horton earned money by composing love lyrics on commission for the students. Local white elites took an interest in Horton's talents, and in 1829 and 1845 collected his verse into bound volumes for sale with the (ultimately failed) intention of buying his freedom and paying his passage to Liberia. In this extraordinary situation, Horton produced a substantial body of love poetry. European Romantics had set romantic love at the center of the social order and understood it as the way to access divinity; Horton took cues from Byron in writing the ways that slavery wrecked those premises. The printed texts of Horton's poems never make clear which were composed on commission and which were drawn from personal experience; often it is impossible to tell the race or legal status of the characters in his work. Like Byron, however, Horton encoded details of his life in his verse, and his vision of Romantic love was sometimes sentimental, sometimes humorous, and often cynical. His work flickers between revealing incursions on white Southern intimacy and innovative representations of Black love in slavery.

In the autobiographical preface to *The Poetical Works of George M. Horton* (1845), Horton notes that, when he was learning to read in Chapel Hill in the 1810s, the undergraduates had shared Byron's work with him. He had come by then to rewrite Byron in a range of ways, especially through his love lyrics and most obviously in his repeated borrowing of the refrain of Byron's widely read poem "Fare Thee Well." First delivered privately in a letter to his wife, Annabella, on their divorce, and later published without his consent in 1816, Byron's "Fare Thee Well" was itself a revision of a traditional English ballad, retuned to the particulars of his dramatic divorce. The speaker reminds his lost love of how her affections will survive their breakup:

> Yet, oh yet, thyself deceive not;
>   Love may sink by slow decay,
> But by sudden wrench, believe not
>   Hearts can thus be torn away:
> Still thine own its life retaineth—
>   Still must mine, though bleeding, beat;

> And the undying thought which paineth
> Is—that we no more may meet.

The seemingly ambiguous "sudden wrench" here was Lady Byron's decision to leave him in response to his sexual misadventures, and secondarily the judgment of English Regency society from which he fled in exile. Whatever one may choose to think of Byron's self-destructive posturing, he made a model for poets who suffered differently under the weight of others' rule. Horton rewrote "Fare Thee Well" repeatedly across some four decades of publishing poetry, reformulating the notion of the "sudden wrench" to accommodate the brutal separations wrought by the slave trade. While his own mobility was severely constrained, Horton's lyrics say goodbye, again and again, seeming, over decades, to continually find new resonance in parting. In these poems, well-wishing at the end of love becomes not only a kind of bittersweet, ironic articulation of detachment, but also an aesthetic theory of fugitivity and a form of wish-fulfillment encompassing world-historical transformation.[12]

Horton often dances around the question of whether slavery is the "sudden wrench" that disrupts love in his versions of "Fare Thee Well." He blurs the racially specific reasons why a love might end in the antebellum South, but this obscurity gives his lyrics antic energy. Like Byron, he played with the anonymity of the ballad tradition to write lyrics that seem universal and yet reflect the character of individual experience. In *Hope of Liberty* (1829), a poem entitled "To Eliza" begins:

> Eliza, tell thy lover why
> Or what induced thee to deceive me?
> Fare thee well—away I fly—
> I shun the lass who thus will grieve me.
>
> Eliza, still thou art my song,
> Although by force I may forsake thee;
> Fare thee well, for I was wrong
> To woo thee while another take thee.

The lyric scene here unfolds as a site where dialogue has broken down; to himself, the poet pleads with his absent lover. Interior monologue becomes a cramped respite from the confusions of attachment. At first, it appears Eliza has misled the speaker; then it emerges that the speaker "may forsake" her "by force." Horton's metrical choices are carefully eccentric; the extra beats on "me" and "thee" emphasize the lovers' out-of-step rhythm. Even in this early work, Horton is a wry and rueful poet of heartbreak, unable to let go and desperate to get away. His poems amplify the bewilderment of love's end through the possibility that it could apply either to the white elites or enslaved people among whom he lived. The historical question of slavery's presence in the poem bleeds into the frustration of romantic ambiguity. The unanswerable question of its racial content makes the poem a kind of optical illusion—from one angle it appears flat, white, unhistorical, and from another it suggests an ineluctably political depth in its Blackness. Where for Byron this trickery would serve to tempt gossips, for Horton it was a matter of life or death.

In his next volume, *The Poetical Works of George M. Horton* (1845), Horton samples "Fare Thee Well" again. He had by then refined the uncertainty about the presence of slavery in his love poems, and made more consistent their uncanny tone, somehow both knowing and overcome. "Farewell to Frances" again condenses the obscure dialogue of couplehood undone in a series of disorienting symbolic entreaties:

> Farewell! is but departure's tale,
> When fond association ends,
> And fate expands her lofty sail,
> To show the distant flight of friends.
>
> Alas! and if we sure must part,
> Far separated long to dwell,
> I leave thee with a broken heart,
> So friend, forever, fare thee well.

The end of the relationship here is more vaguely conditional than the earlier poem, "if we sure must part." Horton's speaker emphasizes the immaterial fictiveness of his own declamations, "Farewell! is but departure's tale." This time, the speaker displaces responsibility onto the "lofty sail" of "fate," a trope in the Black Atlantic imagery of the Middle Passage. This veiled reference to slavery redoubles the vague insecurity of the speaker and his lover's respective desires. Elsewhere in *The Poetical Works*, Horton describes the "dark suspense in which poor vassals stand," during "The Division of an Estate," a poem about the breakup of a plantation on its owner's death. Even in poems more directly addressed to the experience of the enslaved, Horton avoids straightforward documentation, choosing instead to write through densely wrought allegories. The strangeness of his language registers the impossible uncertainty of the situation: "Each mind upon a spire of chance hangs fluctuant." As he discloses Black historical experiences entirely new to the lyric tradition, Horton leaves his readers, like Byron's eager mass audiences, reading between the lines, like lovers looking for a sign. Here again, the seriousness of Horton's need to encode his antislavery sentiments when writing for white clients far outweighs Byron's earlier risking the approbation of his fellow aristocrats. Horton took a privileged libertinism and made it searingly urgent.[13]

In the spring of 1865, the Union Army under General Sherman's command arrived in Chapel Hill just as surrender was negotiated at Appomattox. Sometime in late March or early April, Horton became "contraband," following the Union Army through North Carolina. In the camps, he met a Captain William H. S. Banks of the Ninth Michigan Cavalry, who took an interest in publishing another book of his poems. The resulting volume, *Naked Genius* (1865), his last, documents a period of frenetic creativity, in which Horton, then in his late sixties, responds to the events of the war and the end of his enslavement with a belated, but still deeply ironic, rage. "Hard is the Sentence of Parting Man and Wife, Though They May Have Much Disagreed" finds Horton in a mournful and speculative mood:

Oh! what's like a husband off starting,
　　To look on his wife never more,
'Tis the soul and body fast parted,
　　Is his flight from his own native door.
Art thou hence inclined to leave me ever,
　　Kiss my cheek and move,
If again I see thee never,
　　Fare thee well my love.

Horton's depiction of divorce here is stricken with contradiction. Like the earlier examples, the poem leaves ambiguous the question of who is leaving whom; one line finds the "husband off starting," while another addresses the wife, "Art thou hence inclined to leave me ever." He moves, through the projections and emotional intermittence of romantic argument, from third person to first person, and from alienation to indifference. The Christian metaphor of the enslaving relation between body and soul characterizes the breakup as a kind of transubstantiating liberation. At the same time, the departure from "his own native door" connects the end of love to exile. That sometime in late 1865 or early 1866, Horton had left North Carolina for Philadelphia and then later Liberia, leaving behind his two adult children, Free and Rhody, and their formerly enslaved mother, Martha Snipes, gives the poem its evocative drive.

Elsewhere in the poem it appears that postbellum erotic freedom might paradoxically echo enslavement, as the speaker asks, "If thou art bound to leave me." The cracked rhythm attaches the refrain, "Fare thee well my love," to sight rhymes for mobility, like "move" or the Byronic "rove," suggesting the cross-purposes of movement and romance. Other poems from *Naked Genius*, like "The Southern Refugee," refer more directly to the postbellum circumstances of Horton's "flight" from his "native door." Despite its geographic specificity, that poem still teases the desire for romantic revelation with Romantic cliché: "The verdant willow droops her head / And seems to bid a fare thee well." In weird diction, discordant music, disjunctive grammar, and projective rhetoric, Horton's lyrics illuminate the anxious conditions of Romantic love in slavery and in its transition from slavery to freedom. He put chattel slavery's perversion of romantic love and the lost Black loves of the nineteenth century among the great Romantic stories of the age.[14]

"As epitaph, your mother's curse!"

As the controversy around slavery escalated in the 1850s, free Black activists in the North began to turn to poetry. They did so with a range of intentions, such as to forge a Black national culture, to counter racist arguments about Black people's capacities, and to aesthetically intensify the impending crisis. Like Horton, they took interest in Byron's cracked view of romantic love, but they also found in his longer narrative poems, especially his epics, an account of world history connected to the perversions of intimacy. The invention of the African-American epic tradition in this moment was a part of a collective effort to inaugurate a revolutionary culture only visible in hindsight as "African American." The Black Romantics also saw in Byron's commitment to Greek independence an example of how to pledge oneself to the cause of others' freedom. Byron had, by the early 1820s, decided he would organize for Greek independence—contradicting his earlier advice about freedom and self-determination. He ultimately died in Missolonghi in 1824 during preparations for a military venture against the Ottoman Empire. Overlooking the Eurocentric aspects of Byron's philhellenism, Northern abolitionists identified with this moment of cosmopolitan solidarity in the poet's biography.

In the polemical tract *The Condition, Elevation, Emigration, and Destiny of the Colored People of the United States* (1852), Martin Delany noticed the author of the first epic poem in the African-American tradition, George Boyer Vashon, as one of the antebellum period's most thoughtful Black Byronists:

> In Syracuse, N.Y., resides George Boyer Vashon, Esq., A.M., a graduate of Oberlin Collegiate Institute, Attorney at Law, Member of the Syracuse Bar. Mr. Vashon, is a ripe scholar, an accomplished

Essayist, and a chaste classic Poet; his style running very much in the strain of Byron's best efforts. He probably takes Byron as his model, and Childe Harold, as a sample, as in his youthful days, he was a fond admirer of George Gordon Noel Byron, always calling his whole name, when he named him.

Delany suggests that Vashon's Byronism had little to do with the English poet's humor or his travesty of conventional morality. Instead what comes through is Vashon's moral seriousness, his worldliness, and his accomplishments. Prior to his appearance in Delany's book as a lawyer, poet, and intellectual, Vashon had been denied admission to the state bar of Ohio in the late 1840s. Delany had had a similar experience of racist exclusion from the institutions of incipient white professional culture, having been dismissed from Harvard Medical School at the whims of his white classmates. They had both begun to look outside the United States in the hopes of fulfilling their ambitions. Vashon emigrated to Haiti in early 1848, where he spent the better part of two years, teaching and hoping to set up a law practice.[15]

During this period, Vashon wrote a series of dispatches to *Frederick Douglass' Paper*, under the Byronic pseudonym "Harold," which documented the early years of President Faustin-Élie Soulouque's reign (1847–59). Haiti's creole elite had engineered Soulouque's election as a puppet in 1847, but by 1849 he had betrayed this class, declared the republic an empire, and himself Emperor Faustin I, in Napoleonic fashion. To his readers in the United States, Vashon narrated these events with measured optimism, hoping that "the imperial authority may present a front sufficiently imposing to keep in check the fierce outbreakings, which have for so long a period, saddened [Haiti's] history." Disappointed in this small hope, Vashon returned to the United States in the summer of 1849, and admitted privately that Haiti's "unsettled state ... deterred me from carrying out my intention of becoming a citizen thereof; and I was, in consequence, debarred from the exercise of practicing my profession there."[16]

These experiences of nominal freedom and repressed ambition, in both the northern United States and Haiti, gave Vashon a uniquely ironic perspective on the prospects for Black freedom in the mid-nineteenth century. He had come to view the international and transhistorical dimensions of the abolition movement and the end of slavery with a kind of Byronic detachment. Byron's investment in Greek independence, after all, had come as a result of his disillusion with English freedom, his seeking emancipation from the Protestant moral recriminations of northern Europe in the Mediterranean, and his discovery there of yet another despotism. Byron had taken this experience as the prompt for a wry but also personal vision of the "spirit of the age" and the geographic progress of universal history. Vashon's attitude, having had a similar experience in Haiti, was neither totally disenchanted nor conservative, and he would spend the 1850s and 1860s energetically involved in activism on behalf of antislavery causes in the United States.

Vashon's verse epic "Vincent Ogé" first appeared a few years after his return, in Julia W. Griffiths's two-volume anthology of abolitionist literature *Autographs for Freedom* (1853–54). It centers on the life of the eponymous *homme de couleur libre*, who led a revolt on the eve of the Haitian Revolution. The poem finds Ogé in Paris as the French Revolution began in 1789, where he organized with the Société des Amis des Noirs in the hopes of gaining the suffrage for property-owning free men of color in the new representative government. It then follows Ogé as he returns to Haiti and commandeers a group of several hundred armed men of color who were ultimately defeated by the colonial government of Philippe François Rouxel, viscounte de Blanchelande. Ogé died a brutal death, broken on the wheel in a public square in Cap-Haïtien in 1791. Many accounts suggest Ogé was a poor military strategist, and that his death at the hands of Rouxel was dishonorable. Ogé had avoided allegiances with the enslaved, and had reassured his European collaborators that he had no intention of abolishing slavery. So as a hero for the U.S. abolition movement half a century later, he cuts a strange figure. Vashon drew on the rich body of neoclassical epic poetry written in French about the Haitian Revolution that he would have encountered during his time in the Caribbean. The most famous of these, the anonymously authored *Haitïade* (1827–28?), has Ogé act as a kind of guardian spirit for its protagonist Toussaint Louverture during his imprisonment in Paris. Vashon, however, also draws on Byron's revision of the epic form to handle the contradictions of Ogé's legacy.

Vashon's recognition and redemption of Ogé's tragic dimensions involves a complexly aestheticized theory of history and of revolutionary failure in particular. With a kind of Byronic counterpoint of detachment and sentiment, Vashon tells the story of an ill-conceived African diasporic revolution as a foil to simplistic ideas about historical progress. Describing Ogé's movements from Haiti to revolutionary Paris and back, Vashon treats him as a kind of impermanent embodiment of liberatory idealism, in allegorical terms:

> And the fabric of ages—the glory of kings,
> Accounted most sacred mid sanctified things,
> Reared up by the hero, preserved by the sage,
> And drawn out in rich hues on the chronicler's page,
> Had sunk in the blast, and in ruins lay spread,
> While the altar of freedom was reared in its stead.
> And a spark from that shrine in the free-roving breeze,
> Had crossed from fair France to that isle of these
> And a flame was there kindled which fitfully shone
> Mid the shout of the free, and the dark captive's groan;
> As, mid contrary breezes, a torch-light will play,
> Now streaming up brightly—now dying away.

Vashon represents the French Revolution, and its effect on the political hopes of Black people in Haiti, as a dreamlike chivalric romance, with "the glory of kings" torn down and "the altar of freedom … reared in its stead." He condenses the vast history of freedom's unfolding into the image of a "spark"; revolutionary zeal seems to belong first only to Europeans, then, like it flits "in the free-roving breeze" to Ogé and his band of property-owning free men of color, and finally, beyond his death, it augurs the liberation of the "dark captive." The idea of freedom does not develop in a practical, rational, or linear fashion, but instead like the "play" of a "torchlight ... mid contrary breezes."[17]

To close focus on individuals' wavering commitment to the freedom struggle and thus the intimate consequences of colonial violence, Vashon depicts a brutal moment between Ogé's mother and his men before they go into battle with the French. In a menacing speech driven by matriarchal authority, she warns Ogé and his militia about the ignominy of failure, promising to curse their spirits if they lose their courage:

> But if your hearts should craven prove,
> Forgetful of your zeal—your love
> For rights and franchises of men,
> My heart will break; but even then,
> Whilst bidding life and earth adieu,
> This the prayer I'll breathe for you:
> 'Passing from guilt to misery,
> May this for aye your portion be,—
> A life, dragged out beneath the rod—
> An end, abhorred of man and God—
> As monument, the chains you nurse—
> As epitaph, your mother's curse!'

Like Jacobs's *Incidents*, this scene presents a countertheory of hereditary bondage and the masculinist blow for freedom. Ogé's mother is hardly removed from the action; instead, she is its inspiration and frames its unfolding. Her matriarchal threat approximates eternal justice. The learned Vashon is referring to the relationship in Homer's *Iliad* between Achilles and his dead mother Thetis, who intervenes on his behalf with the gods and consults with him on political plans. Ogé's mother's prophetic posture points to both the personal and cosmological dimensions through which Black abolitionists saw the end of slavery; she reckons the intergenerational trauma of hereditary bondage on a sublime scale.

Vashon's epic historical romance circulated Ogé's mother's warning through the networks of antebellum abolition. It posited a breach through which the historical energy of the heroes of the Haitian Revolution might still inspire new heroes in the struggle against slavery in the United States. It posits Black radicalism as genealogical and spiritual, against the paternal posture of the planter class and their white Northern collaborators and benefactors. Finally, *Vincent Ogé* tells a story of a "blow for freedom" that missed its mark, but that prompted a later, more comprehensive revolution, and that might, via cultural practice and theoretical speculation, do so again.[18]

"That restless and rebellious race"

In the years just after the war, Frances Ellen Watkins Harper made another entry into the African-American epic tradition, and again used Byron to tell a story about Black liberation centered on masculine rebellion, its origins in familial trauma, and its limitations as a mode of leadership. For Harper, even more explicitly than Vashon, the self-determination in the end of "hereditary bondage" cannot come from violence alone. In *Moses: A Story of the Nile* (1869), Harper represented the abolition struggle and the war years in a carefully wrought Biblical allegory. She retells the story of Exodus, focusing on Moses' troubled heroism as a reflection on what Du Bois later called "the Egypt of the Confederacy." The poem is the richest document of Black liberation theology in the nineteenth century, and its treatment of Moses as Byronic gives psychological depth to the comparison of slaveries in ancient Egypt and in the American South.[19]

Harper plays up the complexities of Moses' childhood and family life, darkening her hero's brow with Byronic touches to signal his Blackness. In the Biblical narrative, Moses' mother protects him from a pharaonic order, that all male Jewish children should be killed, by floating him down the Nile, where the pharaoh's daughter Bithiah rescues him. In Harper's retelling, Moses' adoptive mother is called Princess Charmian (renamed after Cleopatra's maidservant). She is jealously protective of her son, who nonetheless grows up acutely aware of his caste. Harper has Charmian worry over Moses' dedication to his people in Romantic vocabulary: "What wild chimera floats across thy mind? / What sudden impulse moves thy soul?... the warm blood of youth flushes thy veins." Sentiment darkens Moses racially, but also marks him as a modern character, embodied and sympathetic, rather than inaccessibly stony-faced and ancient.[20]

Harper's biographer, Melba Joyce Boyd, finds echoes of an array of antebellum heroes in Harper's Moses, including John Brown, Abraham Lincoln, Frederick Douglass, Sojourner Truth, and especially Harriet Tubman, then widely known as "the Moses of her people." The parallel between Moses' murder of the Egyptian he finds beating a Jew and Douglass's fight with Covey, for instance, is unmistakable. Moses' political conversion, like that of Northern abolitionists, involves acknowledging the circumstances of his birth, and detaching himself from the comforts of his childhood. Harper writes of his decision to join the Israelites in a way that condenses psychological commitment and political violence:

> he trampled
> On each vain regret as on a vanquished foe,
> And went forth a strong man, girded with lofty
> Purposes and earnest faith.

This dedication, born not out of circumstance but out of more distant senses of filiation and affiliation, also characterizes Byron's allegiance to Greece and Harper's to abolition and postbellum activism. According to Frances Smith Foster, the poem is, in this respect, "as close to an autobiographical statement as any that Harper ever wrote." The scanty accounts of Harper's life offer tantalizing dramatic possibilities, but because she left behind very little life writing—no memoir, no diary or daybooks, and few letters—her *Moses* stands for her sense of commitment to the battle against slavery and racism.[21]

In an extraordinary swerve on Romantic individualism, Harper applies the characteristics of the Byronic hero to the race of the Jews, as Moses becomes their revolutionary leader. His solitary and estranged fate becomes "our wrecked and blighted fortunes."

When Moses surveys the Israelite slaves building the pyramids, he finds in the furtive glances of his people a kind of secret Byronic coalition:

> There were men whose souls were cast
> In firmer moulds, men with dark secretive eyes,
> Which seemed to say, to day we bide our time,
> And hide our wrath in every nerve, and only
> Wait a fitting hour to strike the hands that press
> Us down.

In Harper's view, collective political action required the control of aggression over long duration and then the pointed release of retributive violence. She suggests that the messianic politics of liberation requires an embodied and exhausting stoicism, in which the Israelites "hide our wrath in every nerve." This movement between interior attitudes and collective culture in Harper's depiction of the Exodus represents a revision of Romantic individualism, tuned up to the circumstances of a people emerging from the many "separate hells" of slavery to a new Black peoplehood, soon to be riven again by segregation. Moses' surrender to old age before reaching the Promised Land figures the generational fatigue of the abolitionists as they lived into the postbellum decades: "It was a weary thing to bear the burden / Of that restless and rebellious race."[22]

Unlike Moses, and many of her abolitionist contemporaries, Harper fought for the fulfillment of abolition democracy into the twentieth century. Black feminist critics have long worried about Harper's capitulation, during the decades after the war, to an apparently simplistic moralism. Tracking the influence of Byron reveals more complex political and aesthetic sensibilities in her work. As a freeborn nineteenth-century Black woman, Harper had little room in her life as an activist for Byron's more sybaritic tendencies. She could never indulge the negativity of his dramatic self-fashioning: "I have been cunning in mine overthrow, / The careful pilot of my proper woe." Because she worked through the emergent, moralizing politics of racial uplift, Harper's dance with the public's appetites was rather different from Byron's. Her tendencies to self-mortification were more straightforwardly saintly and more consistently political. Pauline Hopkins reported in a 1902 profile that "Mrs. Harper was not contented to make speeches and receive plaudits, but was ready to do the rough work, and gave freely of all the moneys that her literary labors brought her. Indeed, it was often found necessary to restrain her open hand and to counsel her to be more careful of her hard-earned income." Byron's politically committed dissipation became in Harper a politically committed indifference to economic self-interest.[23]

"America's coming colored man"

The appearance of Harriet Beecher Stowe's *Lady Byron Vindicated* (1870) stoked antipathy toward Byron among American audiences. The more moralistically inclined in the abolition movement had long harbored suspicions about flaws in Byron's character, but rarely articulated their concerns beyond a stray remark. Stowe managed, however, to stir controversy about the long-dead Byron's philandering by suggesting his charisma disrupted fixed notions of color and gender: "There have been women able to lead their leashes of blinded adorers; to make them swear that black was white, or white black, at their word. Such an enchanter in man's shape was Lord Byron." In the belated public scandal surrounding the publication of Stowe's book, the press consistently drew contrasts between Byron and the enslaved people who had been Stowe's subjects in *Uncle Tom's Cabin* (1852). Recall how Byron had made an early critical intervention on the "medieval morality" James Baldwin later found in Stowe: the culturally entrenched association of Blackness, slavery, and sin.[24]

As poetry became less ubiquitously popular and more "elevating" through the end of the nineteenth century, the embodied politics of Black Byronism became increasingly troubled. Byron became a screen for the sexual politics of what came to be known as the New Negro movement, with its investments in the respectability of Black middle-class communities. Byron's influence thus began to slip into the cracks of what had been abolition consensus: between the incipient Black middle class and the working poor, between women's rights activists and abolitionists, and between gradualists and immediatists. Some Black Romantic writers continued to use Byronic forms to complicate the limiting spectrum of Black masculinity that ran from race man to bad man. Even as Byron's model became riskier to claim, Black activists and poets turned to his work to think outside the distorted notions of Black licentiousness that justified scientific racism, segregation, and lynching terror.

One of the most popular African-American poets of what Charles Chesnutt had called the "postbellum, pre-Harlem" period undertook a sustained post-Byronic poetic project. In a series of lyric epics set on the American frontier, Albery Allson Whitman worked through Byron's influence from his contradictory position as an aestheticist poet and African Methodist Episcopal preacher. Whitman consistently noted "the loftiness of Byron's well wrought rhyme" in acknowledging his influences. He did not write psychologically conflicted Black male characters, however. Instead he set implausibly ideal Black male heroes against the background of the frontier romance, and played on the impossibility of gendered models of conduct in the face of racist state-sanctioned violence. Whitman's protagonists, representatives of what he called "America's *coming* colored man," needed distance from civilization because of their perfection. In the 1870s and 1880s, as Northern industrialists reached a rapprochement with the Southern planter class to roll back Reconstruction, Whitman's Byronic heroes became prototypes of a Talented Tenth that society could not contain.[25]

Whitman was given to what can best be called hysterical flights of postwar patriotic sentiment. In *Not a Man, and Yet a Man*, an epic poem published the same year as the Compromise of 1877 pulled Union troops out of the South and formally ended Reconstruction, Whitman pleads the masculine heroism that had mobilized around Byron in the antebellum period: "Oh comrade freemen strike your hands to stand / Like walls of rock and guard our father-land!" Moments like these read hopelessly false in a moment when the federal government's retreat from the South began to expose Black people to the terrors of rejuvenated white supremacy. With equal intensity, Whitman could express intense rage about the period's disappointments. At his most iconoclastic, he called for an end to the simplistic moralism of racial uplift and its accomodationist representatives among the Black intelligentsia, whom he associated with racial stereotypes derived from *Uncle Tom's Cabin*. He writes in the preface to *The Rape of Florida* (1884): "The time has come when all 'Uncle Toms' and 'Topsies' ought to die. Goody goodness is a sort of man worship: ignorance is its inspiration, fear its ministering spirit, and beggary its inheritance." Here was a late Romantic radicalism, a purgative revolutionary terror to counter the terror visited on Black communities in the aftermath of Reconstruction. Whitman's work, more than his earlier contemporaries, shares with Byron a mercurial quality, a tendency to ill-considered extremes, which sometimes yields a stark beauty and others disappoints. But such disappointments make minor-key echoes of the disappointments of his moment.[26]

As African-American history approached what Rayford Logan called its "nadir" around the end of the nineteenth century, Byron increasingly played the role of a straw man in racial uplift ideology. In *A Voice of the South* (1892), Anna Julia Cooper quotes Byron as a foil to her case for women's equality:

> Man's love is of man's life a thing apart,
> 'Tis woman's whole existence. Man may range
> the court, camp, church, the vessel and the mart,
> Sword, gown, gain, glory offer in exchange.
> Pride, fame, ambition, to fill up his heart—
> And few there are whom these cannot estrange.
> Men have all these resources, we but one—
> To love again and be again undone.

Byron's idea of women's capacity could be much more imaginative than this, but the English critic William Hazlitt had noticed his limitations on this score decades earlier: "Lord Byron makes man after his own image, woman after his own heart; the one is a capricious tyrant, the other a yielding slave." Cooper glosses the above lines in historical terms, distancing herself from the era of exclusively masculine liberal individualism:

> This may have been true when written. It is not true to-day. The old, subjective, stagnant, indolent and wretched life for woman has gone. She has as many resources as men, as many activities beckon her on. As large possibilities swell and inspire her heart.

Cooper sets Byron at odds with progressive-modernist New Womanhood, as it moved away from the doctrine of the spheres to a more self-determined femininity. But Byron had been a watchword for Black men's self-determination a generation earlier. Like Byron, Cooper disguised the autobiographical stakes of her work in her arguments for Black women's perspective as crucial to the

Tintype of a Civil War Soldier. Courtesy of the Smithsonian National Museum of African American History and Culture. Gift from the Liljenquist Family Collection (date unknown).

development of world literature. Byron had fallen out of fashion as an explicit reference for Black writers, but a kind of latent Byronism remained a part of the bedrock of African-American letters.[27]

Like Cooper, W.E.B. Du Bois made a post-Byronic case for Black intellectual life, in opposition to the regime of segregation. In *The Souls of Black Folk* (1903), he imagined his entry into world literature as a kind of eternal palace for canonical writers, claiming: "I sit with Shakespeare and he winces not. Across the color line I move arm in arm with Balzac and Dumas, where smiling men and welcoming women glide in gilded halls." Byron is conspicuously absent from this passage, as if he might upset the genteel atmosphere. Instead, Du Bois quoted the old lines from *Childe Harold's Pilgrimage* as the epigraph to his chapter on Booker T. Washington. There he associates Byron with the "self-assertion" of Black abolitionism, in contrast with Washington's "attitude of adjustment and submission." The recollection of Byron posed a challenge to the moral fussiness and sophistry of racial uplift. Less worried by Byron's chauvinism, Du Bois could read him with wistful nostalgia for the clarity of antislavery politics. He could do so, also, without a sense of intellectual inadequacy in relation to the European culture hero, but instead with an expressive certainty and confidence.[28]

Envoi for Col. Nimrod Burke

> Strike grandly in this hour sublime,
> A blow to ring through endless time!
> Strike! for the listening ages wait!
> Emancipate! Emancipate!
>
> —anonymous, printed in the
> *Liberator*, August 8, 1862

A few months after Lincoln's Emancipation Proclamation, Douglass gave a speech in Rochester, New York, in March 1863, entitled "Men of Color, to Arms!!!," urging his contemporaries to join the fight against the Confederacy. He connected the liberating violence of the lines from *Childe Harold* to the Union war effort:

> Action! action! not criticism, is the plain duty of this hour. Words are now useful only as they stimulate to blows. The office of speech now is only to point out when, where and how to strike to the best advantage. There is no time for delay. The tide is at its flood that leads on to fortune. From East to West, from North to South, the sky is written all over "NOW OR NEVER." Liberty won by white men would lose half its luster. "Who would be free themselves must strike the blow." "Better even die free, than to live slaves."

Some twenty years after Garnet's citation at the Buffalo Convention and ten since he had first cited the lines himself, Douglass returned again to Byron. The formally abstract address to those "who would be free" had taken the form of a real historical possibility. He proceeds from a paradox, first insisting that rhetoric itself, the mode in which he had made his own reputation, was ill-equipped to meet the crisis. Then Douglass finds exceptions, language which can inspire and incite, including Byron's inflaming directive, written in the sky. Insisting on the stakes of the war for Black people, he conscripts the thousands of smaller blows against slavery of the preceding centuries into the epically militarized conflict then reaching its climax.[29]

As readers of Romanticism, Douglass and his contemporaries understood revolution as taking place in consciousness as well as on the battlefield and in history. They sought, in borrowing from Byron, to conceptualize scripts for revolutionary consciousness-raising, and to acknowledge the messiness and complexity of such change on a personal level. Scenes like those between revolutionary leaders and their mothers in Vashon and Harper give emotional and intergenerational density to sublimely heroic historical moments. Despite Byron's occasionally absurd masculinity, Black writers used his work to complicate the gendered politics of liberation. In so doing, the Black Byronic poetry of the end of slavery made its everyday heroism seem both possible and necessary.

Among the many daguerrotypes of Black enlisted men, one image comes closest to representing their quicksilver determination, the decisiveness of their commitment in both its immediately physical and cosmologically historical dimensions. It was for some time thought to represent a Sgt. Nimrod Burke, though it is now listed in the collection of the National Museum of African American History and Culture as an unidentified Civil War soldier. Burke had been born free in Virginia, and was living in Ohio when the war began, so he shared with many of the main characters of this book a sense of political obligation to abolition beyond his own individual experience. In the man's face, the readiness is all the sublime prospect of the end of slavery; his eyes reflect love and radiate potential energy; he appears coiled in anticipation for total historical and spiritual transformation. The Black Byronic writers developed their poetics into and out of his determination, coalescing a Black abolitionist politics that began with striking the first resounding blows. The gun resting on his chest with a deceptively casual softness warns of vengeance, and augurs the industrial civilization with which he threw in his lot. The commemorative encasement frames his hopes in nationalistic iconography, but he could hardly be satisfied by the narrowly conceived citizenship his people won in the war.

2

The Supernatural Avenger

In which George Moses Horton, enslaved near the campus of the University of North Carolina, takes flight into symbolism

Sometime in 1815, George Moses Horton, then in his late teens, arrived in Chapel Hill, North Carolina, on the Sabbath to sell produce from the Horton plantation about ten miles south. With his seemingly spontaneous lyrical effusions, he quickly attracted the attention of the educated elites around the University of North Carolina, the first public institution of higher education in the United States. The students took particular notice of his talent, encouraged his performing, and lent him books. They also took advantage of him, sometimes having fun at his expense, sometimes paying him to perform or to compose love lyrics they would use on their girlfriends, and sometimes involving him in regrettable drunken revelries. The university offered Horton a respite from the surveillance and enforced labor of enslavement; it also offered him access to the Enlightenment ideals and romantic nationalism that justified white supremacy.[1]

Most important, the university was where Horton became a poet. It was there that he learned to write and first set down on paper the oral compositions that he had long memorized. Over the years, the university became a way of life, and he hired his time from his enslavers with the money he earned there among the wealthy sons of the planter class. On Chapel Hill's sylvan campus,

Horton came to understand himself as a genius, with all the cultural significance that entailed. His talents predated his arrival at the university:

> I was early fond of music, with an extraordinary appetite for singing lively times, for which I was a little remarkable. ... At any critical juncture, when any thing momentous transpired, such as death, misfortune, disappointment, and the like, [songs] passed off from my mind like the chanting of birds after a storm, for my mind was then more deeply inspired than at other periods.

The propensity to song, the sympathy with nature, the susceptibility to moments of deep feeling, and the dexterity with death as a spiritual transformation were all qualities associated with the poet in Romantic discourse. Horton found himself in a situation of extraordinary contradiction and precarity: a genius enslaved alongside the elite and enlightened confines of campus life. Borrowing what he could from the first public institution of higher education in the United States, Horton began to formulate a specifically Black Romanticism. His poetry is so anarchic, funny, and deceptive that it seems at first to resist a procedural and ideological definition. But suffice it to say at the outset that the enigmatic coincidence of his talents and his legal status led him to an aesthetic practice that mocks Victor Hugo's equation of Romanticism and liberalism.

Horton encountered liberalism in one of its most acutely paradoxical habitats, the college town, where he carefully navigated a range of profoundly odd social dynamics. He managed to sustain his lucrative arrangement of working for hire around campus through three successive owners in the Horton family. He also maintained relationships with two successive university presidents, Joseph Caldwell (1816–35) and David L. Swain (1835–68). One of Horton's contemporaries recalled: "It was a common saying in Chapel Hill that Poet Horton owned Mr. Horton and all but owned the president of the University." This joke on Southern slavery does not quite capture the fragile complexity of the poet's situation. None of the Horton family could be prevailed upon to let Horton go, even after, at one moment in the late 1820s, the intervention of North Carolina governor John Owen. Later, Swain in particular seems to have been reluctant to assist Horton's own attempts to gain his freedom. Through all this, the poet, rather unsurprisingly, acquired an appreciation for contradiction and for the dialectical ironies of Romantic thought. He benefitted from the attention of the white Northern novelist Caroline Lee Hentz, who acted as an amanuensis for Horton's first collection of poetry in 1829, transcribing his verse before he had learned to write. Given Hentz's pro-slavery sympathies, this collaboration was particularly freighted. She described Horton with a mix of physiognomic racism and philological affection in her 1833 novel *Lovell's Folly*: "Instead of the broad smile of the African, he has the mild gravity of a Grecian philosopher."[2]

Horton's recognition by these elites gives lie to the transatlantic debate about Black people's incapacity for genius that had unfolded across the late eighteenth and early nineteenth century among the likes of David Hume, Immanuel Kant, and Thomas Jefferson. Their conclusions, that Black people were incapable of rational or abstract thought and thus could have no genius, justified slavery and the exclusion of Black people from the privileges of emergent liberal society. W.E.B. Du Bois later pointed to the absurdity of this conversation in light of the reliance of the South on Black labor:

> It is nonsense to say that the South knew nothing of the capabilities of the Negro race. Southerners knew Negroes far better than Northerners. There was not a single Negro slave owner who did not know dozens of Negroes just as capable of learning and efficiency as the mass of poor white people around and about, and some quite as capable as the average slaveholder. They had continually in the course of the history of slavery recognized such men. Here and there teachers and preachers to white folks as well as colored folks had arisen. Artisans and even artists had been recognized.

Transcendental, synoptic, and essentialist interpretations of Black people's supposed inferiority had little to do with everyday life in Southern slavery, which relied in myriad ways on not only on their manual labor but also their technical capacities. In practice, white Southerners' recognition of Black people's abilities was integral to the function of the slave system. Horton, who published two books of poetry while enslaved and a third while escaping as contraband of the Union Army, represents an acutely contradictory case.[3]

The irony at the heart of Horton's work stemmed from the fact that he was recognized as a genius from very early on, and yet this recognition did not yield his liberty. Across forty years as a fixture on campus, Horton performed for white Southerners, to the extent that one unsympathetic early critic worried he was "a forerunner of the minstrel poets." The popular cultural dynamics of racial pride, shame, and desire activated in minstrelsy do not, however, account for the depth, range, or complexity of Horton's work, which was also Black, in and of itself. Horton was no poet at the plow, singing simple-minded plantation pastorals. The uneven, intermittent, and disingenuous appreciations of his audiences inspired him to formulate a recursive form of Romanticism, both solicitous and refusing. Reading Horton means figuring whether he is writing for himself or for his customers, and yet also acknowledging he is always distinctively himself—as distinctive as any lyric poet in the nineteenth century, in fact. Yet rather than taking his originality as verification for a social and political system built around the premise of possessive individualism, Horton turns inward, to an allegorical dream-world in which he sets the repressive apparatuses of slavery and racism against freedoms embodied in strange spirits. Far from what Hölderlin called a "noble, grave genius," Horton was an antic figure; his genius took the form of a fugitive and sometimes freakishly fanciful flight into music and symbolism. Ironizing the available Romantic modes of visionary consciousness, Horton imagined Black genius as a point of departure for a reimagining of the world.[4]

"The receptive gloom"

In late 1844, Horton was preparing a second volume of poetry. His first, *The Hope of Liberty*, had been published fifteen years earlier, and failed to result in his manumission. A year earlier, the planter who held him captive, James Horton, had died, and the poet had been bequeathed to one of the old man's sons, Hall Horton. Emboldened by the change in circumstance, the poet wrote a letter to abolitionist William Lloyd Garrison, seeking support for a new volume:

> Sir i am not alone actuated by pecuniary motives, but upon the whole, to spread the blaze of african genious, and thus dispel the receptive gloom so prevalent in many parts of the country … I faithfully trust a sign that your examination into the facts of my condition will inspire your pleasure to open to the world a volume which like a wild bird has long lain struggling in its shell impatient to transpire to the eye, a dubious world

Horton takes the opportunity of audience with Garrison to set off literary fireworks, in vibrant, strange, and suggestive diction. The tone here is as outrageous as it is obsequious; it is a begging letter, a pitch to an editor, and a prologue to modern Black radical poetics. The idea of "the blaze of african genious" is drawn from Romantic convention: it is Promethean, and situates Horton as a lamplighter, a giver of illumination. The metaphor of his book as a bird breaking out of its shell, "impatient to transpire," also tunes up an old idea, the association of poets with birdsong. The wildness of Horton's imagination, in this setup, intervenes on what he refers to as "the receptive gloom so prevalent in many parts of the country." This phrase captures the mood of Southern slavery that could rely on and at the same time demean the talents of Horton and his Black contemporaries. An oddly funny metaphor for racism, it stages a reversal of the Gothic coordinates of whiteness and blackness; white racists live in the darkness while the Black poet will light the fire of inspiration. The literary history of race, so keenly described by Toni Morrison as "playing in the dark," receives in Horton a thorough and willfully ironic rewiring. Inverting the conventions of Western aesthetic theory, Horton promises illumination by black light, making whites a queasy green and blacks a deep blue.[5]

Garrison does not appear to have replied or purchased a subscription to the volume, which appeared in 1845 as *The Poetical Works of George M. Horton, the Colored Bard of North Carolina*. In the autobiographical preface, Horton again expresses his ardent desire to "remove the doubts of cavilists with regard to African genius." By this point, Horton had grown accustomed to contestation around the question of Black genius. His word "cavilists," meaning a word for people who insult or decry, was not quite obsolete then, and not exactly a malapropism in the minstrel tradition; its use is a stunt, a kind of tall talk, but it also gives a name to "racists" who had not yet been described as such. It suggests that the ideological contest around Black capacity was, of course, a mockery.[6]

Horton may have known the story of enslaved Boston poet Phillis Wheatley's appearance before "the most respectable characters in Boston" to prove her genius in the 1770s; his first book was repeatedly reprinted alongside hers and circulated in abolitionist circles in the North. In an 1838 volume entitled *Memoirs and Poems of Phillis Wheatley, a Native African and a Slave. Also Poems by a Slave*, Margaretta Matilda Odell reports on the tragedy that befell Wheatley in her later life, despite her recognition by the great white men of her moment. It finds her "numbering the last hours of life in a state of the most abject misery, surrounded by all the emblems of squalid poverty!" Such degradations were not uncommon for Black authors in the late eighteenth and early nineteenth centuries, and the recognition that came with print publication was no guarantee of security. Authors of early narratives of slavery often noted their straitened financial circumstances in the wake of escape or manumission. Horton, like Wheatley, had audience with the prominent white men of his day, and yet never managed to sway judgment in such a way that would result in his freedom. The recognition of Black genius by disparate abolitionist or antislavery publics could never ameliorate the totalizing effects of racial slavery or racial capitalism.[7]

Nineteenth-century definitions of genius were categorically complex. In a review of Horton's first book, white abolitionist poet Jonathan Greenleaf Whittier wondered what the enslaved poet might have been capable of given the comforts and advantages of Milton or Robert Burns. Citing some lines from Horton, he asks, "Is there not something of the divine *afflatus* here manifested?" Notions of genius given to spiritual inspiration were common, especially in assessments of the lyric, given its close ties to song and the control of breath. This kind of access to divinity was sometimes assumed to come more easily to differently embodied artists. Horton's performances corresponded to a model of genius associated in European Romanticism with Mediterranean women, that of the *improvvisatrice*. These figures dazzled audiences with the mystical intuition of their poetic performances. In the autobiographical preface to his 1845 volume, Horton tells how the students at Chapel Hill often called on him "to spout," a term long used to describe such poetic improvisation in English. He reports a deep ambivalence about these moments, feeling both truly appreciated and punishingly humiliated by the students.[8]

Spike Lee would have described Horton's role for the students as that of the "magical Negro," whose visionary powers are reserved as adjunct to the success of white characters in recent Hollywood films. Unlike Lee's ironic narrative stereotype, Horton drew on Romantic and transcendental definitions of genius fundamentally at odds with his predicament. Coleridge had defined genius as "eternity revealing itself in the phenomena of time." In Horton's case, the brutally intermittent and selective recognition of his genius gave him a sense of his work as out of step with history, and led him to develop an intensely symbolic and radically oppositional form of aesthetic idealism. Horton used abstraction and allegory as forms of imaginative escape from the corruptions of enslavement. The distance between poetry and the reality of enslavement gave Horton's work its dialectical quality. He contested the "gloom" of slavery and racism with an elating and illuminating inspiration. In this respect, his approach parallels arguments about modernity and the politics of aesthetic autonomy made by some of the most formally radical white poets in Europe and America in the mid-nineteenth century. Yet through the seeming anomaly of his Romantic sophistication, Horton advanced a caustic revolutionary vision of Black modernity.[9]

Poetic irritability

Horton's exceptional talent heightened rather than diminished the fundamental alienations of enslavement. Consequently, he formulated an acutely morbid Black aesthetic and his poetic project involved writing through slavery as what Orlando Patterson calls "social death": an experience of "natal alienation" and "total powerlessness" that substitutes for and thus experientially mimics bodily death. In a late poem, Horton put the problem simply: "Genius seemed leading to a tomb." Along this way, he often expressed his yearning for freedom as a yearning for salvation, although not always of the most strictly Christian terms.[10]

Horton dwelt, for his whole career, in the most trenchant of Wheatley's couplets, the conclusion of "On Being Brought from Africa to America": "Remember, *Christians*, *Negros*, black as *Cain*, / May be refin'd, and join th' angelic train." Horton thought much more extensively about how Black people came to bear the mark of Cain through the trickeration of racist whites. Like many of his contemporaries among the Romantics, he knew wickedness well, both in himself and that projected onto him. Robert Southey had identified this tendency in British Romanticism as the "Satanic School" and found it "especially characterized by a Satanic spirit of pride and audacious impiety, which still betrays the wretched feeling of hopelessness wherewith it is allied." Romantic Satanism involved taking seriously the premise of earthly existence as a form of exile in sin, and reckoning the forces of modernity as products of Satanic energy. Slavery was widely recognized in abolitionist rhetoric as a Satanic force, violating everything it touched. Horton had every reason to see his work as unfolding in relation to the Devil, and his genius as a spirit that rode him, a blaze of Black light through the gloom. He wrote strange lyrics for a secular revelation and a revolution to come.[11]

The idea of the poetic genius working against the crass pre-occupations of his or her historical moment became a criterion of aesthetic judgment in the work of Horton's Southern contemporary Edgar Allan Poe and Poe's French translator Charles Baudelaire. Through Poe, Baudelaire understood modernity not as the result of the progressive spirit of a providential rationality, but as a kind of hell on earth: "The United States were for Poe a vast cage, an enormous counting house." Following this, Baudelaire developed a theory of aesthetic form as a respite from the cruel stupidity of human life and history. In an 1857 introduction to the second volume of his translations of Poe's work, Baudelaire explains the role of art in relation to the afterlife:

> It is both by poetry and through poetry, by music and through music, that the soul foresees the splendors beyond the tomb; and when an exquisite poem brings tears to our eyes, those tears are not proof of excessive joy: rather they bear witness to an impatient melancholy, a bid by our nerves, by a nature exiled in imperfection, which would immediately annex a revealed paradise on this earth.

The poet, in this conception, must cast visions of eternal majesties, but also document his or her everyday "impatient melancholy" for their realization. Baudelaire worked through the opposition between what he called "spleen and ideal," toggling between his bilious response to modern life and his yearning for inaccessibly ideal pleasures. He sometimes found otherworldly delights that fit this scheme via exoticism, especially in his depictions of his long-time Haitian mistress, Jeanne Duval.[12]

Poe's representations of Black people were hobbled by caricature, but he left behind crucially important aesthetic technologies for navigating a society defined by racial terror. In a fragmentary essay entitled "Fifty Suggestions" from 1849, he gives an analysis of the psychology of the artist that could well double for a theory of what we now call microaggression:

> That poets (using the word comprehensively, as including artists in general) are a *genus irritabile*, is well understood; but the *why*, seems not to be commonly seen. An artist *is* an artist only by dint of his exquisite sense of Beauty—a sense affording him rapturous enjoyment, but at the same time implying or involving, an equally exquisite sense of Deformity, of disproportion. Thus a wrong—an injustice—done a poet who is really a poet, excites him to a degree which, to ordinary apprehension, appears disproportionate with the wrong. Poets see injustice—*never* where it does not exist—but very often where the unpoetical see no injustice whatever. Thus the poetic irritability has no reference to "temper" in the vulgar sense, but merely to a more than usual clearsightedness in respect to Wrong:—this clear-sightedness being nothing more than a corollary to the vivid perception of Right—of justice—of proportion.

Borrowing the language of biological taxonomy, Poe defines the poet by his or her heightened aesthetic sensitivity, and gives as the example their perception of injustice beyond the limits of the ordinary. In this view, the poet not only yearns for ethereal Beauty, but remains radically hypervigilant toward the ugliness and unfairness of the present. Because of his own myopia, Poe never considered that such a person might be born in slavery, but his description nevertheless fits Horton rather perfectly.[13]

Horton was nothing if not irritable, and his genius emerged from this basic, resistive sensitivity. What he understood as the eternal dimensions of his genius forced him to struggle against the historical frame of his enslavement. He took slavery as the splenetic modern and freedom as an unknown ideal. In an art practice oscillating between hermetic traps and terrifying ecstasies, Horton elaborated the fractiousness of his subject relation to modernity and to historical time. The typical abolitionist terms "immediatism" and "gradualism" do not easily apply here. A sense of exile beyond the physical desire to emigrate indicated in Horton's biography animates his entire literary production—his is an African-American poetry seeking throughout an escape from the United States, but also any earthly existence defined by slavery.

The premise of aesthetic idealism as a form of fugitivity derived from his engagement with European and American conceptions of genius, progress, and history at the University of North Carolina. The figure of the poet as conceived by the Romantics tended to resist the increasingly workaday division of intellectual labor into disciplines and faculties. The poet, as Coleridge suggested, should "bring the whole soul of man into activity." While he may have appreciated this as an aspiration, Horton expressed in his work the enforced psychic and spiritual fragmentation of enslavement. His flight from his circumstances into the symbolic ultimately made for a lifelong performance of self-annihilation. Herein lies Horton's prophetic contribution to the formation of Black cultural nationalism and Atlantic culture more broadly: his lyrics travesty liberal individualism. But that did not mean for him that there was no alternative, that he and his auditors should be cast wandering in the gloom without guidance or self-certainty.

In *The Souls of Black Folk*, W.E.B. Du Bois formulates a sketch of the figure of "the Priest or Medicine-man" in slavery that resonates with Horton's sense of poetic purpose as much as does any theory of Romantic poetry:

He early appeared on the plantation and found his function as the healer of the sick, the interpreter of the Unknown, the comforter of the sorrowing, the supernatural avenger of wrong, and the one who rudely but picturesquely expressed the longing, disappointment, and resentment of a stolen and oppressed people. Thus, as bard, physician, judge, and priest, within the narrow limits allowed by the slave system, rose the Negro preacher, and under him the first church was not at first by any means Christian nor definitely organized; rather it was an adaptation and mingling of heathen rites among the members of each plantation, and roughly designated as Voodooism. Association with the masters, missionary effort and motives of expediency gave these rites an early veneer of Christianity, and after the lapse of many generations the Negro church became Christian.

Horton's role in antebellum Chapel Hill was similarly ubiquitous, for both Black and white communities. Rather than taking on the institutional and ideological trappings of Christianity, Horton took up the aesthetic prerogatives of Romanticism, and his practice as a poet took into its sweep a range of social functions supplementing the cultural bankruptcy of modern life defined by white supremacy. He became a kind of literary negative of the "Negro preacher" described here; his poems a kind of lyric ritual, his symbolic vision projected into a history wiped out by violence. Horton moved people, and felt the weight of that burden, the frustrations of genius, as too much responsibility.[14]

"Bid me from servitude ascend"

James Weldon Johnson, in his 1922 preface to *The Book of American Negro Poetry*, writes that Horton "expressed in all of his poetry strong complaint at his condition of slavery and a deep longing for freedom." The form of the complaint went back to the Lamentations of Jeremiah in the Old Testament. It took on secular functions in the medieval and early modern period as a vehicle for erotic and occasionally feminist sentiment, as a way to frame romantic bereavement, dejection, abandonment, or mistreatment. It later became enormously important to the Puritans, who reinvigorated the jeremiad as a way to remind New England communities of their spiritual mission. These notes would return in Horton's work in new and pointed ways.

The complaint was also commonly used in English antislavery verse. Poems like William Cowper's "The Negro's Complaint" (1788) and Robert Burns's "The Slave's Lament" (1792) circulated throughout the transatlantic abolition movement. These poems were important early attempts by white writers to figure the subjectivity of Black people in slavery, and they often worked within basically Protestant frameworks. For Horton, wandering in what Baudelaire called a "forest of symbols," there were no given political, cultural, or religious ideals on which he could rely, or to which he could call his auditors. His first collection, *The Hope of Liberty* (1829), contains a poem entitled "The Slave's Complaint," which frames the speaker's condition in terms of his spiritual alienation:

> Heaven! in whom can I confide?
> Canst thou not for all provide?
> Condescend to be my guide
>   Forever:
>
> And when this transient life shall end,
> Oh, may some kind, eternal friend
> Bid me from servitude ascend,
>   Forever!

The address of this poem, its interrogation of "Heaven," suggests the frustrations of a world abandoned by God. Unlike the certitude of Wheatley's "angelic train," Horton's complaint begs the help of some ambiguously unknown "kind, eternal friend." The prospect of salvation as freedom floats unmoored of any doctrinal authority. Horton seems to know eternity, in a lonely way, but to plead on behalf of a collective "all." Elsewhere in the poem, Horton describes himself "groping through this dreary maze."[15]

The Hope of Liberty benefitted from the comparatively liberal Southern attitudes toward slave religion before Nat Turner's Rebellion in 1831. Horton's complaints give a picture of the consciousness of enslavement in a spiritually bankrupt world, through the jangly rhythmic juxtaposition of symbols. "On Liberty and Slavery," also from 1829, sets its subjects in a deeply strange allegorical ballad:

> Oh, Liberty! thou golden prize,
>   So often sought by blood—
> We crave thy sacred sun to rise,
>   The gift of nature's God:
>
> Bid Slavery hide her haggard face,
>   And barbarism fly:
> I scorn to see the sad disgrace
>   In which enslaved I lie.

> Dear Liberty! upon thy breast,
>   I languish to respire;
> And like the Swan unto her nest,
>   I'd to thy smiles retire.

Here again Horton slips between lyric individualism and collectivism, between "I" and "we"; his reference to "blood" grasps for an affirmative racial identification. He orients his poetic gaze away from "the sad disgrace" of slavery and toward the sublimely lovely Liberty. The conceit, of Horton's speaker in a love triangle between the feminized Liberty and Slavery, has a radical erotic quality. Neither antislavery songs of the abolition movement nor the spirituals of the early Black church, both largely anonymous lyric traditions, risked this sort of perversity. Here the bird that would become an icon of aesthetic idealism in Baudelaire—the swan—is identified with Liberty. An eagle would have been a more distinctively American choice, but Horton only knew American freedom as enslaving, and imagined his freedom in an Africa he barely knew. So for him, freedom had to be a bird too pretty to live. The lyric syncopates hope and disappointment; the odd line, "I languish to respire," mashes up two words for the emotional arc of waiting, bends the infinitive, and plays synesthetically on the sibilant mixed connotations of hope and breath. Here, in much more extravagantly vexed language, is the audacity of hope, forged against the near certainty of failure, barely able to believe in its own possibilities.[16]

In these early poems, Horton exploits the lyric as a medium (both spiritual and aesthetic) for an encoded and embodied Black liberation. Another poem from *The Hope of Liberty*, entitled "On Hearing of the Intention of a Gentleman to Purchase the Poet's Freedom," he finds the experience indescribable, and focuses on its sonic quality. He elaborates on the sublimity of freedom in a series of increasingly improbable similes:

> 'Twas like a proselyte, allied to Heaven—
> Or rising spirits' boast of sins forgiven,
> Whose shout dissolves the adamant away,
> Whose melting voice the stubborn rocks obey.

'Twas like the salutation of the dove,
Borne on the zephyr through some lonesome grove,
When Spring returns, and Winter's chill is past,
And vegetation smiles above the blast.

'Twas like the evening of a nuptial pair,
When love pervades the hour of sad despair—
'Twas like fair Helen's sweet return to Troy,
When every Grecian bosom swell'd with joy.

Horton begins again with the familiar association of salvation and liberation, audible first as a figure of prophetic power, the "melting voice the stubborn rocks obey," then the more jubilant but morally perilous sound of "rising spirits' boast of sins forgiven." Horton's grandiloquence takes a further turn to the surreal when the sound of the gentleman's voice makes "vegetation smile[s]." Finally, the third stanza tests plausibility and decorum, comparing Horton's relation to this would-be benefactor with "a nuptial pair," and again hinting at the much more earthly notion of freedom as erotic.

Even in this moment that might otherwise be celebratory, in which Horton would seem to be on the verge of winning his freedom, he manages to be a bit embarrassing. The unknown gentleman did not or could not ultimately purchase his freedom. So that even as it figures hope in outrageous terms, the poem expresses hope's disappointment in outrage. It is the black fire in a receptive gloom. The same could be said of the whole first volume, which takes *The Hope of Liberty* as its eponymous theme, and yet cannot speak of liberty as anything other than a chimera, "a thing with feathers," as Emily Dickinson would have it. Horton had only his estranged own insight, and a troubled but persistent sense of affiliation with an inchoate, enslaved collective. To take up the mantle of the poet in the Romantic period, both exceptional and representative, spiritually and emotionally attuned to freedom, injustice, and history, represented an enormous risk for Horton. The permission he found in Chapel Hill to express complaint against slavery, even in the densely metaphorical language of his poetry, was nothing short of remarkable. This provisional

freedom of expression would not last through the remainder of
Horton's decades in slavery.[17]

"Excoriated deep"

In the aftermath of Nat Turner's Rebellion and the rise of the US
abolition movement, as the South sought to expand the plantation
system into the West, Horton's 1845 volume *Poetical Works* was
more constrained in its direct comment on slavery. He could never
freely express rage in his work, but he increasingly sublimated the
notes of anger in the earlier poems into melancholy and weird
irony. Examples of gallows humor abound in both slave and Black
abolitionist culture, but Horton's work in this vein has a metaphysical and prophetic depth—he finds in the history of American
racial thinking something like what Mark Twain called a "cosmic
joke." In an act of enormous self-sacrifice, Horton makes fun of
his situation as a debased genius, and subjects himself to eternal
laughter; in a series of reversals that look like a dance on a tight-
rope in a strobe-lit room, the joke is always on white supremacy
and the absurd violence visited on Black life by enslavement.

One of Horton's most strange and funny poems, "Troubled
with the Itch, and Rubbing with Sulphur," turns the complaint
to more seemingly mundane purposes. Taking one of the simplest
problems of embodiment as a prompt for metaphysical speculation, Horton works his way up to a countertheory of racialization:

> 'Tis bitter, yet 'tis sweet,
> Scratching effects but transient ease;
> Pleasure and pain together meet,
> And vanish as they please.
>
> My nails, the only balm,
> To ev'ry bump are oft applied,
> And thus the rage will sweetly calm
> Which aggravates my hide.

It soon returns again;
A frown succeeds to ev'ry smile;
Grinning I scratch and curse the pain,
But grieve to be so vile.

In fine, I know not which
Can play the most deceitful game,
The devil, sulphur, or the itch;
The three are but the same.

The devil sows the itch,
And sulphur has a loathsome smell,
And with my clothes as black as pitch,
I stink where'er I dwell.

Excoriated deep,
By friction play'd on ev'ry part,
It oft deprives me of my sleep,
And plagues me to my heart.

Horton takes the experience of itching skin beyond bodily immediacy to psychological, philosophical, and spiritual registers. The
poem begins by setting up a series of oppositions that progress
from the physical aggravation of itching to more affective aesthetic experience ("'Tis bitter, yet 'tis sweet ... Pleasure and pain
together meet ... And thus the rage will sweetly calm ..."). Rather
than indulging demeaning racial caricature that was becoming
popular through blackface minstrel ballads in the North, Horton's
lyric makes an inside-out joke on sonic essentialism, seeking to
reverse the racializing logic Frantz Fanon later referred to as "epidermalization." Horton takes the overdetermination of skin—the
thin material premise that supposedly confirms racial difference—
as his subject.[18]

   In the context of antebellum America, the speaker's burning
skin would have called to mind theories of racial difference,
especially environmental theories of race drawn from the myth
of Apollo's chariot charring the skins of Africans. This burning

moves from the skin to shame, as the speaker laments his dis-
comforts, "with my clothes as black as pitch, / I stink where'er
I dwell." As the emotional and spiritual argument of the poem
unfolds, Horton's humor becomes increasingly serious, and
invests Baudelaire's prescription, "Laughter is satanic," with a
kind of diasporic badness. The laughter is not Horton's—it is in
the thrown voice of a demon, a gloomy, desperate laughter that
becomes ironically humorless. Despite its ostensible superficiality, the poem turns on what would become Douglass's reasoning
in *My Bondage and My Freedom* (1855): "It was not color, but
crime, not God, but man, that afforded the true explanation for
the existence of slavery." Douglass reverses the utility of race as
the reason for slavery, putting blame back on the greed and moral
turpitude of white planters. Horton plays at the same game but
makes it funny, calling in all the affection, intimacy, disgust, and
revulsion of his comic relation with the students.[19]

Horton's meditation has the quality of lyric argument without
Douglass's logical precision. It bends temporality around the
dynamics of exhaustion and compulsion. As the question of
causality begins to coalesce around the association of the devil
and sulphur, the speaker persists through the absurdity of relief
becoming further aggravation: "Grinning I scratch and curse
the pain." The poem experiments with agitation as a temporary
salve and as a precondition for freedom. Horton's philosophical
procedures here are more informal and improvisational. In this
respect, a better reference for thinking through his methods might
be Socrates, who used scratching as a test of the temporality of
freedom in *Gorgias*: "Tell me whether a man who has an itch
and wants to scratch, and may scratch in all freedom, can pass
his life happily in continual scratching." His interlocutor Callicles
refuses to answer, seeing in the question a joke and a trap; he calls
Socrates an "odd person." Socrates' point has to do with his case
for ascetic self-examination, with the distractions of rhetoric, and
the capriciousness of worldly justice, which he was soon to suffer.
Horton amplifies this joking, dialectical suspicion of embodiment determined by the corrupt justice of slave society and white
supremacy.[20]

Instead of grimly marching to face false judgment, "Troubled with the Itch" cuts loose what the German Romantic Friedrich Schiller called the "play impulse," taking "aim at the extinction of time *in time*." Itching is play as a kind of self-scarification, and the lyric has an addictive or obsessive quality, in which the play's underlying aggression comes periodically to the surface. Anticipating Poe and Baudelaire's arguments for aesthetic "autonomy," this sense of play turns deadly radical, inchoately resisting the means-ends rationality and the regimentation of modern work-discipline of enslavement. As an exercise in style, "Troubled with the Itch" seems to take interest in exclusively aesthetic effects; it re-signifies superficiality. The poem's funkiness turns a skin condition into a political style, and makes a study in freedom by its most meaningless gestural negations.[21]

The poem flamboyantly begs attention and recognition, playing on the double significance of "excoriation" as damage to skin and public censure. Another of Horton's influences, Samuel Johnson, once described the need for fame as a kind of itch. He complains about the dawn of what he calls "The Age of Authors" (1753): "so widely is spread the itch of literary praise, that almost every man is an author." Horton's poetic ambitions confirm Johnson's suspicions about the dawning era of print, but the hope he invested in his recognition went beyond a simple self-interested exercise in vanity. The self-abasement of lyrics like "Troubled with the Itch" redounds back on the planter class that ground Horton down. His solicitation of recognition is not self-interested minstrelsy, so much as a reflection on his people's subjugation. Horton wrote through what Paul Laurence Dunbar later called "the mask that grins and lies," to draw attention to the mask of Blackness as conceived by racist whites.[22]

The humor of "Troubled with the Itch" derives from its mercurial displacement of the significance of Blackness. Racism infects the most mundane of everyday experiences, tuning Horton up into madness. He asks, with all the mugging irony of Louis Armstrong, "What did I do to be so black and blue?" And he arrives at the affective paradox Langston Hughes associated with the blues, "laughing to keep from crying." Horton's work, even in the minor key, always touches a prophetic register, joking with political and metaphysical seriousness, but also anticipating the end of slavery in this life or the next. Along this way, he set down lyrics that foretold techniques, attitudes, and theories of twentieth-century African-American culture as it faced the incompleteness of slavery's end.[23]

"Sporting on the current of levity"

In the background of all Horton's poems are the boys—the white college boys who paid him for the poems, especially his love lyrics. Somehow this man whose complaints against slavery they heard, and whose jokes about his condition they laughed at, they also hired to write poems about their girlfriends, their beloveds. The intimacy of these exchanges is no doubt extraordinary, especially because it is so difficult to see his poems as tokens of affection in any straightforward fashion. So many of Horton's love poems concern love's end, it is hard not to conclude that the boys turned to the forlorn expression of the enslaved for consolation. Though they never took enough interest to finally consummate his manumission, the boys turned again and again to his love lyrics for ministration in their own melancholia.

In this respect more than any other, Horton worked through tendencies in American popular culture. The repertoire of blackface minstrel performance was replete with the travails of Black lovers, and racial caricature haunted the popular culture of romantic love in the United States. Horton's intervention on the intimacy of the Southern planter class was both more pointed and more prophetic. At the time, minstrel performers were customarily whites, while Horton was paid directly to facilitate the courtship rituals of students at a predominantly white institution. In this arrangement, Horton's writing in response to the boys' travails spoke more immediately to the unease of the generations that would become the Confederacy. In the published work, Horton left clues about this dark crossroads of interests. In a lyric called "Heavenly Love," Horton imagines a force that could have a curative effect on the legal terrors of slavery:

> Love which can ransom every slave,
> And set the pris'ner free;
> Gild the dark horrors of the grave,
> And still the raging sea.

These reassurances must have struck Horton's Black and white readers and listeners rather differently. The reminder of love's power is dexterously advisory, just abstract enough to salve the wounded and send a more ghostly, crypto-political message to the powerful. Though it seems omnipotent, romantic liberation arrives amid catastrophe; it is defined in opposition to repression, death, and disaster. As the financial panics and territorial conflicts accelerated through the antebellum, Horton's ministrations to the boys came into sharper focus.[24]

In the absence of "heavenly love," the university offered more fleeting, physical pleasures alongside its enlightening effects. In the antebellum period, UNC functioned as a finishing school for Southern gentlemen, as the boys were expected to acquire the distinction that would confirm their place as the heirs of plantation aristocracy. Drinking played an important role in this process; Kemp Battle, an early historian of UNC, writes laconically, "The records show that some of the students were abundantly wild in the early sessions of the University." Accordingly, alcohol played an important role in Horton's interactions with the students at Chapel Hill. In the preface to *Poetical Works* (1845), he blames the students for leading him to drink:

Before the moral evil of excessive drinking had been impressed upon my mind, they flattered me into the belief that it would hang me on the wings of new inspiration, which would waft me into regions of poetical perfection. ... But I have discovered the beneficial effects of temperance and regularity, and fly as a penitent suppliant to the cell of private reflection, sorrowing that I ever had driven my boat of life so near the wrecking shoals of death, or that I was allured by the music of sirens that sing to ensnare the lovers of vanity.

However sincere this grandiose Homeric declaration is, various accounts have Horton giving in to temptation with some regularity. Battle writes of Horton that, "Like Byron, Burns, and Poe, he often quenched the divine spark with unpoetic whiskey." Setting aside the august company of poets, Battle notes that enslaved people near campus often procured alcohol for the students, an arrangement which likely complicated Horton's attempts to stay sober. He often took the moral drama of alcoholism as a prompt for poetic conceits, such as in "The Tippler to His Bottle," where he addresses the drink directly: "Thou canst impart a noble mind, / Power from my tongue flows like a river." He well knew, however, how harmfully such power ebbed and flowed.[25]

Through the 1850s, the conflict over slavery in the territories innervated the campus. Battle reports that everyday life at the university was "unsettled by the portentious rumblings of the coming war and the angry passions of political strife." He tells of incidents of extreme disorder, in which "spirituous liquor was drunk [and] the air was filled at late hours with direful uproars and furious din." In the context of this inchoate political unrest, and in place of his earlier drunken oratorical burlesques, Horton began to turn to prose, and to reconsider his relation to the students—both the influence he had over them and his legal subordination to them. In so doing, he also came to reflect, in Romantic fashion, on the more systemic, world-historical, and cosmological dimensions of these dynamics. In a short essay from the mid-1850s entitled "Individual Influence," Horton worries about the competing spiritual and secular authorities of the period, especially "the feigned power of necromancy" he saw in the Devil's influence. He was, in this increasingly heated atmosphere of crisis, also concerned about his own powers and about the range of his own vision.[26]

In 1859, Horton delivered a complexly theoretical account of the history of human knowledge entitled, "Address: On the Stream of Liberty and Science." The transcription of his speech, taken at the scene by a number of the students, is a fantastically corrupt document. The pages are bent and crumbling from the edges, filled with misspellings in several different forms of handwriting. With a kind of mature swagger, Horton's prose moves through an interdisciplinary account of progress in the West that tests the borders of coherence. He extemporizes radical shifts in focus, sometimes inside a single sentence, from history to astronomy to ethics to Enlightenment philosophy.

The address offers a Romantic theory of progress built on the coeval emergence of political freedom and secular knowledge. Its point of departure is the social function of the university. Horton argues pointedly that the students, in benefitting from the privileges of higher education, were also living the realization of the grandest contemporary principles, and so should not waste their good fortune on booze. He decries "the deplorable catastrophe spreading its veil over the blushing brow of discarded youth," and worries over "mind[s] alienated from the sphere of order and duty by sporting on the current of levity." He sets this warning against his own lack of access to education, and his distance from the figures of nineteenth-century progress, with apologies throughout: "Your unworthy speaker is far from flattering himself with the vain idea of being endowed with the best abilities." Horton betrays these apologies by flamboyantly occupying the attention of the young white Southern elites for upward of an hour, admonishing their dissipation and showing them up with theoretical insight.[27]

As with so much of the period's temperance rhetoric, the high-toned breathlessness of the speech cuts against its sobering message. Horton was not the only enslaved person to notice the ambivalent relation between drunkenness and freedom. Fugitives from slavery consistently reported slave owners' use of alcohol as a means of social control, and Black abolitionists across the North committed themselves to temperance, as part of the larger millennial project of social reform, and in particular reaction to the use of alcohol as a mode of social control during holidays on the plantation. Horton dwelt in the torqued relation between alcohol, freedom and slavery, and he meditated on the civilizational consequences of mistaking debauchery for liberation. As often that he recommended against it, however, drunkenness provided Horton another form of temporary escape from the explicitly white rhetoric of nineteenth-century progress and civilization. He appears to have had little access to or interest in the formal temperance movement, and never adopted the standard use of slavery as a metaphor for alcoholism. Likewise, Horton never drew the conventional comparison between sobriety and self-government; his idea of freedom, in his own struggles with alcohol, required more flexibility. He might as well have gone in for Baudelaire's case for drunkenness as a form of liberation, as in *Paris Spleen* (1869): "It's time to get drunk! Don't be martyred slaves of Time, get drunk; get endlessly drunk! On wine, poetry, or virtue in your style."[28]

"To stay is nothing but disgrace"

The apocalyptic liberation sought by Romantics like Baudelaire arrived soon after Horton's speech in the form of the war. Finally Horton, then in his sixties, tasted the freedom he had long imagined, in the spring of 1865, when he followed the Union Army as a contraband through North Carolina. Having long years of experience playing on the sympathy and unequal fraternity of young white men, he attracted the attention of Captain William H. S. Banks of the Ninth Michigan Cavalry, who assisted in the publication of another collection of his poetry. During this heady period, Horton composed some ninety new poems about the war, and the resulting volume, *Naked Genius* (1865), is his most substantial. The variety of this work, its frenetic humor and deeply felt melancholy, the way that anger, resentment, and disappointment color in the background, all make it nearly impossible to summarize. It is without doubt one of the most compelling documents of Civil War literature.

Some of the comic notes of the 1845 volume remain, especially in a hilarious poem about the hunt for the former president of the Confederacy, "Jefferson in a Tight Place: The Fox Is Caught." The comity Horton felt with enlisted men forms a ground bass of the book, and structures the way he perceived the possibilities presented by the war's end and emancipation. He was capable of extraordinarily charitable sentiment toward the Confederate rank and file, and could articulate a felt need for reunification.

In "Like Brothers We Meet," he tries to fix the wounds of war in familiar symbolic vocabulary: "The blaze of fraternity kindles most sweet / There's nothing more pleasing in life." He longs for a moment "[w]hen brothers no longer lament and complain." However, elsewhere in the book, he took more honest stock of the damage that had been wrought, and the work left to be done. In a poem entitled simply "Weep," Horton demands that his reader "[w]eep for the loss the country has sustained," and warns of "the gloom which still the future waits." In these moments, the grain of Horton's voice sounds the desperate cry of a freedom won in old age and the burden of its national-popular symbolic freight.

Captain Banks, who assisted Horton in the publication of this last volume, attached an advertisement seeking subscription agents to sell the book and any future publications. The language here suggests a kind of soft utopia of postwar optimism, rooted in the interracial male friendship Horton had honed across decades on campus. "Here is a grand opportunity for ENERGETIC YOUNG MEN, especially those who have become disabled by the casualties of war, to build up a fortune for themselves," it promises. Banks and Horton appear to have hoped that in the wake of the war, both those committed to the morality of abolition and those more skeptical could be convinced by his poetry that Black people were ready "to assume the grave responsibilities of that position to which they have been lately called by the proclamation of the

Backpage advertisement from George Moses Horton's Naked Genius *(Raleigh, NC: W. B. Smith: Southern Field and Fireside Book Pub. House, 1865)*

lamented Abraham Lincoln." Horton's hopes were disappointed yet again; the war did not result in the recognition he hoped, and emancipation brought with it new indignities.

When Horton arrived in the North in the aftermath of the war, he continued to work through the mode of the complaint. He did not fit the institutional requirements of free Black life in the North—he never took the temperance pledge, never thought through the constitutionalism of Walker or Douglass, and never acclimated to the bourgeois priorities of the colonization or convention movements. The lyrics he published in Philadelphia in 1866 reveal the aggravations of actually existing freedom and newly retuned fantasies of the future. In "Forbidden to Ride on the Street Cars," Horton finds Philadelphia haunted by slavery, racism, and the Civil War. The poem appeared in the November 10, 1866, issue of *The Christian Recorder*, the national print organ of the African Methodist Episcopal Church, and yet its spirituality remains politically unorthodox, as it addresses a white driver who refuses to pick up Black passengers:

> What retribution wilt though meet,
>   When summoned to the bar?
> Wilt thou not from the call retreat?
> Leave not the traveler on his feet,
>   Alone to watch the car.
>
> Like thee we bravely fought our way,
>   Before the shafts of war,
> Lest thou shouldst fall on the rebel's prey
> Why canst thou not a moment stay
>   And take one on the car?
>
> E'er long, we trust, the time will come,
>   We'll ride, however far;
> And all ride on together home,
> When freedom will be in full bloom
>   Regardless of the car!

Horton echoes the interrogative, complaining millennialism of his antebellum antislavery writing: "What retribution wilt though meet, / When summoned to the bar?" The lyric space in which the cabman comes to judgment is a kind of secular vision, and Horton's speaker demands the role of a confessor. He imagines that the driver fought in the Civil War, and pleads for sympathy: "Like thee we bravely fought our way, / Before the shafts of war."[29]

Horton responds to the speed of modern street life and its stratification along racial lines. The optimism of the poem's conclusion has a collective, messianic dimension: "We'll … all ride on together home." This secular hope suggests the fulfillment of the historical promise of the age of revolutions—"when freedom will be in full bloom"—in postbellum urban life. However, the temporal division of the complaint, between the lived experience of American life and its promised ideals, the lone traveler and the car's riders, here crystalizes around an inequality that would define Black life in the twentieth century. In its everyday, prophetic alienation, the poem predicts the coming effects of Jim Crow racism on American life: train travel was integral to the culture of the Great Migration, and train car segregation was at the heart of legalizing "separate but equal" racial segregation in the 1896 *Plessy v. Ferguson* decision.

Horton's contemporaries had noticed the streetcars as emblematic of racial modernity. Walt Whitman loved the drivers for their democratic access to city life and for their frequent connection to the Civil War, while Emerson commented on their prejudice in his essay "Fate": "The cabman is phrenologist so far: he looks in your face to see if his shilling is sure." Frances Harper, in an urgent speech from the Eleventh National Women's Rights Convention in New York in May 1866, described her own alienation in postbellum Philadelphia as framed by the de facto segregation of streetcars:

> To-day I am puzzled where to make my home. I would like to make it in Philadelphia, near my own friends and relations. But if I want to ride in the streets of Philadelphia, they send me to ride on the platform with the driver … One day I took my seat in a car,

and the conductor came to me and told me to take another seat. I just screamed "murder." The man said if I was black I ought to behave myself. I knew that if he was white he was not behaving himself. Are there not wrongs to be righted?

In her expression of exilic sentiment, in her apprehension of racism as ideologically reversible, and in her sense of the work yet to be done, Harper is close to Horton here in thinking Romantically about the moment after the war. Despite his seemingly expansive patience with white male power, Horton decided not to wait for streetcar drivers to figure out their prejudices and opted for another fantasy he had cultivated for decades: Liberia.[30]

Horton's most elaborate statement on his desire to emigrate has a fantastic and allegorical quality like his protests against slavery. "Let Us Go: A Song for the Emigrant," appears in the January 1867 issue of the American Colonization Society's publication *The African Repository*:

> Let us desert this friendless place,
> To stay is nothing but disgrace;
>   Few are our friends we know;
> LIBERIA! break from every mouth,
> To leave the North and travel South
>   Come, *Sister*, let us go!
>
> Suffer no tear to wet the eye,
> Nor heave a melancholy sigh,
>   For leaving vales of snow;
> There vegetation ever thrives,
> There corn in winter still revives,
>   Come, *Father*, let us go!
>
> LIBERIA, flow from every tongue
> For there the old are waxing young,
>   No lasting pain they know;
> Where milk and honey flow along,
> And murmers kindle into song,
>   Come, *Mother*, let us go!

This place is nothing but a strife,
Distressing all the piece of life,
     We have nothing to show;
Let others scorn me or degrade,
I'll take my hatchet and my spade,
     Come, *all*, and let us go!

Here the notes of complaint are directed at the United States as a "friendless place" that offers "nothing but a strife." The lyric builds around a notion of racial kinship. The refrain addresses the members of an unmarked but implicitly Black and abstractly collective family: "Come, *Brother*, let us go! ... Come, *Sister*, let us go! ... Come, *Father*, let us go! ... Come, *Mother*, let us go! ... Come, *all*, and let us go!" The country's name emerges from a choral, oracular voice: "LIBERIA! break from every mouth ... LIBERIA, flow from every tongue." The poem's critique of American life, composed from the vantage of a Northern, post-bellum city, centers on a resentment of possessive individualism: "This place is nothing but a strife, / Distressing all the piece of life, / We have nothing to show." The word "piece" might be a printer's mistake, a misspelling of "peace," but also calls up the problem of portioning in a United States given over completely to industrial capitalism.[31]

Horton never fit the model of the "Black Yankees" described by Black nationalist intellectual and Episcopal minister Alexander Crummell as suitable for the hard work of colonization. Like many colonizationists, Crummell's Black nationalism made eerie echoes of bourgeois and settler-colonial ambition. As early as 1862, he had already begun the redemptive work of imagining slavery and racism as educative experiences which would help along the way to Black nation-building: "we black men of America who have been trained in the severe school of affliction—we who have been educated amid the free institutions of this country" are best suited to the project of Liberian colonization.[32]

Horton had few such illusions about his experience of slavery, and his crypto-bohemian commitments were hardly likely to prove useful in the work of settlement. His poetic promises of tropical verdure run counter to Martin Delany's firsthand account of Liberia's malarial swamps: "a national Potter's Field, into which the carcass of every immigrant who ventured there, would most assuredly moulder in death." Drunk with the wine of emigrant fantasy, Horton instead asserts an Edenic vision of Africa as an alternative to the gloom of the United States. Reginald H. Pitts's recent scholarship on Horton's time in Philadelphia suggests that the poet left for Liberia on the ship *Edith Rose* at the end of 1866, with the assistance of the Pennsylvania Colonization Society. His vantage, from the first volume in 1829 to his last poems in the late 1860s, remained consistently oriented outside of the nation in which he spent the bulk of his life. Horton's work, and its essential fugitivity, cannot, however, be reduced to a geopolitical desire to escape; he seems also throughout to call for an emigration through time.[33]

Lydia Maria Child, reflecting on Horton's life story in *The Freedmen's Book* (1865), writes, "It would have been better for him if his hopes had not been so highly excited." And yet, like the irritable Poe and Baudelaire, Horton derived an extraordinary poetic practice from the excitement and disappointment of his hopes. His escape from enslavement into aesthetics, his use of the lyric as a site for contemplating the afterlife of freedom, his rewriting the canons of romantic love in the context of racial violence, and his stylization of the diaspora comprise a montage of nineteenth-century dreams deferred. In 1972, the Black Arts poet and critic Sarah Webster Fabio conjures Horton into the present, as she finds him, "transcending that hell-bound scene ... rapping on 'the man,' calling on the ancestors' spirit world." The bluesy estrangement of Horton's genius and the elaborate symbolic forms through which he expressed it became a part of the deep history of Black radical aesthetics. He signaled to his contemporaries the political and aesthetic possibilities of the lyric form. Starting in the late 1840s, a new generation of freeborn Black poets in the North would begin to work through the historic significance of their alienation in verse.[34]

3

The Seething Brain

*In which free-born poet-activists across
the North think and feel their way through
the impending crisis to the Civil War*

American abolitionists sometimes referred to the South as
the "slave Bastille" or the "American Bastille." The figure
of speech involved an uneven comparison and a political wish.
The Bastille was a prison, and slavery a system of enforced labor.
Moreover, the Bastille had been brought down in an act of revolution, whereas elites in the South were seeking to expand slavery.
The Bastille was not an asylum, despite the madness of some of
its more famous occupants. Historians would, however, associate the French Revolution with a collective insanity; the Scottish
Romantic Thomas Carlyle coined the term "eleutheromania" to
describe period radicals' obsession with freedom. In the United
States, abolitionists were widely accused of "monomania": an
implacable and destructive fixation on the end of slavery. George
Moses Horton, writing strange little love poems in Chapel Hill,
North Carolina, was no Marquis de Sade, raving and writing over-
long erotic novels from the towers of the Bastille. But Horton's
genius must have seemed like madness to some of his contemporaries. When the free Black activists of the North began to
write poetry in the late 1840s and 1850s, they took these notions
of political mania as their starting point. The Black Romantics
emphasized the rhythmic heat of their cognition; its warped

sensitivity to nature, to historical crisis, and to haunting, as the augury of historical crisis.[1]

Again, Joshua McCarter Simpson provides an excellent introductory example. Born free in Morgan County, Ohio, Simpson was bonded out as an indentured servant on the farm of two brothers, Robert and John Watson, who beat and starved him in his childhood. Later, freed of his indenture in his late teens, Simpson pursued his education, ultimately attending Oberlin College through the late 1840s. He settled in Xenia, Ohio, where he worked as an herbalist and organized with the Underground Railroad. He published two collections of antislavery lyrics, one in 1852 entitled *Original Anti-Slavery Songs*, and a longer work containing both lyrics and prose called *The Emancipation Car* in 1874. In a prefatory note to the second of these, Simpson reflected on his commitment to abolition and the enslaved:

For many years before the Rebellion, my mind was queerly impressed with the awful condition of my Nation as slaves in the South ... As soon as I could write, which was not until I was past twenty-one years old, a spirit of poetry, (which was always in me,) became revived, and seemed to waft before my mind horrid pictures of the condition of my people, and something seemed to say, "Write and sing about it—you can sing what it would be death to speak."

Simpson experienced the call to poetry as an obsession with images of Black suffering. This lingering recurrence elicits a creative impulse and a sense of Black nationalist solidarity. Simpson set out to write "vivid pictures of the great Babylon of America, American Slavery, one of the ungodliest institutions that ever disgraced the history of a country since the creation of the world."[2]

Simpson's intuition that it "would be death to speak" against slavery in the late 1830s and early 1840s was well founded. He mentions mob violence against abolitionists in the southern Ohio of his adolescence; other threats to antislavery speech included the 1836 gag rule against abolitionist petitions in Congress and the murder of abolitionist printer Elijah Lovejoy in Illinois in 1837.

The widespread, anonymous circulation of "Away to Canada" suggests that Simpson developed a deft sense of how to elude attempts to suppress antislavery activism, and how to work through the period's rapidly expanding Black and abolitionist print networks.

If it was death to speak then, he still could sing. But song, in Simpson's vision, was not just a vehicle for smuggling abolitionism across state lines; it was also a means of intensifying it, aesthetically and prophetically. Nor was it simply the physical act of singing; it was also the writing of lyrics that could move through print to be sung by others well beyond Xenia, Ohio. The facts of slavery were in evidence elsewhere in abolitionist media, but poetry could access psychological and historical registers beyond the reach of straightforward narrative. And singing could reach audiences less affected by the closely argued prose of abolition rhetoric.

Simpson was not alone among his contemporaries in feeling the call to poetry as a call to abolition and Black liberation. He belonged to what Harlem Renaissance–era critic J. Saunders Redding called the "propagandist group" of free Black poets in the antebellum North. The members of this group wrote poetry as an adjunct to other forms of activism. Their works appeared in abolitionist and Black periodicals as well as in innovatively distributed books. They performed poetry for abolitionist audiences as well as for Black community organizations and churches. None of them supported themselves exclusively through their writing. Despite their occasional success in navigating white liberal spaces, their access to the trappings of middle-class life was often stymied by racism. They shared a regional background away from the major cities of the East Coast, living mostly in Ohio, western Pennsylvania, and upstate New York, but also traveling farther west to California, farther north to Canada, or farther south into the Caribbean. They all considered, and some acted on, plans to emigrate from the United States, and the prospect of large-scale Black emigration.[3]

This group thus offers a very different version of the "inner Civil War" than that recounted in George Fredrickson's classic survey of white Northern intellectuals. Simpson's contemporaries, James Monroe Whitfield, Elymas Payson Rogers, George Boyer

Vashon, James Madison Bell, Alfred Gibbs Campbell, and Frances Ellen Watkins Harper, turned to poetry as an activist instrument, which could address the crushing psychological effects of slavery alongside its geopolitical and world-historical consequences. The lyric in particular was then in a period of extraordinary generic expansion across the Atlantic world. Poets had turned eighteenth-century efforts to collect vernacular ballads into aesthetic projects representing the new nationalisms and new political subjects of the age of revolutions. Through its myriad connections between music, speech, and interior monologue, the lyric had become an object of secular ritual performance for recently reimagined communities and elevated individuals. The free Black poets of the 1850s, unmoored from the invented traditions that characterized the rise of nationalism elsewhere, turned to the lyric to articulate their case against slavery and their contradictory affiliation with the unlettered and enslaved. This chapter follows their work across the 1850s and 1860s from where it begins in Simpson, the "mind," or more often the "brain."

Variations on the phrase, "throbbing," "burning," "crazed," and "seething brain" appear throughout Black Romantic poetry of the 1850s, locating an expressive poetic temperament forged in historical crisis. The most immediate prompt for this figure of speech was a passage from Ralph Waldo Emerson's essay "The Transcendentalist" (1849):

> Our American literature and spiritual history are, we confess, in the optative mood; but whoso knows these seething brains, these admirable radicals, these unsocial worshippers, these talkers who talk the sun and moon away, will believe that this heresy cannot pass away without leaving its mark.

Emerson endorses the millennial "heresy" of his contemporaries in the posture of bemused fellow traveler. He does not make clear the connection between abolition in the North and "the optative mood" of his contemporaries. Nor does he mention phrenology explicitly, the racist pseudoscience that nonetheless attracted the widespread interest of antebellum reformers. Emerson borrows the phrase "seething brains" from Shakespeare, who had written in *A Midsummer Night's Dream*, "Lovers and madmen have such seething brains." By the Romantic period, thinkers like Emerson frustrated with the cold system-building elitism of the Enlightenment began to imagine lovers and madmen as the new mythic heroes of democracy. In this vision, "seething brains," subject to states of heightened emotional intensity and irrationality, were integral to and productive of revolutions both personal and political.[4]

The lyrics of the Black Romantics took the temperature of their moment, checking its revolutionary heat, and then turned it up. The songs of the "propagandist group" emphasized emotional cognition, in opposition to racist notions of Black hypersentimentality and the systemic reduction of Black people to what Hortense Spillers called "flesh." They focus on the brain as a machine for processing psychic pain, a place where screams were recorded and resignified. It also functions as an organ for music-making; the Black Romantics represented cognition as rhythmic, and music as ideological. The seething brain also draws its heat from nature, and works through signs from nature that the so-called "white republic" had run afoul of natural law. The brain was thus an instrument for tuning the spiritual, both for mourning the enslaved or abolitionist dead and for anticipating the direction of the spirit of the age. The free-born Black poets of the 1850s hoped the expressions of their seething brains might provoke the long delayed, but now increasingly "irrepressible conflict." They also hoped to communicate, through song, across the divide of freedom and slavery, literate and illiterate. Their work makes up a network of nervous reaction to the atrocities and political tumult of the Civil War era, lamenting the present and calling down God's vengeance on the powerful, in new anthems and epics for nations not yet ratified.[5]

The Music of "Eleutheromania"

The postures and performances of Romantic madness carried additional risks for free Black people of the antebellum North.

While they may have felt a kind of righteous, insurrectionary democratic rage rising up from within, they also had to prove to white authorities their fitness for self-government. The question of their sanity was not merely a medical or spiritual or even political matter; it was also the subject of one of the period's most outrageous public debates about scientific racism. The 1840 Census purported to show that a disproportionate number of free people of color in the North were "insane" or "lunatics." This "discovery" was widely noted in prominent periodicals like the *Southern Literary Messenger*, as well as on the floor of Congress by John C. Calhoun. The data suggested that Black people were ill-equipped for freedom, that it was deleterious to their mental health, and that they required the paternal influence of planter-class cultivation. The independent statistician who first pointed out this phenomenon, Edward Jarvis, later attempted to correct the findings when he discovered that Black lunatics had been counted in towns with no Black people, and that an implausible myriad of disabilities had been attributed to the same Black individuals:

> These disorders exist there in a state of abstraction, and, fortunately for humanity, where they are said to be present, there are no people to suffer from them. But in others the entire coloured population are overwhelmed with these calamities, and now and then they are all afflicted, not with one disease only, but with both blindness and insanity.

Jarvis's correction of this absurd, stigmatizing, and obliterating situation had little effect; John Quincy Adams's efforts in Congress to have the findings revised were stymied by Calhoun. The premise of free Black lunacy fit too conveniently with longstanding associations of democracy, political radicalism, and madness: the "eleutheromania" of revolution and the "monomania" of abolition.[6]

Moreover, scientific racism from the late eighteenth century forward had held that people of African descent were given to extremes of sentimentality. Its proponents relied on convenient assumptions about Black people as disproportionately embodied (thus given to manual labor) and lacking in rationality (thus ill-suited to self-government). In "Diseases and Peculiarities of the Negro Race" (1851), Dr. Samuel Cartwright provided an ostensibly authoritative physiological account of Black racial difference on the issue of sentimentality. He draws the connection to Black music as a way of making his point:

> From the diffusion of the brain, as it were, into the various organs of the body, in the shape of nerves to minister to the senses, everything, from the necessity of such a conformation, partakes of sensuality, at the expense of intellectuality. Thus music is a mere sensual pleasure with the negro. There is nothing in his music addressing the understanding; it has melody, but no harmony; his songs are mere sounds, without sense or meaning—pleasing the ear, without conveying a single idea to the mind; his ear is gratified by sound, as his stomach is by food.

Cartwright does not consider that he might lack access to the intellectual content of Black music, or that that intellectual content might be less divided from sensuality than in Western music. He also fails to wonder whether Black sensuality might form a response to the alienations of slavery and racism. Finally, he relies on an unsustainable and invidious distinction between mind and body that Black Romantic poets would take as explicitly political and exploit to activist effect.[7]

As a Southerner, Cartwright knew the vernacular culture of Black music in slavery; he may have understood the growing importance of music in abolition organizing as well. His remarks make an early entry in the long history of white concern about the enervating and potentially insurgent effects of Black music. Antebellum Black artists and intellectuals had to navigate these prejudices carefully, but they had also come to understand the central role of music in the cultural politics of race. Famous vocalists like Elizabeth Taylor Greenfield ("The Black Swan") and Susan Paul's Juvenile Choir of Boston played key roles in abolition organizing and Black institution-building. Collections of antislavery songs had begun to emerge across the 1840s, including Jairus

Lincoln's *Anti-Slavery Melodies: For the Friends of Freedom* (1843), George W. Clark's *The Liberty Minstrel* (1844), and William Wells Brown's *The Anti-Slavery Harp; A Collection of Songs for Anti-Slavery Meetings* (1848). More literary experiments with lyric form by Black poets like Horton's *Poetical Works* (1845) and Frances Ellen Watkins's (later Harper) *Forest Leaves* (1847) had also appeared before Cartwright's patently false assertions about the lack of intellectual content in Black music.

In response to racism like Cartwright's, the Black poets of the 1850s wrote dissonant and revolutionary lyrics, aimed at both sensuality and intellect. That is, they marshaled poetical and musical forms to contest the limitations set on them by white racism, and took that as the point of departure for visionary political aesthetics. They explored the antiracist effects of mixing cerebral and musical registers, what Emerson had referred to as "metre-making argument." They continued to work through the ballad and hymnal forms that occupied Horton. But they also began to write in marching four-beat tetrameter lines, and they used this talky, martial regimentation to expand interior monologues into epic narrative visions keyed to a time of war. The tetrameter appears so consistently across the Black poetry of this period as to sound with what Langston Hughes later found in jazz: "the eternal tom-tom beating in the Negro soul—the tom-tom of revolt against weariness in a white world." The seething brains of the Black Romantic poets were not, in other words, just seething with heat, but also with a rhythmic pressure, a kind of four-on-the-floor intensity aimed at making a dance at the meeting of mind and body.[8]

Mostly this first generation of Black Romantic writers focused on the seething brains of their Black contemporaries, but they sometimes took aim at the duller minds of racist whites. Elymas Payson Rogers turned the racialized science of the brain into a critique of the failures of white elites in his long poem, *The Repeal of the Missouri Compromise Considered* (1854). An allegory of the breakup of the 1820 arrangement that had kept slavery territorially confined, the poem imagines sectional conflict as a slapstick phrenological exam:

"I want the land," was Freedom's cry;
And Slavery answered, "So do I!
By all that's sacred, I declare
I'll have my just and lawful share.
The Northern check should glow with shame
To think to rob me of my claim:
And if my claim you dare deny,
I'll knock the Union into pi."
The Northern faces did not glow,
Because they were composed of dough:
But such a tall and horrid threat
Their equilibrium upset.
"O gracious heavens!" the patriot said,
As nervously he shook his head,
And quickly moved his tangled hair
To feel the bump of firmness there:
But how distracted was his mind,
When searching long he could not find
This stately organ of the brain,
Nor could the mystery explain,
Or make a fit apology
For this freak of phrenology.
The reason why the bump was low
Was it was fashioned out of dough;
And Slavery's bold and fearless threat
Had crushed the lofty organ flat.

In a cutting joke, Rogers has the white Northerner give himself a phrenological exam and find himself wanting courage and conviction. As Emerson hinted above, many Americans, and especially reformers, were consulting phrenologists in the antebellum decades to see what the bumps of their skulls said about their propensities, but also to contemplate their place within a systemic, though patently bogus, account of racial difference. Rogers finds white Northern politicians suffering from a "freak of phrenology," taking them to task both for the silliness of their scientific racism and the weakness of their political vision. The silly bounce of the poem's rhythm makes the poet's voice sound like the straight man in a comic scenario: "The reason why the bump was low / Was it was fashioned out of dough." This metrical clunk made Rogers's work popular, memorable, and funny to contemporary audiences. In a brief preface, he notes that he had no intention of publishing the poem when he wrote it, that he had initially meant it exclusively as a performance text, but audiences had prevailed upon him to make it available in print. The poem was thus a tool for everyday, vernacular political education.[9]

Rogers returned to the Missouri Compromise in a decisive moment, between its repeal by the Kansas-Nebraska Act in 1854 and the Supreme Court ruling it unconstitutional in the Dred Scott case. His satire targets the shortsightedness and cupidity of free labor and slaveholding interests in territorial disputes. He also understood the violence of Bleeding Kansas, as catastrophic and pivotal:

> 'Tis done! the fearful die is cast,
> The dreadful rubicon is past;
> Nor will the deadly strife be o'er
> 'Till Freedom bleeds at every pore.

Despite this apocalyptic prophecy of imperial crisis, with its deeply surreal terror, Rogers read the poem in public venues, especially churches, around New England in the mid-1850s. Like his contemporaries among the poets, Rogers had been educated in white liberal institutions, in his case the Oneida Institute in upstate New York, with the assistance of wealthy white abolitionist Gerrit Smith. He went on to become the pastor of the Presbyterian Plane Street Church in Newark, and it was in this position that he performed his cartoonish critique of white political ineptitude. William Wells Brown described Rogers in terms that indicate the reach of phrenological thinking across the political spectrum: "Mr. Rogers was of unmixed race, genteel in appearance, forehead large and well-developed, fine figure, and pleasing in his manners." Setting aside for a moment the genteel racialism of this portrait, its buttoned-down tone hardly corresponds with the hilarity or the intensity of

Rogers's poetry. His contemporaries among the poets increasingly let loose the effusions of their seething brains, as the years of the 1850s ticked by, and the impending crisis became increasingly pressurized.[10]

"Thy song of fiercest passion sing"

The Black Romantics used the lyric to articulate their alienation, to make it an aesthetically accessible object of community-building and radical organizing. Of his contemporaries, James Monroe Whitfield was the most preoccupied with registering the psychic cost of the impending crisis around slavery. Born free in New Hampshire, Whitfield lived most of his life in Buffalo, New York, where he balanced his poetic ambitions and his activist commitments with his work as a barber. From those inauspicious circumstances, he produced the most psychologically rich Black verse of the nineteenth century—his work anticipates the "information and energy" Audre Lorde would later find among the "uses of anger." The poems in Whitfield's only collection, *America and Other Poems* (1853), focus on his sense of isolation as a free Black man yearning for his people's freedom. He takes the conventional loneliness of the lyric poet as a political problem. "The Misanthropist" begins:

> In vain thou bid'st me strike the lyre,
> 	And sing a song of mirth and glee,
> Or, kindling with poetic fire,
> 	Attempt some higher minstrelsy;
> In vain, in vain! for every thought
> 	That issues from this throbbing brain,
> Is from its first conception fraught
> 	With gloom and darkness, woe and pain.

Every aspect of this poem is extravagantly estranged. Whitfield refuses the impetus to musicality in lines which nonetheless pulsate: "In vain thou bid'st me strike the lyre." His Elizabethan contractions and complicated syntax seem to oppose the present on principle, disappointed with actually existing democracy. "Poetic fire" here encodes the historical sources of its inspiration in "gloom and darkness, woe and pain." The rhythms of thought, vexed "from its first conception," express at once rage and its suppression. Whitfield exercises sincerity prohibited to the enslaved, whom Frederick Douglass had said, "sing the most pathetic sentiment in the most rapturous tone, and the most rapturous sentiment in the most pathetic tone." This formula certainly applies to certain tonal effects in Horton, but Whitfield's Romanticism, with its urgency of expression and comparatively reduced constraints, had different effects.[11]

Daphne A. Brooks gets closer to Whitfield's procedures when she finds nineteenth-century Black cultural actors "translating alienation into self-actualizing performance"; the poet elaborates this premise in an almost encyclopedic way, his work becoming a compendium of alienations energized and mobilized by his "throbbing brain." Like any good Romantic, Whitfield recalls childhood intimations of his exquisite adult isolation:

> When other children passed the hours
>   In mirth, and play, and childish glee,
> Or gathering the summer flowers
>   By gentle brook, or flowery lea,
> I sought the wild and rugged glen
>   Where Nature, in her sternest mood,
> Far from the busy haunts of men,
>   Frowned in the darksome solitude.

Whitfield finds his "darksome solitude" reflected in nature, and this subtle reversal of devalued Blackness becomes the starting point of revolutionary consciousness. As the poem draws to a conclusion, Whitfield morbidly avows his sense of alienation, even within an intra-racial caste system, as a kind of epitaphic symbol: "And let them on my tombstone trace, / Here lies the Pariah of his race." At this extreme of death-driven, lonely misanthropy, Whitfield reaches for connection to a more generalized condition of subalternity, and reaches outward for transnational solidarity with oppressed classes elsewhere. Later in the volume, this poet, who is so flamboyantly divided from himself and others, includes poems on the occasion of Black churches' founding and poems which memorialize Black and white leaders in the fight against slavery. He draws connections between the gathering storm of US sectional conflict and the end of slavery in the British colonies, as well as the recent history of European revolutions. His lyrics call out from his "darksome solitude" to distant collectives. His cynicism is never simply individual, but instead somehow a gesture in the service of collectivities.[12]

Whitfield's alienation, his status as "the Pariah of his race" and his preoccupation with the seething brain, had to do with his work as a barber—a profession his contemporaries rarely fail to mention, often with a worried disdain. Whitfield had come from a family of Black religious leaders in Boston; his uncles on his mother's side were well-known Baptist ministers Thomas and Nathaniel Paul. Later assessments of his achievements often imply that Whitfield's work demeaned him. Black nationalist Martin Delany writes of Whitfield's work:

> James M. Whitfield, of Buffalo, New York, though in an humble position, (for which we think he is somewhat reprehensible), is one of the purest poets in America. He has written much for different newspapers; and, by industry and application—being already a good English scholar—did he but place himself in a favorable situation in life, would not be second to John Greenleaf Whittier, nor the late Edgar A. Poe.

Delany takes a hard view of the poet's day job. Romantic ideology tended to celebrate poets in lowly occupations, but Whitfield was not a "poet at the plow" in the tradition of John Clare, Robert Burns, or even Horton. The profession consigned him to what might imprecisely be called the lower middle class. Whitfield was among the most "class conscious" of the period's Black poets; his anxiety about his station, and the obscure language in which he articulated it, represents an acute instance of the racialized estrangement of early American labor politics which historians like Eric Foner, Alexander Saxton, and David Roediger have explored in detail. Located somewhere between the emasculated service work often reserved for Black men and the ennobled labor of the artisan, barbering afforded Whitfield a modicum of the independence and perspective lionized by white Jacksonian democratic culture. The barbershop functioned as a space for informal political conversation; its familiarity allowed Whitfield to sell his book to customers he found sympathetic to his views. Barbershops were also important sites of informal music making. Delany's appraisal of Whitfield as "one of the purest poets in America" parallels Poe and Baudelaire's preoccupations with "pure poetry," but Whitfield never sought to extricate his work from the politics of his moment. Its purity was in its seeking liberation. *America and Other Poems* is dedicated to Delany, and the two found in one another a deep, shared commitment to Black nationalism.[13]

In the prefatory note to his only full collection of poetry, Whitfield quotes a line from the eighteenth-century British poet Thomas Gray, promising to "singeth sweetly, and giveth forth the conceptions of his soul in 'words that breathe and thoughts that burn.'" A poem entitled "Yes! Strike Again that Sounding String" makes clear how Whitfield understood the function of these aesthetic priorities. It is another one-sided dialogue about music and the pain of consciousness in the middle of historical transformation. It is also the period's most condensed statement of revolutionary Black lyric theory. Judging by its publication history, the poem was popular among the abolition intelligentsia; it first appeared in the March 15, 1850 issue of *The North Star*, then in *America and Other Poems* (1853), again in an advertisement for the book in the July 15, 1853 issue of *Frederick Douglass' Paper*, and later in Delany's *Blake, or the Huts of America*, during its serialization in *The Anglo-African Magazine* from November 1861 to May 1862. The poem's rhetorical staging is simple enough; the speaker addresses a singer, encouraging and directing him:

> Yes! strike again that sounding string,
>> And let the wildest numbers roll;
> Thy song of fiercest passion sing—
>> It breathes responsive to my soul!

The poem's quatrains echo the musicality of its subject, but also retain a sense of the lyric poem as somehow more interior, more intellectual, and more deliberative than song. This musical conversation cuts against John Stuart Mill's definition of poetry as soliloquy, as "*overheard*": "Poetry is feeling confessing itself to itself, in moments of solitude." By contrast, Whitfield's lyric is half of a call-and-response exchange, an essential form of African diasporic communal culture, here set down in the most meticulously learned but enraged poetic syntax. When Delany interpolated the poem into his novel *Blake, or the Huts of America,* it appears as the work of the Cuban poet Placido, who sings it with eight vocal accompanists and an orchestra, on the eve of a fictional slave revolt.[14]

The speaker elaborates a preference for deep feelings, expressed in "the wildest numbers": a "song of fiercest passion." He argues, counterintuitively, against pastoral music, the "whisperings of the gentle breeze," because it agitates his distemper:

> If thou wouldst soothe my burning brain,
>> Sing not to me of joy and gladness;
> 'T will but increase the raging pain,
>> And turn the fever into madness.

Claiming that happy music enrages him further by contradicting his characteristic misanthropy, the speaker demands emotional mimesis, "responsive" to his "soul." The extra beats on the abstract nouns, "gladness" and "madness," underline the irregularity of the speaker's reasoning. Whitfield's "burning brain" condenses the conventional division of emotion and logical calculation—he is never so overcome that the dialogue breaks down. Instead, anger makes the basis for an aesthetic theory in the "wildest numbers."

The burning brain becomes the storehouse of images of misery and criminality, then the seat of creative action. Whitfield puts anger, rather than misery, at the center of the cultural politics of Black music, and demands lyrics of revolutionary violence:

> Sing of the battle's deadly strife,
>   The ruthless march of war and pillage,
> The awful waste of human life,
>   The plundered town, the burning village!
>
> Of streets with human gore made red,
>   Of priests upon the altar slain;
> The scenes of rapine, woe and dread,
>   That fill the warriors' horrid train.
>
> Thy song may then an echo wake,
>   Deep in this soul, long crushed and sad,
> The direful impressions shake
>   Which threaten now to drive it mad.

Despite the tone of indignation, these lurid scenes have no specific setting, nor any obvious racial content, and thus their threat to slave ownership and white supremacy is veiled. Instead the poem follows a bad mood that develops into a demand for judgment. Whitfield's messianic rhetoric points back to the violent persecutions of seventeenth-century Protestantism, the Terror of the French Revolution and the Napoleonic Wars, and the slave revolts in the New World, but only in the most ambiguous terms. The urgency of his demand innervates the abstract historical scenery, so that its "echo" of Black rage augurs the violence of the Civil War. At the same time, its abstraction outstretches the historical facts of the mid-nineteenth century—the judgment he envisions has not yet come to pass.[15]

"A wailing comes upon the breeze"

In the May 4, 1855 issue of *Frederick Douglass' Paper*, an abstruse essay appeared entitled "The Progress of the Mind in Self-

Investigation." Its author, George Boyer Vashon, was at the time working as a professor of Latin at New York Central College. A year earlier, he had published the first epic poem in what would become the African-American literary tradition, "Vincent Ogé," about a compromised hero of the Haitian Revolution. Vashon had acquired a reputation as one of the most sophisticated Black intellectuals of the abolition movement. Like Horton's "Address" and Whitfield's "throbbing brain," Vashon's essay offers an instance of Black Romanticism in the speculative mode that connected Black interiority to a sublimely vast account of world history. Vashon summarizes "thrice ten centuries" of human thought, and points to racial injustice as the impediment to its universal development:

> When the principles of mind shall all be fully unfolded, and human nature held up as an easily-read scroll to all who are partakers of it, then will he respect right in his brother which he now but too heedlessly and ignorantly tramples upon,—then will he establish governments just in their enactments and righteous in their decisions,—then will he worship his God, not as the creation of his fears, or the sanctioner of his iniquities, but as a being whom his reason demands that he should reverence.

Charting the limits of existing Romantic idealism, Vashon suggests that the history of the human mind is headed toward rights-based recognition across divisions of race, class, or nationality. Vashon's readers would have had little difficulty attributing the "fears" and "iniquities" which stand in the way. They might not, however, have shared his certitude in the messianic arrival of equality, given the expansion of Southern slavery through the early 1850s. Ever the consummate intellectual, even in the middle of the impending crisis, Vashon insisted on the mind's relation to nature and spirituality as the motivating dynamics of transformative social change.[16]

Throughout his career, Vashon contributed a wide range of prose pieces to abolitionist and African-American periodicals, but he consistently returned to poetry as a form of cultural and political practice. He even translated Schiller from the German for publication. His epic poem "Vincent Ogé," which first appeared in Julia W. Griffiths's collection *Autographs for Freedom* (1853–54) alongside work by Whitfield, among others, articulates in verse the relation between the mind, nature, and the spiritual history of revolution. When his hero Ogé, having been in Paris in 1789, returns to Cap-Français, Haiti, and begins to organize among the freemen there, Vashon depicts them as overcome with a collective desire for revolt:

> They speak of wrongs they have received—
> Of freemen, of their rights bereaved;
> And as they pondered o'er the thought
> Which in their minds so madly wrought,
> Their eyes gleamed as the lightning's flash,
> Their words seemed as the torrent's dash
> That falleth, with a low, deep sound,
> Into some dark abyss profound,—
> A sullen sound that threatens more
> Than other torrents' louder roar.

Rather than describe Ogé's revolutionary conspiracy in documentary detail, Vashon turns to metaphor. The minds of the men, as they contemplate their circumstances, become a cloud in which revolutionary storm gathers: "Their eyes gleamed as the lightning's flash, / Their words seemed as the torrent's dash." In a reversal of the racial Gothic, the "dark abyss" into which the rains fall becomes a reservoir of unrequited African diasporic political sentiment. These connections between mind, nature, and revolution work through what the British critic John Ruskin called "pathetic fallacy"—the Romantic tendency to identify human emotion with natural phenomena. In his essay on "The Progress of Mind," Vashon recognized such misidentifications as part of a historical process beginning with "the gibber of the idiot, the maniac's rave, [and] the natural prompting of the peasants' thought." He writes this into Ogé's story to illuminate its utility as organizing rhetoric for collectives of seething brains. The anger of Ogé's men becomes, in its sympathy with nature, not blinding or individuating, but clarifying and unifying.[17]

Ogé's defeat at the hands of French colonial forces was an odd place to start the African-American epic tradition. For Vashon, the act of poetically redeeming Ogé's failure, and of resurrecting him for a new generation of Black leaders to contemplate, is as important as the specifics of the model he provides. The poem ends with an encomium promising its fallen hero a place in the cultural memory of democratic radicalism:

> Thy coming fame, Ogé! is sure;
> Thy name with that of L'Ouverture,
> And all the noble souls that stood
> With both of you, in times of blood,
> Will live to be the tyrant's fear—
> Will live, the sinking soul to cheer!

Vashon reassures Ogé's spirit that he has made his mark on history. He borrows this insistence from Wordsworth's address "To Toussaint L'Ouverture": "There's not a breathing of the common wind / That will forget thee." Whitfield uses the same gambit, and insists on making music of his subjects' names in poems for John Quincy Adams and Joseph Cinqué. Vashon's choice was a more complicated test of the moral and political capacity of Black revolutionary thinking. Ogé's new poetic afterlife would quickly get caught in the contradictions of the period's Black nationalisms.[18]

After his own sojourn in Haiti, disappointed by the emergence of the authoritarian Emperor Faustin Soulouque, Vashon's life would become an argument against emigration in an 1854 note in *Frederick Douglass' Paper*: "Our people ... need not migrate, nor trans-migrate, to become an honorable, as well as useful people." Despite this conviction, his epic of diasporic leadership would go on to support the opposing case. In 1857, Bishop James Theodore Holly quoted the above lines on Ogé's fame in his plea for emigration to Haiti, *A Vindication of the Capacity of the Negro Race for Self-Government and Civilized Progress, as Demonstrated by the Historical Events of the Haytian Revolution; and Subsequent*

Acts of that People Since Their National Independence. Holly casts "Oje" as a "right hearted, noble and generous man" who made an "error of the head." He also makes the case for Soulouque's empire, which had so disappointed Vashon: "There is far more security for personal liberty and the general welfare of the governed, among the monarchical negroes of Hayti ... than in this bastard democracy."[19]

Unlike Holly, Vashon came to see the potential of the "bastard democracy" with a committed and Byronic irony. Black intellectuals of the 1850s grew certain of the reckoning on the horizon, but their disagreements about the prospect of emigration indicate a deeper uncertainty about what the aftermath of slavery might, would, or should look like. Vashon articulated his careful, prophetic sense of its possibility through poetic connections between psychological pain, sympathetic nature, and the history of revolutionary change. Vashon's work as an activist through the period was energetic and optimistic, even as his work as a poet held out a more studied and nuanced melancholy. In the late 1850s, he moved back to Pittsburgh to work in that city's Black public schools, and in the wake of the Civil War he was involved in the Pennsylvania State Equal Rights League's legislative efforts on behalf of the freed people. His poetry from this same period continues to focus on the politically alienated relations between the mind, nature, and spirituality.

In "A Life-Day" (1866) Vashon tells a tragic tale of interracial love, of an unnamed young enslaved woman who nurses her sick white master back to health, marries him, and then is sold back into slavery after his death. The poem figures the protagonist's arc allegorically as the parts of a single day, "Morning," "Noon," and "Night." He depicts her as enmeshed in the environment while caring for her master in the "Morning" section: "Her sweet smile is the sunshine bright / That floods the landscape wide with light." In the "Night" section, her identification with nature multiplies her pain:

> A wailing comes upon the breeze,
> That sighs amid the orange trees;
> And she is there, and all alone,
> Oh, linger, night!

Here Vashon turns to another Romantic trope, the "correspondent breeze," a classic instance of the pathetic fallacy, to represent the entanglement of slavery, sentiment, and the natural order. The striving toward universality he finds in "The Progress of Mind" takes the form here of a passionately ecological antislavery. The mind of nature thrums with desperation for the woman, but also a quiet, knowing, and more universal hope. Vashon insists in a note to the poem that it is based on real-life events, and that the unnamed judge who oversaw the woman's re-enslavement "has recently figured in President Johnson's plan of reconstruction." For Vashon, the progress of mind, in its heated sympathies with nature, with spirituality, and with Black collectivity, did not end with the Civil War.[20]

The "Aliened American" Breakdown

Looking back on the decades in the prefatory note to his 1874 collection, Joshua McCarter Simpson took a certain pride in the "flashes of prophecies" he had made and then lived to see come true. Like many of his contemporaries, Simpson's prophetic posture obligated him to an audience he knew and another he imagined, hoping to vouchsafe his dreams of freedom for what Walt Whitman called "generations hence." The Black Romantics embedded their speculations and interventions in lyrics, with the idea that rhythms would move across the regional, racial, and educational differences of contemporary audiences, and penetrate the consciousness of their readers and listeners more deeply. In this effort, Simpson was not the only one of his contemporaries to borrow flagrantly from popular song.[21]

Abolitionist lyricists often took on Samuel Smith's 1831 anthem "America," later known as "My Country, 'Tis of Thee." Scores of versions of this song appeared in antislavery and African-American periodicals across the antebellum decades, each one playing on the cognitive dissonance of singing about slavery to a patriotic tune. The movement, in "My Country 'Tis of Thee," between individual and collective, its sketch of the relations between music, land, and

freedom, all appealed to the heated brains of abolitionist radicals. One version, entitled "A Parody" and credited to "the Bangor
Mechanic," was repeatedly reprinted by the abolition press from
1838 to 1861. This version matches the rhythm of the original,
beginning:

> My country! 'tis for thee,
> Dark land of slavery,
> For thee, I weep;
> Land where the slave has sighed,
> Land, where he toiled and died,
> To serve a tyrant's pride—
> For thee, I weep.

"The Bangor Mechanic" touched a nerve, and several of the Black
Romantics took their turns at Smith's song. Whitfield's long poem
"America," from his 1853 volume, begins with a satiric revision
of Smith as well:

> AMERICA, it is to thee,
> Thou boasted land of liberty,—
> It is to thee I raise my song,
> Thou land of blood, and crime, and wrong.

Whitfield takes closer aim at the hypocrisy of Smith's "sweet freedom's song" and the bogus chromatic resolution of his "liberty." He
goes on to explore the failed promise of the American Revolution;
the parallels between Biblical, Christian, and US chattel slavery;
and finally the likelihood that "patriot blood" will spill again as
punishment for the sin of slavery. Here again, Whitfield turns his
alienation from song into lyric poem, cataloguing the sources
of his intuition of a historical reckoning on the horizon. In this
instance, his seething brain achieves a synoptic vision, a prophecy
about the distance between real and ideal democracy, scored by its
echo of Smith's anthem.[22]

Simpson's version seems at first to hem closely both to the
original and to the widely reprinted "Parody." His "Song of the

'Aliened American' " first appears in his retrospective postwar collection, *The Emancipation Car* (1874), but it was very likely written before the war. The word "aliened" in the title draws ironically on the Jeffersonian concept of "inalienable rights" and Roger B. Taney's 1857 decision in the Dred Scott case, which represented descendants of the enslaved as "alien" and thus not citizens. Taking the contradiction of the "aliened American" as its starting point, the song begins by simply substituting "slavery" for the original's "liberty":

> My country, 'tis of thee,
> Dark land of Slavery,
>   In thee we groan.
> Long have our chains been worn—
> Long has our grief been borne—
> Our flesh has long been torn,
>   E'en from our bones.

This lyric certainly fulfills Simpson's aesthetic intention to "change the flow" of popular song. The movement between possessive individualism—"my country"—to national collectivity—"to thee we sing"—in Smith's original becomes collective Black suffering in Simpson—"in thee we groan." National integration devolves into torn flesh.[23]

In contrast to Taney's attenuated, legalistic, and dehumanizing conception of Black people as alien, Simpson works through the choral voicing of the first-person plural "we," orchestrating the exilic dissonance of period Black nationalisms. He turns to a metaphor of communal awakening:

> No! No! the time has come,
> When we must not be dumb,
>   *We must awake.*
> We now "Eight Millions Strong,"
> Must strike sweet freedom's song
> And plead ourselves, our wrong—
>   Our chains must break.

Sleep appears here as a figure of political inactivity. Simpson makes his song a kind of internal alarm clock, a collective self-awakening. He uses the term "strike" to mark the physical act of music-making, suggesting song can substitute for the violence Black abolitionists found endorsed in Byron. The lyric becomes a tool for breaking chains, and for unifying Black people. Simpson refers to a Biblical scene in Acts (16:25–31), in which Paul and Silas, imprisoned in Philippi, sing a prayer to God, and an earthquake breaks their chains and destroys the prison. The story of Paul and Silas became a popular spiritual entitled "Paul and Silas Bound in Jail." The Black Romantics also hoped to call down earthquakes with their songs, but, much more than the spirituals, they focused on the problem of fusing psychic interiority with political and historical change.[24]

The metaphor of political complacency as a kind of national sleep appeared across transatlantic Romanticism, for instance in Blake's *Jerusalem* (1804–20), which calls for a national uprising: "England! awake! awake! awake! / Jerusalem thy Sister calls!" But for Simpson and his contemporaries, collective dreaming also offered a window onto future freedoms. The archives of early African-American literature and culture contain myriad examples of dream interpretation as a form of political theory by proxy, a kind of abolitionist unconscious. In a short prose piece collected in *The Emancipation Car*, Simpson records three dreams he had in 1860, each auguring the onset of the Civil War. The first involves a map peddler trying to sell Simpson a map of the United States, all in red, and cut in "two from West to East." The second features an enormous, "queer looking" furnace fought over by two armies of white people, reframing sectional conflict as dispute over the control of Black labor. In the third, Simpson contemplates the coming of a massive storm:

> An awful black cloud over-shadowed the whole continent. Men and women were out conjecturing the meaning of the dark day and the black cloud. I thought some one said to me "Mc. come out and look, and tell us what is going to happen." [...] I said to those standing by, "there will be a Universal Storm. It will extend all over the United States."

Joshua McCarter Simpson, undated, Norris Schneider
Collection, Ohio Historical Society

Simpson takes on the role of a dream interpreter and an omen reader, linking his Romantic ambitions with what Du Bois calls the "bards" of diasporic slave culture. Biographical notes on Simpson often suggest that he worked both as a Christian minister and as an "herbalist" or "herb doctor." He is listed in the Oberlin College "Catalogue and Record of Colored Students, 1835–62" as having "taught & preached in Zanesville" while also working as a "grocer & provision dealer." The only extant photo of him, arrayed in books and scientific apparatuses, suggests the range and modernity of his intellectual ambition. His music was also a form of vernacular political education, and a kind of medicine for curing ailments of seething brains suffering from nightmares of history.[25]

"Final Abolition"

The monomania of abolitionists and the eleutheromania of the enslaved were realized and displaced in the war years. As war broke out between the states and then wore on, the Black Romantics sought to reconcile their prophecies of God's vengeance on the slaveholders' republic with the grim realities of news from the front and through the grapevine. The figurative promises of the seething brain, that it could resolve the bodily objectification of Black people, that it could rationally direct Black historical outrage, and that it could draw on nature in revolutionary music, all seemed near fulfillment. The Black Romantics began to tally the deadly toll of the war and the many thousands gone in the wake of slavery. As they contemplated the prospect that the war might not yield freedom, their work increasingly took an interest in the question of haunting. The Black Romantic mind, in that singular, generalizing way, became subject to ghostly presences and horrific visions. The work of James Madison Bell and Frances Ellen Watkins Harper during and immediately after the war especially articulated this emphasis. Bell shared a great deal with his contemporaries in the abolition movement: like Douglass, he worked as a plasterer; like Simpson and Rogers, he served as a church leader; like Vashon and Simpson, he lived in Ohio, and benefited from the liberality of Oberlin College in his education (in his case, attending the Oberlin-associated Cincinnati High School for Colored People). Bell was involved in the most explicitly revolutionary actions of the abolition movement, especially from 1854 to 1860, when he moved his family to Chatham, Ontario, and organized alongside John Brown. Like Whitfield, he spent the war years in Northern California. During this period, Bell wrote the work for which he was best known, a series of long poems in response to the Civil War and Reconstruction, which he regularly performed in public, and which set the events of the period against the backdrop of vast, spectral historical landscapes.

In a long poem entitled *The Day and the War*, Bell marked the first anniversary of the Emancipation Proclamation; he performed it at Platt's Hall in Cincinnati in January 1864. In this work, he calls for "final abolition" as the outcome of the war, thinking with Douglass and others about the necessity of ensuring Black freedom in the chaos:

> If Slavery lives, the Union dies;
> And if the Union's e'er restored,
> 'Twill be when Freedom is secured;
> And liberty, man's rightful due,
> Is not proscribed by grade nor hue.
> Hence he that would avert the doom,

> And rescue from sepulchral gloom,
> His freedom, must, with sword in hand,
> March 'gainst the slavery of this land.

Though the work's prophetic aims lie close, with the end of slavery on the horizon, Bell still works through the "sepulchral gloom" that Black writers had used to characterize slavery and racism for decades. Likewise his references to violence put symbolism —"sword in hand"—against historical facticity. The pressure of the seething brain and the expansiveness of prophetic vision fluctuate in Bell's demand, as the epochal debts of centuries-long enslavement came due in daily news from the front. The antiquated diction, imagery, and syntax come up against an unabashedly contemporary orientation: "of the present we would sing." The hopes and demands of the last decade and a half now had an answer in the form of the war, but what freedom it would bring remained to be seen.[26]

Like her contemporaries, Harper took an especially circumspect view of the likelihood that the violence of the war would bring real freedom. She had been working toward abolition since the 1840s. During the war, she recuperated from chronic illness, married, and had a child in rural Ohio. Then as the war was coming to an end, her husband died, and she returned to public life as an itinerant activist, speaker, and performer. In the January 14, 1864 issue of the *Liberator*, she published "Bury Me in a Free Land," a stunning and strange lyric that expresses her total commitment to what Bell called final abolition, but also anticipates the haunting residues of slavery in its aftermath.

"Bury Me in a Free Land" takes off from intimations of mortality Harper seems to have experienced in this period as she recovered from the exhaustion of her antebellum activism. The lyric conceit is simple enough: the speaker imagines her spirit awakened in the grave by the suffering of the enslaved, unable to rest in death. In taking this as her subject, Harper retools conventional associations of slavery with death and freedom with salvation. Instead, she formulates a haunted conception of the historical relation between freedom and slavery:

Make me a grave where'er you will,
In a lowly plain, or a lofty hill;
Make it among earth's humblest graves,
But not in a land where men are slaves.

I could not rest if around my grave
I heard the steps of a trembling slave;
His shadow above my silent tomb
Would make it a place of fearful gloom.

I could not rest if I heard the tread
Of a coffle gang to the shambles led,
And the mother's shriek of wild despair
Rise like a curse on the trembling air.

I could not sleep if I saw the lash
Drinking her blood at each fearful gash,
And I saw her babes torn from her breast,
Like trembling doves from their parent nest.

I'd shudder and start if I heard the bay
Of bloodhounds seizing their human prey,
And I heard the captive plead in vain
As they bound afresh his galling chain.

If I saw young girls from their mother's arms
Bartered and sold for their youthful charms,
My eye would flash with a mournful flame,
My death-paled cheek grow red with shame.

I would sleep, dear friends, where bloated might
Can rob no man of his dearest right;
My rest shall be calm in any grave
Where none can call his brother a slave.

I ask no monument, proud and high,
To arrest the gaze of the passers-by;
All that my yearning spirit craves,
Is bury me not in a land of slaves.

Harper imagines making arrangements for her own death as a kind of late abolitionism. She warns of the political circumstances in which she "could not rest," and threatens to haunt the "bloated might" of any surviving planter aristocracy. Predicting how her soul will respond, in the grave, to the muffled echoes of suffering, the poem dwells on sound, the "step of a trembling slave ... and the mother's shriek of wild despair." The densely rhythmic quatrains indicate the otherworldly sonic experience of hearing from underground. Southern slavery appears a synesthetic nightmare, with whips "drinking" mothers' blood and babies taken like "trembling doves from their parent nest." The poem's sensuality is systematically disoriented, and the coordinates of life and death, mind and body, fundamentally scrambled.

Marx's famous figure for haunted history in *The Eighteenth Brumaire of Louis Bonaparte* assumes a shared burden: "The tradition of all dead generations weighs like a nightmare on the brains of the living." Harper's lyric makes this premise literal and everyday: she seems to talk frankly to her mourners and passersby alike, and to carve a warning about slavery on her tombstone. Beyond its strange intimacy, the poem demands a geopolitical and cosmological reckoning of white guilt. In its rattling, accusatory spirit, "Bury Me in a Free Land" seeks to ventilate the pressurized brains of her contemporaries with soul. The lyric's morbidity works from a radical interiority to a kind of historical inclusivity. It would become an important part of Harper's repertoire after the war; postbellum audiences would thrill to its threat of haunting. Read today, it forces the question, can her spirit really rest here? Harper's postbellum work, in either case, took a new turn outward; she would go on to write her epic on Moses, the first dialect poems in the African-American tradition, and a series of panoramic novels about the Civil War era. Meditating on death, Harper found the capacity to sing, in the postbellum, what she called "songs for the people."[27]

In the years after the war, Bell returned to the lyric premise of a song against song. At an August First festival in Toledo, Ohio, in 1868, celebrating the anniversary of the 1833 abolition of slavery in the British colonies, Bell read a poem entitled "The Dawn of

Freedom." Such festivals were common in free Black communities both before and after the war as collective affirmations of diasporic sentiment in the face of slavery and racism. Bell uses the occasion to revisit "My Country 'Tis of Thee," remaking it as an anthem of negation:

> 'Tis not of thee my native land ...
> 'Tis not of thee, though worthy thou
> Of many a song and plighted vow.
> 'Tis not of thee that we have ta'en,
> Our *harp* to wake its humble strain;
> But of a land and far away,
> Bathed by the ever restless sea;
> A land where freedom's sons' to-day,
> Are met in gladsome jubilee
> With them we would commemorate
> An epoch in the march of years,
> An epoch ever proud and great,
> The chief of freedom's pioneers.

Black Romantic poetry in general might well be understood as a "plighted vow." Bell marks the unmet promise of the moment with pointed irony, praising the British Commonwealth as "freedom's pioneers" and fulminating about the dawning Gilded Age: "All partial justice is unjust, / And merits man's profound distrust!" The Black Romantics would need, in the years after the war, to develop new tools for negotiating the hypocrisy of white leadership, with its counterfeit promises about their rights to citizenship.[28]

In another long postbellum poem, *Modern Moses, or "My Policy" Man* (1867–68?), Bell casts a bitter satire of the leadership of Andrew Johnson. He makes jokes about Johnson via racial science, now inflected by Darwinism, finding him "as much unfit to rule, / As apes and monkeys are for school." Bell anticipates Du Bois's interpretation of Johnson as "the trans-substantiation of the poor white," in which the ambitions of a politically ambivalent, uneducated, and unhappy class find their expression in a charismatic leader. The Black Romantics, having spent the better part of the past two decades taking measure of slavery as a moral crime and anticipating the reckoning of the war, turned quickly, issuing caution against the cooptation of freedom by corrupt redeemers. At the same time, they began the immense work of building the institutional supports for Black freedom, the schools and churches that would make Black community. In these contexts, the seething brain, with its connections to nature, history, music, and the spirit, would continue to play a role, but its attempted resolution of rationality and racial anger would, like so much of the period's promise, be left behind.[29]

4

The Uprising of Women

*In which Frances Ellen Watkins Harper
writes, speaks, and sings against sexual
objectification and economic exploitation*

As the war came to an end, Frances Ellen Watkins Harper turned forty years old, and lost her husband, Fenton Harper, to whom she had been married for only a few years. She had been writing and organizing for two decades and had used the war years to recuperate from chronic illness and to have her only child, Mary, in 1862. She returned to public work in the middle of the 1860s, and quickly fell into the political fight of her life: the breakup of the coalition between abolitionists and women's rights activists over the question of suffrage.

The richest known account of Harper's performance style comes from this period, written by a white American woman of letters who went by the pseudonym Grace Greenwood. Describing a series of lectures by abolitionist heroes like Douglass and Garrison in Philadelphia in the spring of 1866, Greenwood effuses over Harper. From the vantage of a heartfelt but insecure solidarity, she articulates what Harper represented to Northern white liberals in their moment of victory:

Next on the course was Mrs. Harper, a colored woman; about as colored as some of the Cuban belles I have met with at Saratoga. She has a noble head, this bronze muse—a strong face, with a shadowed glow upon it, indicative of thoughtful fervor, and of a nature most femininely sensitive, but not in the least morbid. Her form is delicate, her hands daintily small. She stands quietly behind her desk, and speaks without notes, with gestures few and fitting. Her manner is marked by dignity and composure; she is never assuming, never theatrical.

In the first part of her lecture, she was most impressive in her pleading for the race with whom her lot is cast. There was something touching in her attitude as their representative. The woe of two hundred years sighed through her tones. Every glance of her sad eyes was a mournful remonstrance against injustice and wrong. Feeling on her soul, as she must have felt it, the chilling weight of *caste*, she seemed to say,

> I lift my heavy heart up solemnly
> As once Electra her sepulchral urn.

Yet, after all, Mrs. Harper's greatest power lies in her wit and humor. There is something very peculiar about her here. She makes her best points, utters her keenest satire, with a childlike simplicity, a delicious *naiveté* I have never seen surpassed. She is arch, yet earnest; playful yet faithful. She shoots sin with a fairy shaft; she pierces treason through the joints of his armor with the bodkin of a woman's wit.

As I listened to her, there swept over me, in a chill wave of horror, the realization that this noble woman, had she not been rescued from her mother's condition, might have been sold on the auction-block, to the highest bidder—her intellect, fancy, eloquence, the flashing wit that might make the delight of a Parisian *salon*, and her pure Christian character all thrown in—the recollection that women like her could be dragged out of public conveyances in our own city, or frowned out of fashionable churches by Anglo-Saxon saints.

I am glad that the colored people have such a *Harper*; and I hope she will continue to harp on the one grand string till the nation listens and grants the only reward she asks, the only "hush-money" she will take—justice to her people.

Later discussions of Harper rarely fail to cite Greenwood's paradoxical description of the poet as a "bronze muse"; it so suggestively fixes her as an object of contemplation and effaces her objectifying work as an artist. In a series of cosmopolitan metaphors for Harper's complexion and racialization, Greenwood describes the poet-activist playing virtuosically on her audience's expectations of Black performance. Harper strikes her notes with a fearsome and uncanny precision that becomes a kind of militancy: "She shoots sin with a fairy shaft; she pierces treason through the joints of his armor with the bodkin of a woman's wit." The poet embodies the plight of her people both in and beyond her physical presence: "The woe of two hundred years sighed through her tones." Harper would continue to pluck the "one grand string" of Black liberation for some forty more years, even as it threatened to come unraveled under the pressures of reorganizing white supremacy, patriarchy, and capitalism.[1]

Put simply, Greenwood's description of Harper is objectifying. It is not, however, objectifying in the way that Black women were commodified and sexualized in slave markets. Instead, Greenwood's account frames Harper in white feminist terms, drawn from the cosmopolitan Romanticism of the abolition movement. At this decisive moment in the aftermath of the war, as Northern intellectuals debated the significance of the Union victory and emancipation, Harper's performance signaled opposition to modes of gendered oppression and liberation that had interested antebellum reformers, like the resistance to such cultural problems as alcoholism, corsetry, and "domestic slavery" that would recede into the background of the explicitly political concerns of the day. Matters like Black men's access to citizenship and the distribution of the Western lands took precedence over the more ephemeral, embodied, and cultural concerns of previous generation. Across the length of Harper's career, and the breadth of her prophetic vision, she carried the critique of slavery's racial, sexual, and economic objectification forward to attack the new ways Black bodies were objectified in the postbellum.

This chapter finds Harper thinking her way from abolition to what would become Black feminist critique of political economy.

The first section focuses on Harper's interpretation of the Free Produce movement, a consumer activist wing of abolitionism that animated her approach to literary language and ideas of domesticity for decades. The second section turns to Harper's self-conception as a Black woman of letters, writing against the brute sexual objectification of enslavement, but also aiming toward a theory of Black feminist pleasure. The third section focuses on Harper's sense of the postbellum revolutionary role of women's work, which she reconceived not as a set of ideas about the doctrine of the spheres, but as a mode of internationalism. The chapter concludes with a discussion of Harper's literary experimentation as an attempt to generalize feminist and antiracist modes of objectification. Poetic language and lyric performance, in her practice, become a means to effect the transvaluation of Black objecthood. To testify to the importance of this seemingly abstract consideration, Frederick Douglass quoted the British Romantic poet and philosopher Samuel Taylor Coleridge in the epigraph to his *My Bondage and My Freedom* in 1855: "By a principle essential to christianity, a PERSON is eternally differenced from a THING; so that the idea of a HUMAN BEING, necessarily excludes the idea of PROPERTY IN THAT BEING." The Black Romantics understood the totally brutal effects of enslavement as objectification on consciousness and the spirit. Harper sought to reverse these effects through activist aesthetic practice. The prophetic possibilities of this project, as a counter not only to slavery, but also its implications in capitalism and patriarchy, made her a crucial foremother to twentieth- and twenty-first-century iterations of Black feminism.[2]

"I wear an easy garment"

In the middle 1850s, Harper became involved in "Free Labor" or "Free Produce," an abolitionist effort to create a marketplace for goods made without the assistance of enforced labor. Modelling their efforts on the British abolitionist sugar boycotts of the late eighteenth century, Free Produce advocates ran into significant practical difficulties: Free Produce consumers struggled to avoid the plantation supply chain, and Free Produce goods tended to be more expensive and of lower quality. Like styles of "ethical consumption" in the twenty-first century, Free Produce worked on consumers' guilt and ascetic ambition as much as on their desire for sensual pleasure. Free Produce had little economic impact on plantation slavery, but it had significant symbolic and ideological utility as an organizing strategy. In a letter dated October 20, 1854, Harper wrote to her friend and confidant, the Underground Railroad conductor William Still, of her feelings about the consumer politics of slavery:

> Oh, how we can pamper our appetites upon luxuries drawn from reluctant fingers? Oh, could slavery exist long if it did not sit on a commercial throne? I have read somewhere, if I remember aright, of a Hindoo being loth to cut a tree because being a believer in the transmigration of souls, he thought the soul of his father had passed into it. ... Oh, friend, beneath the most delicate preparations of the cane can you not see the stinging lash and clotted whip? I have reason to be thankful that I am able to give a little more for a Free Labor dress, if it is coarser. I can thank God that upon its warp and woof I see no stain of blood and tears; that to procure a little finer muslin for my limbs no crushed and broken heart went out in sighs, and that from the field where it was raised went up no wild and startling cry unto the throne of God to witness there in language deep and strong, that in demanding cotton I was nerving oppression's hand for deeds of guilt and crime.

Very little of Harper's correspondence has survived, but like other men and women of letters in the nineteenth century, she used her letters to work out ideas which she would later employ in more public venues. Here she exercises the possibilities of Free Produce rhetoric. She mentions elsewhere in the letter that a reading of Solomon Northup's recently published *Twelve Years a Slave* (1853) prompted her commitment with its detailed descriptions of slavery as a system of economic production and its terrifying account of the thin line between Northern freedom and Southern slavery. She already recognized the ways Free Produce would fail on a practical level—it could not displace slavery as a mode of production. Its rhetoric could, however, bring the facts of plantation slavery into Northern homes, or more specifically, it could illuminate to ostensibly virtuous Northerners their unconscious dependence on the products of enslaved labor. It could make obvious the institution's reach, its global implication beyond the South.[3]

In the letter to Still, Harper draws attention to the human labor "congealed" in everyday objects, as Marx would have it over a decade later in *Capital, Vol. 1* (1867). From her different vantage on the Atlantic world-system, Harper imagines an aesthetic reversal of commodity fetishism via Free Produce, making obvious rather than obscuring the brutality that went into producing her food and clothes. Marx characterized the commodity as "a very queer thing, abounding in metaphysical subtleties and theological niceties." He focuses on the ways that commodities obscure and conceal but nonetheless contain alienated labor. His use of the term "fetish" refers ironically to Hegel's *Lectures on the Philosophy of World History* (1822–30), where the term is used to disparage African religion as falsely objective and falsely pretending to spiritual knowledge. Marx turns Hegel's prejudice into a critique of capital, using it as a figure of the objective delusions of industrialized production. In Harper's poetics, the fetishism of the commodity becomes a medium for the animation of enslaved makers and thus a critique of slavery as an economic institution. Through a kind of secular conjuration, Harper calls up the "wild and startling cry" of the enslaved amid the ambiance of Northern domestic consumption.[4]

She began to develop this poetic reversal of commodity fetishism in a series of activist interventions on abolitionist public culture. Within a year of sending the letter to Still, Harper published a piece advocating for "The Free Labor Movement" in the June 29, 1855 issue of *Frederick Douglass' Paper*:

One of the saddest features of American Slavery, is its mournful reaction upon the whole country, both north and south. Its influence surrounds us like the atmosphere; we gather around the social board, and one of the first things which meets our gaze, is some luxury wrung from the reluctant, trembling hands of the crushed and weary slave. We enter the wardrobe and the sighs and groans of the slave are lingering around the seams of our clothes, and floating amid the folds of our garments. But who will say, when Carolina's rice, with snowy whiteness, tempts the taste, perhaps the hands that gathered this were severed from some loved and lost embrace? Who will gaze upon the manufactured cotton, and see the stain, the stain of blood and tears upon its warp and woof? Who will look beneath the delicate proportions of the sugar cane, and see the stinging and clotted lash, and on their surface, trace the agony of years?

Here Harper imagines that the traffic in goods produced by enslaved labor has an influence over a kind of national ambience or mood—the most mundane of everyday things implying a vast historical wrong. Ordinary rice, sugar, and cotton are haunted by the systemic brutalities of their production. Harper notes a "mournful reaction" among the ambiguously collective "we" of abolition periodical culture. She wonders "who" among her audience might be conscious of the crimes of slavery embedded in their everyday "wardrobe" and "board." Twelve years later, Marx would describe the commodity fetish as a "fantastic form" in which the "relations between persons" are obscured. Harper's rhetorical procedures seek to reverse this process, to make the "seams of … clothes" broadcast Northern dependence on Southern slavery, and to bring the atmosphere to crisis.[5]

The first-person plural of this editorial involves a significant presumption on Harper's part—it subtly sets her on the level of white readers who shared, and perhaps might even feel, her guilt about consuming the products of slavery. Both Black and white readers of *Frederick Douglass' Paper* harbored a range of inchoately bourgeois ambitions, so they would have understood the audacity of Harper's claims to a place within the cultural politics of genteel domesticity. She takes on the role of a spirit guide through the object world of the Northern middle class, as she tours closets and pantries, finding blood and pain in the place of comfort and nourishment. She plays on the refined whiteness of the staple crops produced by enslaved labor, making them bloody through aesthetic trickery. Little wonder, in the context of this weird vision, that Grace Greenwood found in Harper such strange and contradictory provocation.

When she returned to it a few years later, in a ballad entitled "Free Labor" in the 1857 edition of her collection, *Poems on Miscellaneous Subjects*, Harper amplified the gendered risks of this gambit. The opening stanzas dramatize her dual role as consumer and political poet-seer:

> I wear an easy garment,
>   O'er it no toiling slave
> Wept tears of hopeless anguish,
>   In his passage to the grave.
>
> And from its ample folds
>   Shall rise no cry to God,
> Upon its warp and woof shall be
>   No stain of tears and blood.
>
> Oh, lightly shall it press my form,
>   Unladened with a sigh,
> I shall not 'mid its rustling hear,
>   Some sad despairing cry.

Here, as in the letter, Harper sets her enjoyment of Free Produce clothing against the suffering of enslaved people. Her speaker expresses a *sprezzatura* pleasure derived from the absence of the ghost pains and guilt associated with enslaved labor: "Oh, lightly shall it press my form." The verb "shall" gives the poem a strangely displaced effect, a mix of hope, desire, and commandment. The lyric voice calls up slave labor synesthetically and through paraleipsis, noting that she does not hear "some sad despairing cry" rising from the garment. Harper uses the lyric to collapse the distances that defined the market revolution and the obfuscations of the commodity relation. She calls up the sensual gratification of a liberated object and the torture of the enslaved simultaneously, staging the life of the object as a paradox. Her posture is both prophetic and sexy, indulging the sensual pleasures of everyday freedom and demanding an abolition that extends to all things. The lyric gives aesthetic substance to what in Marx would become the cornerstone of his general theory of capital.[6]

Harper's thinking about Free Produce extended from the spiritual-philosophical and political-economic ideas associated with Hegel, Coleridge, and Marx to theories of Romantic aesthetics. Her rendering of Free Produce in poetic language derives from notions of genre and medium which had been a preoccupation of Romantics since Gotthold Ephraim Lessing's *Laocoön: An Essay on the Limits of Painting and Poetry* (1766). Lessing argues for poetry's potential to disrupt fixed ideas about materialism: "In poetry, a garment is not a garment; it conceals nothing, our imagination sees right through it." Nearly a century later, Harper turns this poetic effect to antislavery purposes. Following Romantic notions of the power of the imagination, she sought to bring abolition into the everyday lives of people for whom it might otherwise have been a distant and vague injustice.

Harper's self-celebration via Free Produce clothes makes a bid for a totalizing and transformative political aesthetic. In this aspect she revises what Thomas Carlyle called "the dandiacal body" in *Sartor Resartus* (1833–34). For Carlyle, the dandy represents an apotheosis of clothedness as the flimsily defining feature of the human. In satirically overheated rhetoric, he claims the wearing of clothes is an act of civilizational and apocalyptic significance: "And now, for all this perennial Martyrdom, and Poesy, and even Prophecy, what is it that the Dandy asks in return? Solely, we may say, that you would recognize his existence; would admit him to be a living object; or even failing this, a visual object, or thing that will reflect rays of light." Carlyle's dandy is an absurd figure, but he articulates the conditions of self-expression in the dawning age of fashion. Harper again presses this Romantic notion into service as a critique of capitalism and slavery. If her dress can emblematize slavery as a form of systemic oppression, then wearing it well can foreshadow that system's apocalyptic end; if clothing can make people recognizable, then clothing can mark the entry of Black women into the privileges of liberal selfhood and recognizable political protest. The pleasures of the "easy garment" anticipate the pleasure of slavery's imminent end.[7]

Harper's performance of satisfaction with Free Produce clothing takes a number of risks. In one gesture, she plays up the autonomy of Black women's pleasure and at the same time shames the consumption habits of the white middle class. With an extravagant and contradictory decadence, the poem reserves the possibility for a Black feminist politics of pleasure. As an advertisement of the pleasures of Free Produce garments, the lyric parallels the trend among white women abolitionists who wore kerchiefs and other visible emblems of their involvement in the movement. Beyond Northern modes of ethical and conspicuous consumption, Harper's enjoyment of Free Produce clothing as a Black woman expresses a kind of solidarity, again by negation, with enslaved Black women forced to wear rough and uncomfortably revealing "negro cloth" or "linsey woolsey" garments. In a likewise negative dialectical way, the lyric hints at the so-called "fancy trade," with its performative sexualization of black women in slave markets.

In the decades leading up to the Civil War, abolitionists increasingly turned to the knotted metaphorical relation between clothing, slavery, and sexuality to articulate the role of sexual violence and breeding practices in the sustenance of slavery as a system. James W. C. Pennington's oft-cited formulation of the "chattel principle," in his 1849 narrative *The Fugitive Blacksmith*, demonstrates the centrality of these associations to the Victorian culture of the abolition movement:

> The being of slavery, its soul and body, lives and moves in the chattel principle, the property principle, the bill of sale principle; the cart-whip, starvation, and nakedness, are its inevitable consequences to a greater or less extent, warring with the dispositions of men.
>
> There lies a skein of silk upon a lady's work-table. How smooth and handsome are the threads. But while that lady goes

out to make a call, a party of children enter the apartment, and in amusing themselves, tangle the skein of silk, and now who can untangle it? The relation between master and slave is even as delicate as a skein of silk: it is liable to be entangled at any moment.

Pennington's domestic metaphor represents the consequences of slavery for ostensibly pure white spaces of home and hearthside. The "nakedness" he associates with the "being of slavery" and the suggestively "smooth and handsome" silk on the "lady's worktable" hint at the myriad sexual violence of slavery. Pennington goes on to illustrate his point with an anecdote about the fate of Rachel, "a beautiful girl about twenty-four" owned by his enslaver, and ultimately sold, along with "her few articles of clothing," after his enslaver's son coerces her into a sexual relationship. Harper dwelt on the generalizing function of metaphorical language like Pennington's, and pressed its potential to transform political consciousness.[8]

By the end of the 1850s, Harper had begun to write in more speculative ways through clothing to an apocalyptic perception of slavery's omnipresence. In "The Triumph of Freedom—A Dream" (1860), she returns to the image of the blood-soaked garment in a complex allegory of US politics in the moment between the failure of John Brown's raid and the outbreak of the Civil War. Appearing in *The Anglo-African Magazine*, the piece might as well be described as a short story, a fairy tale, or a prose poem. The narrator begins on "a beautiful day in spring" in "a state of dreamy, delicious languor." She finds herself in a pastoral landscape, and meets a spirit who guides her to the goddess, "a presiding genius of glorious beauty ... seated on a glittering throne ... She wore a robe of flowing white, but it was not pure white, and I noticed that upon its hem and amid its seams and folds were great spots of blood." This unsettling detail does not bother the throng of worshippers that surround the goddess, except one young man, who risks their "tumultuous fury" to reveal that the throne is built on "piles of hearts laid layer upon layer." He tallies "the hearts of a hundred-thousand newborn babes ... the hearts of desolate slave mothers, robbed of their little ones ... the hearts out of which manhood has been crushed; and ... the hearts of young girls, sold from the warm clasp of their mothers' arms to the brutal clutches of a libertine or profligate." Recall the "commercial throne" on which Harper said slavery sits in the letter to Still; in this dreamlike scenario, the spiritual, economic, political, and sexual implications of slavery come together in a prophetic vision. Harper unfolds her allegory with scholastic precision—the serial logic of the dream becomes a catalogue of the institution's sins, and the "congealed labor" in the "seams and folds" of the goddess's robes becomes political. The goddess begins to fear the young man, and demands her followers shield her with the armor of state and religious authority: "Hide me beneath your constitutions and laws—shield me beneath your parchments and opinions. ... Hide me ... beneath the shadow of your pulpits; throw around me the robes of your religion." The tale culminates in an abstractly described yet extraordinarily violent spiritual battle with losses on both sides, a bloody "baptism of Liberty," which ends in the installation of a new goddess of Freedom.[9]

After the death of her husband in 1864, as the end of the war came into view, Harper returned to work, and began to experiment with longer forms, not just in poetry but also in prose fiction. The end of the 1860s and the 1870s were an enormously creative period, as she published three more books of poems, *Moses: A Story of the Nile* (1869), *Poems* (1871), and *Sketches of Southern Life* (1872), and two serial novels in *The Christian Recorder*, entitled *Minnie's Sacrifice* (1869) and *Sowing and Reaping* (1876–77). Harper completed these works while also keeping up an enormously busy schedule of touring, speaking, and other organizing activities. In both her writing and activism, she made a crucial adjustment in the decade after the war, from addressing audiences of Northern white liberals to focusing her energy on recently freed Black people. In so doing, she extracted Free Produce tactics from their engagement with white bourgeois domesticity to arrive at a more general sense of the role of objectification in slavery and its aftermath.

Free Produce was never the only way in which Harper had thought objectification, but a prompt to explore an integral aspect of the system. The role of Free Produce rhetorical devices in her repertoire long outlasted the movement's impact as a form of direct action. These poetic experiments work through the objectification of Black labor and Black people to arrive at ideas of material agency, autonomy, and subjectivity which test extant notions of individualism. The world of objects may bear the marks of sublime historical suffering, but Harper's characters also remake the world by remaking themselves; that is, re-appropriating themselves from ownership by others. In the early 1850s, Harper had written to William Still of encountering some "passengers on the Underground Railroad": "These poor fugitives are property that can walk." This re-articulation of objectification involved a systemic perception of nineteenth-century American political economy, but also a richly complex understanding of its symbolism. The capacity of figurative language to reverse slavery's objectification became the cornerstone of Harper's poetics. The focus of postbellum politics on expansion of citizenship, in the form of voting rights, tended to set limits on the more fulsome, philosophical notions of self-determination which appear here in Harper. Despite the utility of Lessing, Carlyle, and Marx in explicating her intentions here, what she sought to express is best understood in retrospect as Black feminism.[10]

"The women, restive 'neath our rule"

By the time Harper began her career in the 1840s, a number of Black women public intellectuals had begun to make contributions across the North—Jarena Lee's preaching in the African Methodist Episcopal churches of the Philadelphia area and Maria Stewart's more secular lecturing in Boston in the 1830s were followed by the publication of Ann Plato's essays in early 1841. Harper's use of fiction and poetry as a part of her public work, her posture and performance as a woman of letters, also drew on Anglo-American sentimentalists like Anna Leticia Barbauld, Felicia Hemans, Lydia Maria Child, and Harriet Beecher Stowe. Harper's interventions across genres rank her with the charismatic feminist intellectuals of the age of revolutions, such as Mary Wollstonecraft, Mary Shelley, Madame du Staël, and Margaret Fuller. The sexual objectification of women had been a concern among these women at least since Wollstonecraft's dispute with Rousseau in *A Vindication of the Rights of Woman* (1792): "Rousseau declares that a woman should never, for a moment, feel herself independent, that she should be governed by fear to exercise her *natural* cunning, and made a coquettish slave in order to render her a more alluring object of desire, a *sweeter* companion to man, whenever he chooses to relax himself." To have a career as a woman of letters in this era, then, mandated opposition to this objectification, and to what was widely known through the nineteenth century as "domestic slavery." But entry into the public sphere—especially as a Black woman—involved enormous risk.[11]

Black feminist scholars of the late twentieth century who turned to Harper as a foremother have emphasized her approach to the contradictory expectations facing Black women activists. Deborah McDowell finds Harper reacting to Jezebel stereotypes of Black women and the cult of white domesticity by formulating what she calls a "countermyth" of Black feminist heroism. Darlene Clark Hine finds the uplift-oriented feminists—organizations like the National Association of Colored Women's Clubs and the women's clubs at new Black colleges and universities—relied on a "culture of dissemblance" to maintain the impossibly "super-moral" ideal of Black femininity of the postbellum period. Harper's contemporaries often saw her work in heroic terms; the Black journalist and fiction writer Pauline Hopkins, for instance, claimed: "By personal effort alone she has removed mountains of prejudice." Later twentieth-century Black feminist critics, emerging from the difficult work of the Civil Rights movement, would view praise like this as setting unreasonable, indeed unlivable expectations. Barbara Christian observed, in a cutting remark, the embodied sacrifices of Black women in public life: "The problem was not whether black women were heroic, but whether they were women at all." The careful play between pleasure and domestic ideology in Harper's "Free Labor" lyric suggests that Harper sought to complicate, and help her audiences navigate, the period's ideological constraints on Black womanhood.[12]

During the fight for suffrage in the aftermath of the war, Harper broke ranks with white women's rights advocates, who saw the opportunity of the war's end to demand the franchise alongside the newly freed people. Just a few months after Greenwood's account of her performance in Philadelphia, Harper offered her views, not only on the extension of suffrage but also of the more transhistorical claims of white feminist domestic ideology, in a speech at the Eleventh National Woman's Rights Convention in New York, May 1866. Entitled "We Are All Bound Up Together," the speech is bombastic, deeply personal, urgently political, and speculative. Harper reports the discrimination she faced as a Black farmer's widow and as a travelling Black woman lecturer, to indicate the distance the country had yet to go to make good on its ideals. She shuttles between the promise of a universal American exceptionalism based on its commitment to freedom and the grinding political reality of the coming split between abolitionists and white feminists over the vote:

> This grand and glorious revolution which has commenced, will fail to reach its climax of success, until throughout the length and brea[d]th of the American Republic, the nation shall be so color-blind, as to know no man by the color of his skin or the curl of his hair. It will have no privileged class, trampling upon and outraging the unprivileged classes, but will be then one great privileged nation, whose privilege will produce the loftiest manhood and womanhood that humanity can attain.
>
> I do not believe that giving the woman the ballot is immediately going to cure all the ills of life. I do not believe that white women are dew-drops just exhaled from the skies. I think that like men they may be divided into three classes, the good, the bad, and the indifferent. The good would vote according to their convictions and principles; the bad, as dictated by prejudice or malice; and the indifferent will vote on the strongest side of the question, with the winning party.

Harper counters the abstracted moralizing of arguments about women's "influence," and disputes rhetoric of the cult of true womanhood. The ironic figure of white women as "dew-drops" emphasizes their estrangement from the materiality of women's work. Her sharp language here reflects the broader conflict among women's rights activists and abolitionists, who decisively split over the Republican Party's making Black men's enfranchisement a priority and the inclusion of gendered language in the Fourteenth Amendment.

The implications of the breakup of the antebellum reform coalitions were far-reaching—women would wait until 1920 for the right to vote and African-American civil rights would be severely abrogated by the end of the century. Prominent women's rights advocates like Susan B. Anthony and Elizabeth Cady Stanton would take explicitly racist positions during decades after the war, further alienating Black women. The cultural politics of the antebellum women's movement, with its metaphorical connection to abolition through the concept of "domestic slavery," would set such embodied concerns aside in pursuit of the franchise. By the late 1860s, Harper can be found speaking to the universal prospects of abolition as a gendered project in her fiction and taking an expedient position in the service of suffrage for Black men in more explicitly political contexts. Quoted secondhand in reports of the 1869 meeting of the American Equal Rights Association, the poet's break with Susan B. Anthony and Elizabeth Cady Stanton, who opposed adoption of the Fourteenth Amendment because it excluded women, appears complete:

> Mrs. Harper then proceeded with her remarks, saying that when it was a question of race she let the lesser question of sex go. But the white women all go for sex, letting race occupy a minor position ... If the nation could only handle one question, she would not have the black women put a single straw in the way, if only the men of the race could obtain what they wanted.

Meanwhile, in her novel *Minnie's Sacrifice*, published in serial form that same year in *The Christian Recorder*, Harper includes a dialogue echoing the debate at the convention and recasting it in a more universalist and idealist critique:

> I cannot recognize that the negro man is the only one who has pressing claims at this hour. To-day our government needs woman's conscience as well as man's judgment. And while I would not throw a straw in the way of the colored man, even though I know that he would vote against me as soon as he gets the vote, yet I do think that women should have some power to defend herself from oppression, and equal laws as if she were a man.

Framing the issue one way for the pressing occasion and mixed audience of the convention, and another way altogether for the literate Black audience of the AME Church periodical, Harper struck a delicate balance between her prophetic commitments to revolutionary emancipation and her political commitments to short-term gains for Black people.[13]

While it took aim at the white supremacist leanings of her collaborators, Harper's critique of the cult of true womanhood in "We Are All Bound Up Together" echoed some of her white male contemporaries. Novels like Nathaniel Hawthorne's *The Blithedale Romance* (1852) and Henry James's *The Bostonians* (1886) satirized early feminism for its spiritual and utopian pretensions. In what may be the most condensed instance of this tendency, Edgar Allan Poe objectified the cult of true womanhood in a short poem in his late essay "The Rationale of Verse" (1843):

> Virginal Lilian, rigidly, humblily dutiful;
>   Saintlily, lowlily,
>   Thrillingly, holily
> Beautiful!

Here is Harper's "dew-drop" white woman in crystalline musical form. Poe's Lilian appears impossibly both earthbound and ethereal. The outrageously silly adverbs, the lilies of this grammatical garden, echo her name, hint at her whiteness, and yet insist on her activity. The guiding principle of Poe's argument, that "*Verse* originates in the human enjoyment of equality," requires that Lilian be creaturely, engaged, and at work, unlike more genteel forms of feminine idealization. At the same time, her symbolization of principle becomes a kind of morbidity; Poe had written elsewhere: "the death ... of a beautiful woman is, unquestionably, the most poetical topic in the world." Harper's women are like photographic negatives of Poe's. Their embodiment of principle makes them the heroes of tragedy, but in more historically mimetic narrative contexts. The metaphysical alienations that horrify and mortify Poe's women become the ground of activism in Harper's. She finds women's work, from the drudgery of domestic labor to the artistic, intellectual, and political pursuits associated with genius, at the center of postbellum reunion and Black community-building.[14]

In an 1870 poem, "Vashti," Harper addresses the problem of women's sexual objectification as an impediment to this work. Based on the Book of Esther, the lyric imagines the exchange between King Ahasuerus and his wife Vashti, as he requests that she present herself naked before a banquet, and she refuses. Harper makes explicit the king's sense of ownership over his wife:

> "Each gem that sparkles in my crown,
>   Or glitters on my throne,
>   Grows poor and pale when she appears,
>   My beautiful, my own!"

In the king's view, Vashti is a cherished part of the system of objects, like his crown, which define his status as the monarch. Vashti's refusal to appear in the nude, however, comes from a distinctly nineteenth-century sense of herself as a representative woman. Her principles echo the associations between freedom, slavery, and death characteristic of abolitionism and the age of revolutions:

"A queen unveil'd before the crowd!—
Upon each lip my name!—
Why, Persia's women all would blush
And weep for Vashti's shame!

"Go back!" she cried, and waved her hand,
And grief was in her eye:
"Go, tell the King," she sadly said,
"That I would rather die."

Refusing to perform as a sexual object, Vashti instead expresses her self-possession and her claim to autonomy on behalf of Persia's women. The king's advisers underscore the political problem of Vashti's disobedience:

"The women, restive 'neath our rule,
Would learn to scorn our name,
And from her deed to us would come
Reproach and burning shame."

Through Biblical allegory, Harper declares her commitment to a longer durational and universal struggle against patriarchy, just a year after seeming to cut her ties with white feminism in the service of racial equality. The lyric expresses the formerly revolutionary dimensions of abolitionists' protest against Black women's sexual exploitation in slavery, just as their immediate political impossibility came into view. However, Vashti also anticipates Black women's historical intervention on the late nineteenth century. The lyric sounds like Anna Julia Cooper's oft-cited line from *A Voice From the South* (1892): "Only the BLACK WOMAN can say 'when and where I enter.'" Both Harper and Cooper frame the ambitions of early Black feminism as world-historical, and direct their work against white supremacist objectification and idealization. Black women's peculiar place both in and out of nineteenth-century history made the prospect of their self-determination dramatic, vital, and decisive.[15]

"I want to be a poet"

Another of Harper's contemporaries, Fanny Barrier Williams, articulated the apparent elusiveness and ephemerality of Black female genius even more frankly. Speaking alongside Harper at the World's Congress of Representative Women in 1893, Williams declared, "Less is known of our women than of any other class of Americans." Despite Harper's heroically representative status as a woman of letters from the middle decades of the century onward, Williams's line is sadly even true of her. The dearth of sources on Harper's biography forces us to face her as her British contemporary Algernon Swinburne recommended: "knowing as you do the dates and sequence of my published books, you know every event of my life." Throughout her career, Harper wrote Black women as fictional characters with cultural and political ambition, repeatedly and across several genres. This had the effect of generalizing, or democratizing her genius, especially in her series of semi-autobiographical short fiction pieces about a young Black

Frances Ellen Watkins Harper, frontispiece to her
Poems *(Philadelphia: George S. Ferguson Co., 1898).*
Image courtesy of the Library of Congress.

poetess entitled "Fancy Etchings" or "Fancy Sketches," published in *The Christian Recorder* between 1873 and 1874.[16]

This episodic narrative offers a *künstlerroman* of a young Black college graduate named Jenny, unfolding her ambitions in dialogues with her family. In the first of these, Jenny announces her lofty intentions to her aunt:

> I want to be a poet, to earn and take my place among the poets of the nineteenth century; but with all the glowing enthusiasms that light up my life I cannot help thinking, that more valuable than the soarings of genius are the tender nestlings of love. Genius may charm the intellect, but love will refresh the spirit.

Jenny articulates a desire to write modern poetry but worries that a literary career might alienate her from the sentimental benefits of domesticity. Her adolescent equivocation anticipates Cooper's sense of Black women's entry into history and Barbara Christian's critique of early Black feminism as desexualized. Jenny takes her choice as a question of grand philosophical idealisms, "intellect" versus "spirit," but she also faces the dilemma within the temporal frame of a Black, female, human life in late-nineteenth-century America: should she marry or should she write?[17]

In a later installment, Jenny avows an activist approach to aesthetic practice and a sense of herself as avant-garde. Her Aunt Jane goads her by asking, "What do you expect to accomplish among our people by being a poet?" Jenny's answer marks a beginning for a theory of politicized aesthetics:

> It is just because our lives are apt to be so hard and dry, that I would scatter the flowers of poetry around our paths; and would if I could amid life's sad discords introduce the most entrancing strains of melody. I would teach men and women to love noble deeds by setting them to the music of fitly spoken words. The first throb of interest that a person feels in the recital of a noble deed, a deed of high and holy worth, the first glow of admiration for suffering virtue, or thrill of joy in the triumph of goodness, forms a dividing line between the sensuous and material and the

spiritual and progressive. I think poetry is one of the great agents of culture, civilization, and refinement. What grander poetry can you find than among the ancient Hebrews; and to-day the Aryan race with all the splendor of its attainments and the magnificence of its culture; still lights the lamp of its devotion at Semitic altars. Ages have passed since the blind beggar of Chios was denied a pension, in his native place, but his poetry is still green in the world's memory.

Jenny begins with a notion of poetry as an antidote to the disenchantment of modernity—"entrancing strains of melody" making beautiful the "hard and dry" aspects of life. She then imagines how poetry could affect its audiences' ethics, inspiring "throb[s] of interest" in "noble deeds" and "suffering virtue." From there, she considers the possibility of a poetry that can range across history, pointing out how Anglo-Saxon culture still prizes the "splendor" and "magnificence" of the Old Testament and Homer's epics. Through Jenny's developing consciousness, Harper offers a lyric theory of ethical and political modeling beyond national chauvinism. Her work, in poetry, fiction, and prose argument, makes Jenny's inchoate ambitions programmatic.[18]

Frances Smith Foster points to this intergenerational dialogue as an important Black feminist intervention on period theories of progress: "Both the new black woman and her foremother were potential agents of change." Rather than seeking to overpower her ancestors, Jenny swerves from the conventional Romantic association of youth with progress, and instead stops to learn from her aunt. She engages with the experience of age in a moment of crisis. The story thus offers a racial sense of revolutionary time, in which ancestors and descendants work together to transform the future. Poised on the cusp of adulthood at a moment of unprecedented opportunity for Black people, Jenny's revolutionary youth, tempered by her aunt's revolutionary experience, stands ready to articulate the spirit of the age, the sublime enormity of Emancipation. The Black intergenerational collaboration here compensates for the interracial collaboration of abolition sisterhood, largely abandoned by the early 1870s, well before the official end of Reconstruction efforts. Harper would, however, keep the radical possibilities of collaboration between what had been abolitionism and what would become feminism in her memory and in her prophetic rhetoric, even as segregation set in toward the end of the century and the incremental gains of white feminism seemed increasingly disconnected from the ambitions of Black women.[19]

"The threshold of a woman's era"

Harper had participated in the grassroots organization of Black Reconstruction: speaking at conventions, in churches, school-houses, and sometimes backwoods fields. She played key roles in the institution-building efforts of the African Methodist Episcopal Church and the National Association of Colored Women. Even as the expansive hopes that had attended abolition and Reconstruction began to fade, and reformers refocused on temperance and urban poverty, Harper saw herself as participating in a revolution, with unwavering certainty. Speaking at the World's Congress of Representative Women during the 1893 World's Columbian Exhibition in Chicago, Harper made the gendered aspects of her perspective more clear, and declared the late nineteenth century the "woman's era":

> Through weary, wasting years men have destroyed, dashed in pieces, and overthrown, but today we stand on the threshold of a woman's era, and woman's work is grandly constructive. In her hand are possibilities whose use or abuse must tell upon the political life of the nation, and send their influence for good or evil across the track of unborn ages.

Harper marks the historical moment in relation to the Civil War, then decades over, and posits that its violence was distinctly masculine. She sets this recent history against a projected new society based on women's work, reframing the doctrine of the spheres and notions of women's "influence" as a polemic for their leadership.

Harper's conception of women's work as "grandly constructive" turns quotidian acts of making, organization, and social reproduction into expansive ideals. She imagines a radical women's work that could transform rather than reproduce the immiseration, injustice, and inequality that had begun to set in after the collapse of Reconstruction.[20]

In appraising the moment after nearly forty years as a public intellectual and poet-activist, Harper drew on a range of readings and historical perspectives. The idea of the "woman's era" had roots in the white liberal strain of republican motherhood, but most directly it came from the French Romantic poet and novelist Victor Hugo. In an 1888 essay about the Woman's Christian Temperance Union, Harper makes her citation explicit:

> Victor Hugo has spoken of the nineteenth century as being the woman's era, and among the most noticeable epochs in this era is the uprising of women against the twin evils of slavery and intemperance, which had foisted themselves like leeches upon the civilization of the present age.

Harper recalls her readers to the antebellum collaboration between abolitionists and temperance advocates. In this late period, Harper worked alongside white feminists in the so-called Colored Section of the Woman's Christian Temperance Union—she also did so in her continued organizing efforts toward women's suffrage. The connection between temperance and abolitionism dated back to the early nineteenth century, when arguments about Black people's capacity for the responsibilities of freedom seemed to depend on their sobriety. This argument about embodied citizenship held particular interest for Harper, in its linking scenes of individual consumption with systemic, political questions. Her thought and practice as a poet-activist pushed the imaginative limits of what Black feminist historian Evelyn Brooks Higginbotham has called "the politics of respectability." The revolutionary rhetoric here, Harper's focus on "the present age" and women's "uprising," suggests that her interest in bodily regulation was rooted in struggle and aimed at historical transformation.[21]

The reference to Hugo implies that Harper saw these struggles as international, and that she understood poets as integral to historical transformation. Hugo's original language appeared in English in the *New York Times* in 1875:

The Society for the Improvement of the Condition of Women have sent an address to Victor Hugo appealing to him in the name of right, to lend the aid of his valuable voice. The poet replies in the following characteristic letter:

MESDAMES: I have received your address, which does me honor. I am aware of your noble and legitimate demands. In our society, such as it has been made woman suffers. She is right to claim a better fate. I myself am only a conscience, but I understand your rights, and to obtain them is one of the duties of my life. You are, therefore, not wrong to rely on my good-will and assistance. Man was the problem of the eighteenth century; woman is the problem of the nineteenth. And who says woman, says child—that is, the future. The question thus put appears in all its profundity, and on its solution depends the fate of the supreme social battle. What a strange and anomalous situation! In reality, man depends on you, for woman holds the heart of man. Before the law she is a minor, incapable, without civil action, without political right—in short, she is nothing; before the family altar she is everything, because she is the mother. The domestic hearth is what she makes it; at home she is the mistress of good and ill. Sovereignty complicated by oppression; woman can do all against man, but nothing for herself. It is imprudent of the law to make her so weak when she is so strong. Let us recognize that weakness and protect it; let us recognize that strength and counsel it. There lies the duty of man, and there is also his interest. No, I shall never cease to say it, the problem is laid down, and it must be solved. She who bears half the burden ought to have half the right. Half of the human race is deprived of equality; it must be given to them. This will be one of the grand glories of our grand century. Let the right of woman

counterbalance the right of man—that is to say, let the laws
be placed in conformity with the morals and manners of the
country. Accept, mesdames, my respects.

Hugo's French feminism echoes Atlantic traditions of republican
motherhood, Christian ritual, and democratic revolution. He notes
women's power within their limited sphere ("let us recognize this
strength and counsel it"), and complains against their exclusion
from the full privileges of period liberalism: "woman can do all
against man, but nothing for herself." Lending his voice, so long
associated with the revolutionary spirit of the age, to the cause
of women's political enfranchisement, Hugo makes an epochal
demand in the service of gendered liberation. His notion of "sovereignty complicated by oppression" found an audience across the
Atlantic of the 1870s, during heated postbellum debates about
the extension of suffrage. The French poet's wording, "Man was
the problem of the eighteenth century; woman is the problem
of the nineteenth," however, also sounds like Du Bois's famous
claim: "The problem of the Twentieth Century is the problem of
the color-line." Harper and Du Bois both confronted the unfulfilled promise of the Reconstruction through Hugo's posture of
secular prophecy: "I shall never cease to say it, the problem is laid
down, and it must be solved." Despite the vatic certainty of this
declaration, it would take decades for American women to win
suffrage, and African Americans' access to the vote is still under
attack today. The echo of these three voices across the Atlantic of
the late nineteenth century sound out cultural, political, and economic chasms still not securely bridged nearly 150 years later.[22]

Both French and American readers of the mid-1870s would have
understood Hugo's comments in reference to the Paris Commune
of 1871. Women had played a disproportionate role in the organization of the Commune, as well as in the scenes of violence
entailed by its fall. Rumor had it that enraged activist women
later known as *pétroleuses* burned public and private buildings
in the last days of the Commune. Hugo was especially taken with
the so-called "Red Virgin" of the Commune, Louise Michel, with
whom he had corresponded and to whom he dedicated a poem,

"Viro Major." Hugo took Michel's activism and leadership as disruptive of nineteenth-century gender norms; the Latin title of his poem about her can be translated either as "Greater Man" or "Greater Than Man." Paralleling the concerns of postbellum African-American communities, Michel advocated for a notion of "integral education" balancing manual and intellectual models of development to discourage class division in the schools and to make Commune society more flexible. She had famously (and this is the subject of Hugo's poem) demanded to be executed at her trial, only to be exiled to the French colony New Caledonia, where she continued her activism in an expanded anticolonial context. Michel's request set the utopian possibilities of the Commune against a Second Empire she associated with something like social death. She recounts the events of spring 1871 in her memoirs as a dream of freedom dislodged from history: "The Commune, surrounded from every direction, had only death on the horizon. It could only be brave, and it was. And in dying it opened wide the door to the future. That was its destiny."[23]

Alongside the apocalyptic transformation of gender and class wrought by the Commune, contemporary observers cast its implications in terms of race. Michel's memoirs recall poignant moments of collaboration with French Africans, and the Commune's opponents associated it with ethnic savagery. Men of letters like Alphonse Daudet depicted the Commune as "Paris in the hands of the blacks," and Théophile Gautier compared Communards to "savages, a ring through their noses, tattooed in red, dancing a scalp dance on the smoking debris of society." More sympathetic commentators like Karl Marx made an analogy between the Commune and the end of US chattel slavery. In his pointedly titled report, *The Civil War in France* (1871), Marx continually refers to the Thiers government (overthrown by the Commune) as a "slaveholders' conspiracy." American politicians and public intellectuals debated the Commune, and drew it into parallels with US current events, especially Reconstruction, throughout the later decades of the nineteenth century.[24]

The idea that Harper might have felt the appeal of the Communards is not so far-fetched. She had, in the antebellum period, expressed heartfelt solidarity with the "sublime sacrifice" of John Brown, to whom she wrote: "You have rocked the bloody Bastille; and I hope that from your sad fate great good may arise to the cause of freedom." William Still testifies to her fluency in European political theory:

> Mrs. Harper reads the best magazines and ablest weeklies, as well as more elaborate works, not excepting such authors as de Tocqueville, Mill, Ruskin, Buckle, Guizot, &c. In espousing the cause of the oppressed as a poet and lecturer, had she neglected to fortify her mind in the manner she did, she would have been weighed and found wanting long since.

Both Tocqueville and Guizot are relatively conservative respondents to the Revolution, and Still may have felt the need to conceal Harper's interest in more current events. Black intellectuals made conspicuously rare mention of the Commune, despite its appearance across US periodical culture of the period. Yet it must have held some appeal as a form of revolution that encompassed civil rights as well as modes of production, gendered conceptions of work, and the problem of colonialism.

Harper's claims for the "women's era" at the outset of Jim Crow look conservative in hindsight, seemingly embedded in the bourgeois, Victorian concerns of racial uplift. Yet she continued to understand herself in terms of the revolutionary, Romantic, and international ambitions of abolitionist feminism. The foreshortening of these aims in the late Victorian culture of the clubwoman movement in the last decade of the nineteenth century should not obscure from memory the more radical dimensions of Harper's vision. The reorganization of white supremacy and patriarchy around lynch law and the professional managerial class effectively deferred her dreams of a revolution refocused on women's work. Separate but equal social and corporate policy curtailed the influence and ambition of new Black women like Harper's Jenny. The integration of domestic ideology with industrial society managed to delay the crises of care and service, of production and accumulation, and of sexuality and nourishment, which Harper found linked to the system of slavery. But as she foresaw, these cannot be delayed forever.[25]

"We are all bound up together"

Iola Leroy (1892), the novel by which Harper is best known, depicts slavery, the war, and its aftermath in panoramic form. As in her oratorical appearances over the same years, the novel reflects on emancipation, Reconstruction, and the onset of segregation as a part of the same revolutionary moment. In a brief note at the novel's end, she claims to have written it on "behalf of those whom the fortunes of war threw, homeless, ignorant and poor, upon the threshold of a new era." The book returns repeatedly to the concerns of abolitionist feminism—the afterlives of slavery in the everyday objects of domestic life and in the familial traumas of sexual violence. One of the main characters, Robert Johnson, tells an anecdote about "a poor old woman who couldn't bear to hear any one play on the piano." His interlocutor, a white captain in the Union Army, asks:

> "Is that so? Why I always heard that colored people were a musical race?"
>
> "So we are; but that poor woman's daughter was sold, and her mistress took the money to buy a piano. Her mother could never bear to hear a sound from it."
>
> "Poor woman!" exclaimed Captain Sybil, sympathetically; "I suppose it seemed as if the wail of her daughter was blending with the tones of the instrument. I think, Robert, there is a great deal more in the colored people than we give them credit for."

The dialogue here is surely didactic and sentimental, but it also works through the symbolic reversals of commodity fetishism which underpin Harper's most radical poetics, her songs of fiercest passion. The captain expresses respect for the woman's sensitivity, the way she can see through the piano as an object to its role in a brutal system of exchange. The piano, like so much of the object world of nineteenth-century America, acts as a doubled fetish, animated both by capital and by the soul disappeared within it.[26]

The image recalls the Romantic figure of the Aeolian harp. In Coleridge's poem on the subject, a young man argues with his Christian lover for pantheism, inspired by the sounds of wind on the otherwise unplayed harp. He hears the "rhythm in all thought, and joyance every where." The woman in Harper's anecdote can rely on no such universal comforts, or in her case, the totality represented in the harp is negative, a world abandoned by God, in which even the spirit of things is haunted by dispossession. Percy Shelley's use of the figure in his "Defense of Poetry" makes the association between "man" (abstractly conceived) and the lyre, both of which have the capacity for sensibility and the ability to harmonize sentiment. Shelley finds in the Aeolian lyre an image for the ways that "Man in society, with all his passions and his pleasures, next becomes the object of the passions and pleasures of man." Harper was capable, in other moments, of imagining (especially) women's objective work as directed away from enslaving and toward emancipating forms of use and pleasure. Here, however, Harper's anonymous enslaved woman does not have the autonomy of Shelley's abstracted "man"; her aversion to the piano constitutes a reaction to white men's apparent control of the spirits embodied in the object. In this moment, Harper fixates on the personal, historical, and excruciating losses that resulted from chattel slavery. The eternality that sounds through the Aeolian harp threatens to become slavery's open-ended legacy—how long might that piano sound the wail of the woman's daughter? As always, Harper has her eyes on both the immediacy of her moment and larger scales of time.[27]

Elsewhere in the novel, Harper returns to the image of the bloodstained garment. The main character's mother, Marie Leroy, comments on the political struggles of Reconstruction:

> I do wish the attention of the whole nation could be turned to the cruel barbarisms which are a national disgrace. I think the term "bloody shirt" is one of the most heartless phrases ever invented to divert attention from cruel wrongs and dreadful outrages.

The phrase "bloody shirt" has origins deeper in history than Free Produce rhetoric. It derived from Mark Antony's eulogy for Julius Caesar, during which he waved Caesar's bloody tunic at the crowd to remind them of his violent end. Its usage in the United States comes from a speech by Benjamin Franklin Butler in the House of Representatives in 1871. Butler waved at Congress the bloody shirt of a carpetbagger nearly beaten to death by the Ku Klux Klan. The phrase became a Southern cliché for grandiloquence about Black and Northern suffering. In the spirit of Free Produce, Harper's Marie Leroy argues against rhetorical caricature and for sentimental attention to objects bearing the stain of violence. *Iola Leroy* itself is a literary "bloody shirt," a document of violence against Black people, but also a symbol of national crisis and the moral heroism of Black protagonists. Harper understood her novelistic characters as objectifications, "living epistle[s]" against slavery and racism. Late in the novel, she has Iola argue in favor of this aesthetic strategy: "Every person of unmixed blood who succeeds in any department of literature, art, or science is a living argument for the capability which is in the race." Here Harper arrives at the apotheosis of the fugitives as "property that can walk." She mixes racial uplift with the process of objectification, in search of the emancipation that eluded her people at the end of Reconstruction. Objectification is turned, here more succinctly than in her earlier work, into political subjectivity.[28]

Harper had by then long understood the relation between literary experimentation and symbolic emancipation. The family sagas of her novels represent one sort of attempt to project the phenomenological immediacy of objectification outward toward the national landscape. Other forms approach the same problem differently. In her 1871 publication of *Moses: A Story of the Nile*, Harper included a short companion piece, "The Mission of the Flowers," which imagines the conflicts of Reconstruction through ecological metaphor. Like "The Triumph of Freedom—A Dream," it is one of the more unabashedly strange and intellectually adventurous allegories in early African-American literature. "The Mission of the Flowers" has no human characters at all, and instead begins with a rosebush at the center of "a lovely garden." Harper makes the plant her main character:

> Now the rose was very kind and generous hearted, and, seeing how much joy she dispensed, wished that every flower could only be a rose, and like herself have the privilege of giving joy to the children of men; and while she thus mused, a bright and lovely spirit approached her and said, "I know thy wishes and will grant thy desires. Thou shalt have a power to change every flower in the garden to thine own likeness. When the soft winds come wooing thy fairest buds and flowers, thou shalt breathe gently on thy sister plants, and beneath thy influence they shall change to beautiful roses."

Under the pretense of service to the spirit's ideal, the rose sets out to change the nearby tulips, verbenas, and poppies into roses. Harper's language here draws directly on period notions of women's influence, but emphasizes the melancholia of the roses' imposed conformity: "The violets, whose mission was to herald the approach of spring, were averse to losing their identity. 'Surely,' said they, 'we have a mission as well as the rose;' but with heavy hearts they saw themselves changed like their sister plants." Harper plays with color symbolism, emphasizing the defeated self-regard of the snow drops, "emblems of purity and innocence," and the rebelliousness of the dahlias, who "scorned submission." The racial significance of the allegory is at once blatant and oblique. The roses' takeover resonates with colonialism, monopoly capitalism, and ethnic nationalism alike. Likewise, the sexual implications of the roses' supremacy play lambently but threateningly below the surface of the story. The apocalypse of roses activates anxieties about slave-breeding, eugenics, and miscegenation, and the story's end provides little relief.[29]

Once the entire garden has become a "perfect wilderness of roses; the garden had changed, but that variety which had lent it so much beauty was gone, and men grew tired of roses, for they were everywhere." The rose awakens to realize it had all been a dream:

But an important lesson had been taught; she had learned to respect the individuality of her sister flowers, and began to see that they had their own missions,– some to gladden the eye with their loveliness and thrill the soul with delight, some to transmit fragrance to the air; others to breathe a refining influence upon the world; some had power to lull the aching brow and soothe the weary heart and brain into forgetfulness; and those whose mission she did not understand, she wisely concluded there must be some object in their creation, and resolved to be true to her own earth-mission, and lay her fairest buds and flowers upon the altars of love and truth.

The concept of "earth-mission" mixes Christian and astronomical registers, taking the coordinates of women's work from the unknown. The rose learns to accept the limitations of her vision and the inaccessible political-allegorical complexity of the garden. In her 1866 speech anticipating the breakup of the abolition feminist alliance, Harper made a similar plea for broad, democratic equality: "We are all bound up together in one great bundle of humanity, and society cannot trample on the weakest and feeblest of its members without receiving the curse upon its soul." In both visions of interracial comity, a certain tension remains unresolved, indeed suspends a more inclusive community. Even under the most revolutionary circumstances, objectification, as a basic philosophical and physical procedure, continues. Harper saw how aesthetic practice could make objectification emancipatory rather than enslaving. Meanwhile, the garden, as quaint metaphor for the nation, would become increasingly difficult to sustain as Reconstruction came to an end, amid pitched battles for the last of the unsettled Western lands and new spatial constraints on Black life.[30]

5

Freedom Is an Empty Name

*In which Albery Allson Whitman imagines a
collaborative resistance of Black and Native people
to US empire in the aftermath of Reconstruction*

In his discussion of the postbellum prospects for "abolition
democracy" in *Black Reconstruction*, Du Bois credits Thaddeus
Stevens, the white Radical Republican congressman from
Pennsylvania, with prophetic vision, referring to him as a "seer."
He cites Stevens's plan to confiscate and redistribute the assets of
the planter class, laid out in a speech at Lancaster, Pennsylvania,
on September 6, 1865. At the end of the summer after the surrender at Appomattox, the total wealth of the Confederacy might
have become the economic base of a new social organization:

> There are about 6 million of freedmen in the South. The number
> of acres of land is 465,000,000. Of this those who own above 200
> acres each number about 70,000 persons, holding in aggregate—
> together with the States—about 394,000,000 acres, leaving for
> all the others below 200 each about 71,000,000 acres. By thus
> forfeiting the estates of the leading rebels the government would
> have 394,000,000 of acres, besides their town property, and yet
> nine-tenths of the people would remain untouched. Divide this
> land into convenient farms. Give, if you please, forty acres to
> each adult male freedman. Suppose there are 1,000,000 of them.
> That would require 40,000,000 of acres, which deducted from

394,000,000 leaves 354,000,000 of acres for sale. Divide it into suitable farms, and sell it to the highest bidders. I think it, including town property, would average at least $10 per acre. That would produce $3,540,000,000. Let that be applied as follows.

Stevens's calculations elaborate on General Sherman's "Special Field Orders No. 15," which sought to divide 400,000 acres of Southern territory along the coastline between Florida and South Carolina among freed people in parcels of forty acres each. For Du Bois, Northern leaders' refusal to take plans like this seriously allowed what he called "the counter-revolution of property" and the retrenchment of white supremacy in the decades after Reconstruction.[1]

Stevens's plan for the South did not come to pass, of course, and neither did other abolitionist proposals focused on land ownership for the recently freed. The radicals' grand plans for land redistribution, however, did parallel the settlement of the West over these same years. Horace Greeley's 1854 prescription, that "The public lands are the great regulator of the relations between Labor and Capital, the safety valve of our industrial and social engine," had come to justify the federal dispossession of Native land and its sale to white settlers and railroad corporations via the Homestead Acts in 1862 and 1866. Early twentieth-century literary historian Vernon Parrington described this process as "the Great Barbecue," noting the "inconspicuous persons" who had not received invitations. Among these were the freed people. In lieu of real reparations, the rhetoric of possessive individualism came to disguise the usurious and exploitative debt-peonage arrangements that defined the economics of Black life in the New South. The premise of Black yeomanry became an important ideological mechanism for the management of Black people, especially in the South but also in the West, in the decades after the war. The industrialization and incorporation of the American West had made the Jeffersonian fantasy of a continent of small freeholders untenable, while the entrapment of newly freed African Americans in profitless relation to agricultural production succeeded only in remaking the planter class as rentier elites.[2]

Literary critic Houston Baker sums up African Americans' alienation from the frontier myth and the yeoman ideal: "Tales of pioneers enduring the hardships of the West for the promise of immense wealth are not the tales of black America." This categorical claim does not, however, mean that Black people had no frontier myths of their own. Greeley's safety valve may not have liberated Black people, but the spatial facts of North America still generated alternative forms of Black romance. Melvin Dixon contends that during slavery, "the wilderness" functioned "as a place of refuge beyond the restricted world of the plantation." After the war, African Americans formulated a range of visions of the American landscape, the West, and the frontier that suggest they saw in its vastness some hope of reprieve. The Black Romantic poets, as they reckoned the problem of slavery in the middle decades of the century, played a key role in articulating African Americans' relation to New World spaces, places, and homelands. Some, like James Monroe Whitfield and James Madison Bell, moved to California during the war, and looked directly on the foreshortened prospects for Black people at the culmination of Manifest Destiny. Others, like George Moses Horton and Martin Delany, imagined emigrationist or colonizationist pastorals beyond the reach of US territory, which nonetheless eerily recapitulate settler/planter understandings of land and nature.

In the middle of these contradictions around Black relations to the land as the mythic basis of US national identity, the most popular African American poet in the wake of Reconstruction, Albery Allson Whitman, wrote vast lyric epic romances about frontier history in which Black and Native characters take center stage. Whitman was unique among his contemporaries in considering Indigenous communities and experiences at length, and this perspective led him to what can best be described as an impossibly radical depiction of American life.[3]

Whitman's most creative period, during which he came to be known as the "Poet Laureate of the Negro Race," overlaps with a catastrophic phase in both African-American history (from the Compromise of 1877 to *Plessy v. Ferguson* in 1896) and Native American history (from the Great Sioux War of the late 1870s through the Dawes Act of 1887 and Wounded Knee in 1890). His two most important long poems project the brutal disappointments of this moment back onto scenes of colonial violence that took place some fifty years before their publication. *Not a Man, and Yet a Man* (1877) focuses on the Blackhawk War (1830–32), while *The Rape of Florida* (1884, reprinted as *Twasinta's Seminoles* [1885]) represents the First and Second Seminole Wars (1816–18, 1835–42). In these vast and richly aestheticized romances, Whitman puts Jacksonian historical subjects and antiquated poetic forms to the service of an aesthetic critique of postbellum colonialism, racism, and capitalism. Because of their length, subject matter, and rhetorical complexity, these works did not have the obvious activist utility of the short lyrics of Harper or Simpson. However, Whitman was deeply involved, through the African Methodist Episcopal Church, in post-Reconstruction Black community-building across the South and Midwest. He saw his poetry as an extension of revolutionary abolition.

The romance as an American form had long worked through the cultural norms of US frontier life and the contradictions of settler colonialism. Whitman's romances linked slavery to Native American genocide, and thus the onset of segregation to the reservation system, and led him to apocalyptic conclusions about postbellum reunification and the consummation of Manifest Destiny. The historical dissonance of his formal choices made for an insurrectionary response to the end of Reconstruction. In mid-nineteenth-century America, historical romances had made the violence of settlement a literary tradition to rival the national histories of Europe. In its more deluded and self-aggrandizing forms, the antebellum historical romance justified the brutality of planter aristocracy. Mark Twain diagnosed the South and especially the Confederacy with what he called "the Sir Walter disease"; he finds its "jejune romanticism of an absurd past ... in great measure responsible for the war." Whitman's historical romances do not suffer from the disorientation of an entrenched elite; instead, they depict moments of interethnic resistance on the antebellum frontier in protest of Jim Crow social policy. This gesture to moments of Black and Native anticolonial struggle recalled to

Whitman's audiences the role of Western lands in exacerbating the conflict around slavery, and to collaborations between abolitionists and activists against Indian removal. The concatenation of antiquated forms and subjects in his work queries narratives of civilizational progress; the echo between border wars of the ante- and postbellum calls attention to white supremacy's reinvented dominion over people of color after the end of slavery.[4]

The historical romance in the US context had long focused on the ways captivity and sexual violence result from territorial disputes. Whitman sets this preoccupation of the genre against the ideals of character that drove racial uplift. In his compulsive digressions from the complex plots of his epics, Whitman poses aesthetic and ideological challenges to uplift, shading in the contrast between sexual violence as a historical fact of settler slavery and sexual "hygiene" as a mode of social control in emergent industrial society. He rewrites the frontier myth to center the opposition between white rapacity and anticolonial love. His experimentation with narratives of Black and Native collaboration contradicts the seeming inevitability of US empire's consolidation, forcing the question of nonwhite futurities inside, outside, and along its borders. The vertiginous movement of his work between historical pasts and the tumultuous present, as well as between the vast machinations of empire and its intimate effects, made him the most popular African-American poet of the 1870s and '80s.

Happy Hunting Grounds

Whitman read into the epic and romance traditions at Wilberforce University in southern Ohio, where he was educated in the late 1860s and early 1870s, and where he first imbibed the ideas of racial uplift. Wilberforce was founded by members of the African Methodist Episcopal Church, and aimed to provide a classical education to its students. Frances Harper was involved in its early days, having taught at Union Seminary, which later became Wilberforce, in the early 1850s. Whitman would have read her earlier epic

Moses: A Story of the Nile (1869) with significant interest. Beyond Harper's poetic prompting, and after Whitman had graduated, William Sanders Scarborough, the great African-American classicist, came to Wilberforce to teach in 1877. Scarborough reflects on his arrival on campus in his autobiography: "My young professor's imagination was at once captured by the situation as well as by its history which I soon learned here. I saw magnificent possibilities which should have been utilized to the utmost making it the 'Mecca' of Negro education." He mentions the institution's proximity to the birthplace of the Shawnee chief Tecumseh, and its "situation" on what had once been "the happy hunting grounds of the Shawnee Indians." Long historical perspective thus framed the uplift orientation of Wilberforce; Whitman would take this as the background of a lifelong poetic project.[5]

After his time at Wilberforce, Whitman became a preacher and an agent of the AME Church, first in Springfield, Ohio. James D. Corrothers, another alumnus of Wilberforce and an important poet and novelist in the generation after Whitman's, recalls the idylls of interracial life in 1870s Ohio after it had played host to the Underground Railroad:

> No better class of coloured people, surely, has ever been produced in this country, anywhere, than those who lived in Springfield, Ohio, at that period. They were industrious, progressive, and intelligent. A large percentage owned homes, and a few were in business. They had beautiful churches, intelligent ministers, and competent school teachers. There was not a disreputable Negro in the city. A splendid feeling of mutual respect and trust existed between the races there, and colour was not an absolute bar against advancement. ... Of the Rev. Albery A. Whitman, too, then the acknowledged coloured poet of America, Springfield was especially proud. ... He was sometimes invited to preach in white pulpits, in Springfield, and frequently had a group of white visitors in his own congregation.

Here was a virtuous augury of abolition-democracy: the freed people succeeding in assimilating to small-town life in the Middle

West. Whitman began, in this period, to gain a national reputation as the "Poet Laureate of the Negro Race" or the "Poet Laureate of the Church" through his regular appearance in the pages of the African Methodist Episcopal Church's periodical, *The Christian Recorder*. No copies of his first book, *An Essay on the Ten Plagues and Miscellaneous Poems*, published sometime in the early 1870s, have survived; his second, *Leelah Misled*, a white woman's seduction narrative in verse, appeared in 1873. Corrothers goes on to say that, by the 1880s, lynch law had come to Southern Ohio, and "terrible holocausts of race hate" disrupted this "progressive atmosphere." By then, Whitman had left Ohio; it appears he had a talent for founding AME Church congregations, which he did as far south as Georgia and Florida and as far west as Arkansas and Texas, where he also helped found Paul Quinn College. Through these same years, Whitman also became increasingly disillusioned with the supposed virtues of white settlers.[6]

In 1877, Whitman, twenty-six, published his third book. *Not a Man, and Yet a Man* was put out by the Republic Print Company of Springfield, Ohio, an outfit otherwise responsible for the publication of college catalogues, association minutes, and local histories. Whitman dedicated the work to "the abolition fathers," setting abolition within the patrilineal tradition of American democracy. In the preface, he makes clear that he published the work by subscription with the intention of contributing the proceeds to Wilberforce: "Our canvassers get ONLY such part of the sales as will help them honestly to live. Purchase, therefore, remembering that your mite goes to the aid of a noble cause." He commits the book to the service of the institution's educational mission:

> My object in placing these verses before an intelligent people is, First, to carry to their minds the purpose of the founders of Wilberforce. That purpose, as stated in the last Catalogue of the Institution, is "An aim to inspire and increase in the pupil self-respect, self-control, and self-development ..."
>
> The production of NOT A MAN, AND YET A MAN, whatever it is, is owing to that spirit of "self-development" which Wilberforce inspires.

Whitman's purposes compare intriguingly with Horton's; here again a male poet, closely associated with an institution of higher education, writes poems with the intention of soliciting charity. However, Whitman commits his readers to the principles of the education of Black youth, and the grand educational experiment at the heart of Black Reconstruction efforts. He shares Horton's appreciation for dialectical irony, and his book focuses on the challenges slavery and colonialism pose to its ideals of gendered character. Though *Not a Man, and Yet a Man* was regularly mentioned in *The Christian Recorder*, the paper's contributors often apologize for its "queer" title.[7]

Following Walter Scott, Whitman sets his ordinary characters' heroism alongside that of a major historical figure, in this case, the Sauk warrior Black Hawk. Popular interest in the Sauk people had been piqued by the popularity of the memoir *Life of Black Hawk* (1833) and its revision in a number of texts by white authors across the period. Whitman casts Black Hawk as "the red Napoleon of solitude," combining the Romantic characters of the noble savage and the "great man" theories of Hegel, Carlyle, and Emerson. Like Vashon's foray into the Caribbean, Whitman's representations of Native society are exceedingly thin in terms of the emergent anthropological concept of "culture." He describes the Northern Midwest Sauk tribes in *Not a Man, and Yet a Man* in remixed clichés of noble savagery. However, the multiracial inclusiveness of his perspective means his play with racist convention points all the more clearly to the moral and political corruption of white settlement. He commends Black Hawk for his vision of the onset of capitalism: "He saw neath mammon's desecrating tread, / The turf-green dwellings of the sacred dead." These lines recall a moment in Black Hawk's memoir; after the Sauk leader has been captured by a young Jefferson Davis, he takes stock of the antebellum US landscape:

> I surveyed the country that had cost us so much trouble, anxiety, and blood, and that now caused me to be a prisoner of war. I reflected upon the ingratitude of the whites, when I saw their fine houses, rich harvests, and everything desirable around them; and

recollected that all this land had been ours, for which me and my people had never received a dollar, and that the whites were not satisfied until they took our village and our grave-yards from us, and removed us across the Mississippi.

Whitman's epic echoes this sense of American civilization as enrapt with "mammon," and links white American greed to disrespect for the dead. His antiquarian subjects and formal choices have a haunted quality, and his work can flash between a burial ground and a battlefield.[8]

The plot of the poem is packed with incident, a picaresque tour of the American borderlands with slave-owning pioneers as the antagonists of virtue at every turn. The action focuses on Rodney, a biracial man enslaved to a white settler in Illinois named, improbably, Sir Maxey. In an impetuous fit of territorial ambition, Sir Maxey attacks a nearby Sauk tribe, whose members retaliate by kidnapping his daughter Dora. Maxey then promises Dora's hand in marriage to whoever can rescue her, and he is surprised and dismayed when Rodney achieves this feat of knight-errantry. Whitman makes risky, veiled suggestions that Rodney succeeds in winning Dora's affections; a prospect foreshadowed in a subplot about the Sauk chief Pashepaho's daughter Nanawawa falling in love with *their* Black slave White Loon. To avoid keeping his promise, Maxey sells Rodney down south to Florida, where the handsome and capable hero quickly attracts the attention of Leeona, who, like him, is enslaved and biracial. Rodney's new owner, Aylor, rapes and impregnates Leeona, so the two lovers escape to Canada, where they find idyllic refuge. At every turn, white men's sense of ownership over both Native land and Black bodies yields sexual violence.

In Homeric fashion, the characters make declamatory speeches elaborating their heroic ethics, but Whitman insists repeatedly on showing how border skirmishes complicate his characters' principles. Early on, the otherwise forceful but sagacious Sauk chief Pashepaho gathers the nearby tribes of the region to implore them not to respond to Sir Maxey's incursion: "Be peaceable my children, / dwell in friendship's tents together." When a small band ignores him and attacks a white hunting party in retaliation, Rodney lectures the white elites of the frontier town about how they should take up arms against the Natives:

> Had I a single treasure to me dear,
> A single home joy bright, or, even were
> I owner of my life, my arm I'd bare,
> And thrust my fingers into peril's hair.

The spectacles of a Native leader pleading union and an enslaved person scolding white settler cowardice both cut against the myth of frontier violence as a test of white American masculinity. Although he takes interest in the ethical parallels of Black and Native experience, Whitman had not yet, in this volume, arrived at a narrative of Afro-Indigenous solidarity. Rodney's bravery echoes Black intellectuals' claims about the battle heroics of Black enlisted men, against both the Confederacy and Indigenous insurgents in the West, as support in the fight for citizenship rights. Besides this buffalo-soldier bravado, Rodney's jeremiad recalls Whitman's Romantic sources, like Walter Scott's *Lady in the Lake* (1810), from which Frederick Douglass also took his name. Scott writes that one of his heroes has "the will to do, the soul to dare, / The sparkling glance, soon blown to fire, / Of hasty love or headlong ire." Rodney's self-righteousness leads him into trouble, as his heroism runs afoul of racial and sexual mores of frontier communities. Whitman's emphasis, however, falls not on his tragic flaw, so much as how Jacksonian historical circumstances conspire against him tragically.[9]

When Rodney is sold down the river, Whitman emphasizes his distinction from ordinary members of the slave community. He sets Black vernacular music in opposition to Rodney's implicitly Westernized epic character:

> The cabin dance, the banjo and the song,
> Are courted yet by Afric's humble throng.
> They drown their sorrows in a sea of mirth,
> And crush young griefs as soon as they find birth

> Neath dance's heel; and on the banjo string
> A theme of hope, that forces woe to sing.
> But one is there, to them a stranger born,
> Whose manly brow the marks of thought adorn.
> The low inventions of poor darkened mind,
> Can never in the threads of nonsense bind
> This mental Sampson; tho' by Slav'ry shorn
> Of rightful manhood, weakness he doth scorn.

The appellation "mental Sampson" puts a classical gloss on Rodney's "seething brain." Like his earlier contemporaries, Whitman explored the political dynamics between Black interiority and Black collectivity through the representation of music in lyric poetry. Here he takes Rodney's resistance to the songs of slavery as an indication of his uplifted character; "the marks of thought adorn" his "manly brow," and so he takes no interest in "the low inventions of poor darkened mind." Rodney's rational but grandiloquent dismissal of Black music does not stand for Whitman's whole corpus; the poet vacillated in this elitism throughout his life, and he participated with studied energy in the popular music of the Black church. Even *Not a Man, and Yet a Man* shifts between the above heroic couplets and the tetrameter that appealed to earlier Black Romantics as means to a more musical lyric poetry. In this moment, however, and throughout his career, Whitman focused on the problems and prospects of an elite Black vanguard, what Du Bois later called the "Talented Tenth."[10]

Whitman sometimes underscores Rodney's distinction from his Black peers with a blunt and impossible racialism, noting the "eighty-five per cent. of Saxon in his veins." On the whole, however, *Not a Man, and Yet a Man* tends to overload these clunky essentialisms with paradox and casuistry. Descriptions of Rodney's natural, nearly white masculine perfection inevitably run into contradiction:

> A lover of fair women, and as blind
> To her weaknesses as Egyptian night,
> A fondler with soft childhood, and as kind

To its mistakes, as if mistakes were right;
Skilled in the feats of backwoods life adorn,
Although a stranger to the backwoods born,
The shelly clamor of the autumn trees,
Or howl of beasts, or savages alike can please.
And he a slave? Ah Saville, can it be
That such a noble heart can not beat free!

Despite his apparent whiteness, Rodney's virtue emerges as a series of Byronic incongruities. Whitman associates his inability to see the "weaknesses" of women with the darkness of "Egyptian night." Rodney's indulgence of children presses the limits of rationality, "as if mistakes were right." Whitman goes on to suggest that the hero knows the ways of the wilderness despite having all the qualities of a civilized man. Finally he arrives at the problem of Rodney's enslavement, at odds with the character of his "heart." Through the twists and turns of Whitman's logic, Rodney's virtue, first associated with his whiteness, becomes Black, on the basis of his sentimentality and his comfort with confusion, what Keats would call his "negative capability."[11]

Whitman takes the same digressive and dialectical approach to his description of Rodney's lover Leeona, "the fair Creole":

Ah! She was beautiful, tho' not
So *fair* as lovesick rhymers plot ...
Ah! not so fair, but a rich rose,
And brilliant as the stream that flows
From Summer hills, with meadows sweet,
And dewy corn-fields at their feet;
While bleating pastures peaceful lie,
Beneath an azure canopy.

Here again Whitman's Byronic vamping rewires color symbolism. He suggests that Leeona's coloring, "not so fair, but a rich rose," is more beautiful for being closer to nature than the ethereal whiteness that preoccupies lesser "lovesick rhymers." The pastoralism of this passage hints at a Romantic nationalism in Leeona's beauty—its organic roots in, and claim on, the land. Her "fair" coloring reflects an array of natural similes that approaches a full landscape. Elsewhere in the poem, he describes Leeona more tragically as, "By heaven forsaken, and denied by earth, / As if too crime-stained to deserve a birth." In this gloss, Whitman hints at Leeona's history as the child of rape—contrapuntal to the "virgin land" that mid-twentieth-century cultural historian Henry Nash Smith found at the heart of the mythology of the frontier. Both Rodney and Leeona's biracial heroism results from embedded national and territorial contradictions and alienations that resist simple assertions of moral principle.[12]

After Rodney and Leeona escape to Canada, Sir Maxey's daughter Dora, the white "heroine of Saville," in a rather extraordinary contrivance, arrives at their door, and offers him "the white hand of recognition":

His great stern face of simple fidelity and manhood brave,
Was now lighted up with a glow exceeding portrayal,
And in its effulgence approaching those who stand in white robes
Ever, within the tidal glory of the Throne Eternal.

Earlier on, Whitman's hints of the possibility of romance between Rodney and Dora risked miscegenation. Here in this concluding scene, Whitman exsanguinates their implied erotic connection, relighting it in a white spiritual "glow." Dora's recognition promises a deracinating and spiritually chaste uplift out of tune with the poem's harrowing depiction of rapacious settler colonialism. Pleading to his sense of moral rectitude, Dora draws Rodney back to the United States, where along with his and Leeona's grown sons, he becomes a hero yet again fighting for the Union in the Civil War. The action of the epic ends here, sealing the connection between Rodney's mixed-race masculine virtue and US nationalism.[13]

In a concluding section entitled "The End of the Whole Matter," Whitman makes Rodney's chivalric enlistment symbolic of Black allegiance to the postbellum Union. Through a dense array of metaphors and paradoxes, Whitman implores his Black contemporaries to keep vigilant watch over the free institutions of the postbellum Union:

> Oh comrade freemen strike your hands to stand
> Like walls of rock and guard our father-land!
> Oh guard our homes and institutions free,
> The price of blood and valor's legacy.
> Awake and watch ye sovereign sons of toil!
> If despot feet e're touch our country's soil,
> Fly to the standard that by freeman born,
> The glory of a hundred years has worn,
> Blood-stained, yet bright, streaming, but battle torn,
> And *rally* till the last drop from the veins
> Of free America flows on our plains.
> Eternal vigilance must light the tower,
> Whose granite strength can bide the evil hour,
> Whose wave-dashed base defies the tempest's shock,
> Builded upon the everlasting rock ...
>
> Free schools, free press, free speech and equal laws,
> A common country and a common cause,
> Are only worthy of a freeman's boasts—
> Are Freedom's *real* and intrinsic costs.
> Without these, Freedom is an empty name,
> And war-worn glory is a glaring shame.

Whitman's critique of American exceptionalism comes to an improbable crescendo. Rodney's fugitive, biracial heroism has been thoroughly assimilated; his Blackness, which once pressed him into the wilderness beyond American civilization, is now a kind of reserve of sustenance on which the Union will draw in perpetuity. Blood has ceased to function as the measure of racial difference and instead becomes, through war, the currency by which violence pays for free institutions. The romantic anticapitalism Whitman found earlier in Black Hawk haunts this exchange, however, and his histrionic patriotism suggests an underlying anxiety about Black assimilation to American democracy that would worsen, with good reason, in the late 1870s and early 1880s. The extravagance of Whitman's language makes his declarations of national allegiance seem absurd, and his rhetoric amplifies the brutal coincidence of centennial celebration and the collapse of Reconstruction.[14]

The Interlude of "Eternal Bass"

The charged political ambivalence of Whitman's epic takes into its sweep racial and national identifications; its most difficult moments involve his heroes' seeming estrangement from Black community and Black culture. Whitman's thinking on this question was complex and evolving. Collected alongside the epic in the print volume of *Not a Man, and Yet a Man* is an elegy, entitled "The Lute of Afric's Tribe," which takes a very different view of Black music than his hero Rodney seems to while enslaved in Florida. Dedicated "To the memory of Dr. J. McSimpson, a colored Author of Anti-Slavery Ballads," the poem is unique in the period for its address to another Black poet. It is a crucial document in establishing the internal coherence of Black Romantic aesthetics, and in connecting Black Romantic lyrics to longer-term conceptions of African-American culture. Simpson had lived most of his life just a few miles from Wilberforce in Xenia, Ohio, and Whitman had apparently come to appreciate his work in the struggle to end slavery. Extraordinarily ornate in both its prosody and its interlacing Biblical, diasporic, and US histories, his elegy makes a museum case for Simpson's antislavery songs.

In contrast with the antic uncertainty of Whitman's epic, this short work consecrates Black Romanticism as a movement around the figure of the poet. It offers another theory of cultural politics in the form of a lyric poem, now three decades after the coalescence of African-American literature alongside the abolition movement. Through a profoundly abstracted historical narrative of Black music, it also makes clear Whitman's messianic and revolutionary conception of the end of slavery:

When Israel sate by Babel's stream and wept,
The heathen said, "Sing one of Zion's songs;"
But tuneless lay the lyre of those who slept
Where Sharon bloomed and Oreb vigil kept;
For holy song to holy ears belongs.

So, when her iron clutch the Slave power reached,
And sable generations captive held;
When Wrong the gospel of endurance preached;
The lute of Afric's tribe, tho' oft beseeched,
In all its wild, sweet warblings never swelled.

And yet when Freedom's lispings o'er it stole,
Soft as the breath of undefiled morn,
A wand'ring accent from its strings would stroll—
Thus was our Simpson, man of song and soul,
And stalwart energies, to bless us born.

When all our nation's sky was overcast
With rayless clouds of deepening misery,
His soaring vision mounted thro' the blast,
And from behind its gloom approaching fast,
Beheld the glorious Sun of Liberty.

He sang exultant: "Let her banner wave!"
And cheering senates, fired by his zeal,
Helped snatch their country from rebellion's grave
Looked through brave tears upon the injured slave,
And raised the battle-arm to break his gyves of steel.

But hushed the bard, his harp no longer sings
The woes and longings of a shackled mind;
For death's cold fingers swept its trembling strings,
And shut the bosom of its murmurings
Forever on the hearing of mankind.

The bird that dips his flight in noonday sun,
May fall, and spread his plumage on the plain;

But when immortal mind its work hath done
On earth, in heaven a nobler work's begun,
And it can never downward turn again.

Of him, whose harp then, lies by death unstrung—
A harp that long his lowly brethren cheered,
May'nt we now say, that, sainted choirs among,
An everlasting theme inspires his tongue,
Where slaves ne'er groan, and death is never feared?

Yes, he is harping on the "Sea of glass,"
Where saints begin, and angels join the strain;
While Spheres in one profound, eternal bass,
Sing thro' their orbs, illumined as they pass,
And constellations catch the long refrain.

Here Whitman complicates the categorical view of Black music attributed to Rodney; he explores in greater depth the so-called "low inventions of poor darkened mind." He traces Black music back to its historical roots, drawing connections between Africa and the Biblical scenery of the ancient Mediterranean. The poem glosses the Middle Passage and the experience of enslavement in tersely artful language, comparing the suppression of diasporic culture to the silencing of an instrument. The titular "lute of Afric's tribe" functions like the Aeolian harp of Romantic thought, a medium for the enactment of Black liberation, like the "one grand string" Grace Greenwood recognized in Frances Harper's commitment to abolition. Whitman imagines Simpson's rise as a correspondent breeze, "Freedom's lispings" across the strings of that lute, and his music thus performing the self-realization of Black peoplehood. The poem seeks to reconcile, through song, the moral elevation of Whitman's heroes with the voice and experience of Black people as a mass.

The poem's history is more speculative than accurate, to say the least. The "wild, sweet warblings" of Black music in slavery could hardly be said to have "never swelled." Given Simpson's anonymity, the claims Whitman makes for his voice in the movement to end slavery are extraordinary, that "His soaring vision mounted thro' the blast," and that he "[h]elped snatch their country from rebellion's grave." When the poem turns to Simpson's passing, it insists on his immortality with characteristically redemptive frenzy. Whitman identifies the permanence of Simpson's lyrics as "nobler work"—the "eternal bass" and the "long refrain" draw the Black freedom struggle out of the particularity of the end of slavery in the United States and into the speculative idealism of universal history. The bewildering syntactic and prosodic complexity of the lyric worries the line between the postbellum present and heavenly emancipation—one must read it over and over to hear the music of the spheres. The late 1870s and early 1880s saw the "sun of Liberty" darken and the costs of freedom skyrocket, with little compensation for the recently freed. Whitman's music would increasingly fall out of rhythm with history, but this had become his method, to make, for a people forced back from the revolutionary vanguard to pre-modern containment, a syncopation of old and new as an expression of the elusive spirit of the age.

"An apocalypse of sentiment"

The title of Whitman's next poem would attract even more controversy than his last. *The Rape of Florida* (1884) was published by the Nixon-Jones Print Company in St. Louis—whose list otherwise featured unliterary material like the proceedings of the Missouri Bar Association, records of local urban planning efforts, and the catalogue of a mercantile library. The volume attracted enough attention in its first printing to be republished the following year under a less incendiary title, *Twasinta's Seminoles* (1885), again with notices in the *Christian Recorder*. In the preface to the second edition, Whitman apologized vaguely for the previous title: "Youth thinks extravagantly and often speaks more so, but sober experience comes to correct us." Otherwise, Whitman kept the firebrand rhetoric of the 1884 preface, which had declared: "The time has come for all 'Uncle Toms' and 'Topsies' to die."

Whitman had plenty of reason, in the seven years since *Not a Man*, to become disillusioned with the veiled white supremacy of racial uplift and what he calls the "empty name" of American freedom. Against the drift of history, he mounts a critique of assimilation a decade before Booker T. Washington urged Southern Black laborers to "Cast down your bucket where you are."[15]

The historical perspective which rendered the end of *Not a Man, and Yet a Man* so extraordinarily strange had only intensified. The emergent middle-class periodical culture of the 1880s had begun to represent the Civil War in sepia tones. Edmund Wilson described the process as a medical procedure: "the old issues must be put to sleep with the chloroform of magazine prose"; historian David Blight described it as the jettisoning of a story of racial reckoning for a story of national reunion. Whitman's preface describes the moment in abstract terms, avoiding the specific historical prompts for his epic. Instead, he lays out a Romantic anticapitalist theory of poetry:

> I cannot think that money-getting is the whole business of man. Rather I am convinced that the whole world is approaching a poetical revolution … I think poetry is the language of universal sentiment. Torch of the unresting mind, she kindles in advance of all progress. Her waitings are on the threshold of the infinite

Albery Allson Whitman, frontispiece to The Rape of Florida *(St. Louis: Nixon-Jones Printing Co., 1884).*

where, beckoning man to listen, she interprets the leaves of immortality. Her voice is the voice of Eternity dwelling in all great souls. Her aims are the inducements of heaven, and her triumphs, the survival of the Beautiful, the True, and the Good.

Between the vague resistance to "money-getting" and the paean to "progress," this has the ring of Romantic boilerplate. However, set against the emergent middle-class conception of poetry as genteel high culture, Whitman's rhetoric appears more bombastic. His language echoes Walt Whitman's earlier prose work *Democratic Vistas* (1871), which also called on poetry as an antidote to Gilded Age corruption. Where the white Whitman hoped the postbellum consummation of Manifest Destiny would provide an opportunity for national regeneration, the Black Whitman found white territorial ambition at the root of US corruption. His suggestion, that the best political and poetic impulses of the period are feminine, and that these impulses should be the real source of future-orientation, echoes contemporary Black feminists like Harper and Anna Julia Cooper. It challenges the period's less reflective, and often imperial investments in perfected masculinity. In sum, the preface to this formally complex long poem announces its pitch in the direction of revolution against both capital and patriarchy.[16]

Whitman establishes the Blackness of *The Rape of Florida* in its opening "canto," which centers on the voice of an anonymous "negro slave" who "by the Swanee river sang," before escaping down to Florida. The plot of the poem, like that of *Not a Man, and Yet a Man*, focuses on captivity, fugitivity, and sexual violence as the inevitable results of border war. It follows the capture of the aging Seminole chief Palmecho; his rescue by the heroic Afro-Seminole Atlassa; the subsequent capture of Ewald, Palmecho's beautiful daughter; her rescue; and finally the displacement of its main characters to a Seminole settlement in Mexico. These events take place mostly during the Second Seminole War, especially through future President Zachary Taylor's command of the US Army in Florida in the late 1830s. The plot is at every turn made difficult to follow, and its historical context difficult to ascertain, by Whitman's digression, rumination, and improvised abstractions.

The poem continues Whitman's attempt to write an ethnic American epic poetry and returns to the model of Scott's historical romances, balancing the fate of ordinary characters alongside the doings of great men—this time the Creek-Seminole resistance leader Osceola. Whitman describes Osceola as a kind of latter-day Achilles, "the hidden terror of the hommock, he / Sat gloomily and nursed his bitter hate." Osceola's motivations are framed by the sexual politics of settler colonialism:

> From the wizard caverns of despair,
> Came a voice and groan, reminding o'er and o'er
> The outrage on his wife so young and fair;
> And so, by heaven and earth and hell he swore
> To treat in council with the white-man never more.

Representations of Osceola's life were popular across the nineteenth century, but Whitman likely drew on Joshua Reed Giddings's *The Exiles of Florida* (1858). Giddings had been a vocal abolitionist in the federal legislature as representative from Ohio's Twentieth District, which included Wilberforce, and he opposed the Seminole Wars from an abolitionist perspective. Of the galvanizing incident with Osceola's wife, Giddings notes, "She was the daughter of a chief who had married one of the Exiles; but as all colored people by slaveholding laws are said to follow the condition of the mother, she was called an African slave." He describes her rape as an example of the "slaveholding pollution," just the sort of euphemism characteristic of the period's radicals on the subject of sexual violence. For his part, Whitman draws the scene into a thick network of Euro-American cultural references, from Homer to Edmund Spenser and Walter Scott. The "wizard caverns of despair" situate Osceola as a Byronic hero, with the landscape echoing his bereavement.[17]

The Rape of Florida does not fixate on its characters' blood quantum; instead Whitman makes a virtue of Seminole ethnogenesis and juxtaposes the joy of Afro-Indigenous romantic relations with the sexual violence of captivity. This poetic argument involves a turn from his earlier bio-essentialist notions of ethnic character to an interest in ethnic cultural practice, specifically Seminole hospitality toward fugitives from slavery. In conventional epic fashion, Whitman understands these dynamics through the Homeric notion of *xenia*, or guest-host relations. He describes encounters between what Giddings calls "exiles" and the Natives of Florida in elaborately aestheticized terms:

XXVIII.
The poorest black that came upon their shore,
To them was brother—their own flesh and blood,—
They fought his wretched manhood to restore,—
They sound his hidings in the swampy wood,
And brought him forth—in arms before him stood,—
The citizens of God and sovran earth,—
They shot straight forward looks with flame imbued,
Till in him manhood sprang, a noble birth,
And warrior-armed he rose to all that manhood's worth.

XXIX.
On the dark front of battle often seen,
Or holding dang'rous posts through dreadful hours,—
In ranks obedient, in command serene,
His comrades learn to note tested powers
Which prove that valor is not always ours,
Be whomsoever we: A common race
Soon from this union flows—soon rarest flowers
Bloom out and smile in beauty's blending grace,
And rivals they become for love's sublimest place.

XXX.
The native warrior leads his ebon maid,
The dark young brave his bloom-hued lover wins;
And where soft spruce and willows mingle shade,
Young life mid sunniest hours its course begins:
All Nature pours its never-ending dins
In groves of rare-hued leaf without an end,—

> 'Tis as if Time, forgetting Eden's sins,
> Relents, and spirit visitors descend
> In love's remembered tokens, earth once more to blend.

Whitman casts racial mixture as a sublime counterpoint to the sexual violence at the center of the New World contact narrative. In the first stanza, the masculinity of the fugitives is restored through the recognition of native warriors, whose "looks with flame imbued" reinvigorate Black men emasculated by enslavement. A kind of antiracist relativism colors these encounters between men, in which interethnic solidarity depends on the acknowledgment that "valor is not always ours, / Be whomsoever we." Whitman then depicts the sexual results of these encounters in a series of metaphorical tricks on nature's "rare-hued leaf" and "beauty's blending grace." This suggestive mix of race and nature helps Whitman avoid his earlier overdetermination of multiracial identity, so he finds in Afro-Seminole relations a place "where soft spruce and willows mingle shade." This alternate myth of origins for an imagined community of the borderlands reconceives the "virgin land" through Afro-Indigenous sexuality, cleansed of colonial "sins."[18]

Whitman takes Seminole hospitality toward fugitives, their shared relation to the land, and their erotic union, as prompts for a Romantic revisionist philosophy of history. In the passage above, this takes the form of prelapsarian longing: "'Tis as if Time, forgetting Eden's sins, relents." Elsewhere, Whitman elaborates the aestheticism and decadence of his poetic interest in righting historical wrongs:

> Oh! would the muse of history rend the veil,
> And bring her hidden instances to light;
> How many standards of the soul would trail,
> As thousands all unknown would rush in sight!
> From steepled vale and celebrated height!
> Wherever civilization spreads her name,
> Nations that perished in the scourge and blight
> Of wars would rise, and in the book of fame,
> Record their struggles and their heroes' deeds proclaim.

Playing yet again on the "eternal bass," Whitman imagines the struggle for freedom as not just world-historical, but cosmological. Hard as it may be to square with the unabashed sexuality and violence of his poetry, Whitman's working life as an itinerant preacher reappears in this messianic liberation theology. The figure of the "veil" anticipates Du Bois's *The Souls of Black Folk*, with its mix of secular and theological prophecy. In Whitman's reckoning, what he calls at the poem's outset an "apocalypse of sentiment," historical romance can unveil the victims of colonial progress. In this distinctly syncretic and aesthetic moment of judgment, the claims of contemporary "civilization" would be settled against the "nations that perished" on its rise. *The Rape of Florida* itself acts as a symbolic fragment of the revelations promised in "the book of fame" which would record the heroism of the conquered. In telling stories of Indigenous and maroon communities in residual literary forms, Whitman's historical romances make an aesthetic argument against settler-colonial theories of progress. He rewrites the self-aggrandizing invented traditions of American frontier mythology to begin with slavery and dispossession.[19]

The poem's conclusion follows its Seminole protagonists to settle in Mexico, and thus makes a kind of historical ellipsis, in which Black, Indigenous, and mixed-race characters find an ill-defined freedom outside the United States. Through the antiquated forms of verse epic and historical romance, Whitman's *The Rape of Florida* imagines a kind of interethnic sovereignty from below. Other works of African-American literature at the end of the nineteenth century took similarly weird and revelatory liberties with the time and space of diaspora: Pauline Hopkins's *Of One Blood* (1902–3) makes a time-traveling detour to ancient Ethiopia, for instance, and Sutton Griggs's *Imperium in Imperio* (1899) imagines a Black nationalist shadow government based in Waco, Texas. The onset of Jim Crow had made speculative writing more urgent. Whitman anticipated these trips through time and across space in sometimes impossibly beautiful language, his aesthetic idealism set against the horrors of colonial history. In *The Rape of Florida*, he offers an exquisitely condensed figure for the agonized ambivalence of Black postbellum US nationalism:

"at patriotism's shrine, / The ardor of exile is divine." Whitman's movement, in his life and work, around the country and across time, sought to counter the suspended animation of Black life at the end of Reconstruction. The distance between real and ideal freedom feels, in his work, both spiritual and erotic, a kind of ecstasy resulting from meditative poetic practice. In Florida, Whitman found a political yearning beyond fantasies of racial purity or cultural elevation that he would struggle to sustain.[20]

"New world greatness, drawn from ev'ry human race"

Despite the ambivalence displayed in his frontier epics, Whitman headed west to Kansas in the 1880s. William J. Simmons noted in *Men of Mark* (1887): "The poet is still living in ill health in the West, in Kansas." He would have been, at the time, 36 years old. The next year, bishop in the AME Church and one of the founders of Wilberforce, Daniel Payne, complained in his autobiography about the poet's drinking: "O Whitman, Whitman! canst thou not break the chains that bind thee to the chariot-wheels of intemperance? Why boast of thy freedom from the white man, and yet be the slave of alcohol?" It appears Whitman went to Kansas out of some combination of desperation and commitment. African Americans moving out of the South to Kansas in the late 1870s and 1880s had become known as Exodusters. In an 1879 essay entitled "The Negro Exodus from the Gulf States," Douglass associated migration to Kansas, "the modern Canaan," with earlier efforts at Black nationalist emigration. Whitman's epics may have explored the corruption at the heart of settler mythology through detours to half-century-old conflict, but Kansas was his later work's real background. Kansas offered the hollow promise of land not yet swallowed up by railroad speculators and industrial agriculture, and of towns not yet the gleaming cities of the industrial North which would draw Black migrants in the coming decades. In other words, Whitman's confused rage about Black people's stake in the promise of American life would only intensify through the end of the 1880s and '90s.[21]

At the same time, he remained capable of operatic patriotism. On the occasion of the Chicago World's Fair of 1893, Whitman wrote what would become his most well-known shorter poem, "The Freedmen's Triumphant Song." This lyric condenses the geopolitics of the epics into a jeremiad on Black belonging in the US national community. It returns to the "granite" strength of Black soldiers, the sacred contribution of their "blood" to the Union cause, and their spiritual relation to the glories of New World nature. The poem is a gorgeous piece of poetic speculation, moving across the American landscape with the facility of that other Whitman, but in more wrought tetrameter couplets. Taking the mantle of a nineteenth-century poet-statesman, Whitman seeks to resolve tensions around the World's Fair, which was widely protested by figures like Frederick Douglass and Ida B. Wells for excluding Black people from its so-called "White City." He recalls Black enlisted men's contributions to American modernity, and seeks to quiet regional animus:

> Let caste's old mouth
> Keep still about the "North and South"
> The Negro's dark intrepid brow
> Shall wear the hero's laurels now.

Later sections of the poem struggle to keep "caste" at bay. At one moment, Whitman insists that African Americans "*will not* yield" to immigrant labor "just hailed from foreign coast." In another he wonders about still looming prospects of Black emigration: "Shall the Negro turn away / And leave his native land for aye?" For the occasion, Whitman imagines an inclusive American nationalism in response: " 'No!' every home industry cries," but the World's Fair itself had made clear that white American manufacturing was not yet open to Black labor. The poem struggles to disguise the historical frustrations of Black Americanization, even as it makes high-flown patriotic claims: "Oh! may Columbia forever reign, / The pride of worlds, with empires in her train!"[22]

A tantalizing newspaper item hints at the shakiness of Whitman's patriotism and his closely held ethnic nationalism. The

Wichita *National Reflector* of February 8, 1896 reprinted a letter that originally appeared in the *Lawrence World*, contesting a planned colony in Central America:

I see that Albery A. Whitman, the octoroon poet and evangelist, is the author of a scheme to colonize Gautamala or Yucatan with quadroons and octoroons, and to establish an independent government. This great Jonah said that it has been a dream of his life to found a nation, which shall be composed exclusively of the quadroons and octoroons of the United States, whom he denominates the "New Race."

Albery A. Whitman proposes to lead this new race of his to Central America, where he will be crowned lord of all. I would like to know about how many members of this new race of Whitman's live in the city of Lawrence, and are getting ready to go with him to Central America, where he will not need the light of the sun, nor the stars and moon to shine at night, for the light of all those quadroons and octoroons that Whitman will carry over there will light up Central America. This man Whitman said, "We hold no affiliation with the kinkey race any more than we do with the whites." He goes on to say, "We are a beautiful race, superior to both." If anyone can see anything about Whitman that is beautiful, it is more than I can do.

The origin of this kinkey race Whitman speaks of, is definitely known. I would like for Whitman to tell us something about the origin of this new race of his. This man Whitman goes on to say, "We do not encourage the blacks, and do not want them." The devil makes no distinction between men on account of color. But do not understand me to say that this man Whitman is worse than the devil. But think over the matter. I want no hypocritical, sycophantic, cowardly, dirt-eating religion. Any Christian organizing any scheme that points to the separating of husband and wife, mother and children, brothers and sisters, is a hypocrite and a cowardly scoundrel. Whitman must remember that he will find the kinkey race anywhere in the world that he may go, and there will be kinkey races on earth when he is dead.

Across a prolific and lifelong career as a poet, Whitman had performed an African-American patriotism, while also harboring a plan of escape from the United States. That Whitman was an emigrationist is surprising, but that he was also quietly developing a theory of multiracial nationalism is truly strange. Given the poet's preoccupations, profession, and reputation as "the Poet Laureate of the Negro Race," his apparently antiblack attitude towards the "kinkey race" makes for a brutal historical irony. How does one reconcile this moment with Whitman's poetic pleas for Black inclusion in the US national community? With his painstaking depictions of Black character and Black heroism? With his ardent expressions of frustration with racial uplift leadership's accommodation of white supremacy? The letter poses to Whitman the question of "the origin of this new race of his," as if the poet had not been writing about sexual violence and captivity for more than twenty years. From the vantage of Whitman's unerring focus on African-American life as a product of diaspora, indigeneity, and white rapacity, perhaps the paradoxes of this belated illusion are not so irreconcilable. The coincidence of the "nadir" of African-American history and "the golden age of Black nationalism" had produced in Whitman a fantastic celebration of collaborative Black and Indigenous resistance in the epics, but also a bizarre, reactionary fantasy of ethnic nationalism divorced from actually existing ethnic community.[23]

A few years later, Whitman would combine the national theme of "The Freedmen's Triumphant Song" with his post-national fantasy of mixed ethnic colonialism. In "The Southland's Charms and Freedom's Magnitude" (1901), Whitman gives yet another allegorical account of the Civil War and Reconstruction, and again finds the United States inadequate to its own dream of freedom. Late in the poem, he contemplates the "Sovran Rockies," casting the mountain range as "the standard of triumphant Equal Rights" and "the temple dome of Liberty." Forgetting the violence of the frontier, Whitman turns the moralized landscape of the West into a dream of an interracial paradise:

> I saw a city in the setting sun,
>   Superb and vast, that crowned a noble height;
> It was the city of the Yellowstone.
>   In New World greatness, from its ancient site
> Removed—the future's Washington.
>   And guarded round, in its unconquered might,
> By leagues of fortress, was a populace
> Unnumbered, drawn from ev'ry human race.

This multiethnic neverland, "the future's Washington," has more specific utopian stipulations than one finds elsewhere in Black Romantic literature. Here Whitman sets his insistently archaic vision of, and spelling of, sovereignty, alongside a proper science-fictional utopia. Within the securitized terrain of the Rockies, he imagines a system of apprenticeships so that "no children roamed the streets at will," and legal mechanisms to prevent marriage "when there was presence of a known disease, / Hence, no divorces, no adulteries." In this nightmare of social engineering masquerading as a dream, the sexual strictures of racial uplift, which otherwise emphasized self-surveillance, now become enforced eugenics.[24]

At the close of the poem, as migrants arrive at his Western city upon a hill, Whitman subtly recapitulates the antiblackness of his planned mixed-race colony:

> There from the South I saw the blue-eyed blonde,
>   And from the North the Junoesque brunette;
> From Hawaii the olive maiden fond,
>   The dainty Cuban with her eyes of jet—
> And Octoroon whose beauty was beyond
>   Description, in a swirl of glory met,
> Through mazy depths of flow'rs and lace to stream—
> A symphony of lovely forms—My Dream.

Most of the ethnic representatives at this female congress of the races stand in for colonial mixture. The Blackness of the Octoroon and the Cuban is adulterated by whiteness, like Rodney with his "eighty-five per cent" Saxon blood. Setting aside the earnest beauty of this "symphony of lovely forms," Whitman's shortsightedness disappoints. His racism and frantic US nationalism represent real failures of vision on the part of a poet who otherwise wrote some of the most popular and compelling political poetry of the late nineteenth century. Likewise, the feminist tendencies of his other work seem qualified here by a frankly sexual fantasy of anonymous women presented in the round. The radicalism of his approach, his errands in the wilderness of history aimed at poetical revolution, also led him to his worst conclusions. So invested in capturing the historical confusion of his people, Whitman became, at the late peaks of his creative intensity, confused.[25]

Whitman's long poems, with their antiquated diction, could never thrive in the magazine culture that took up dialect poetry in earnest in the 1890s. Paul Laurence Dunbar became a nationwide celebrity as a poet in this period, through prestigious and widely circulated national (and white) periodicals like *Harper's* and the *Saturday Evening Post*. Dunbar and his contemporaries' Romantic historicism represented Black folk life on the antebellum plantation in subtly critical but also idealizing ways that played well with white audiences. By the early years of the first decade of the twentieth century, Dunbar had taken Whitman's mantle as the "Poet Laureate of the Negro Race." In a 1903 essay entitled "Representative American Negroes," Dunbar riffed on Shakespeare in a line that encapsulates the ironies of Whitman's career: "Some men are born great, some achieve greatness, and some lived during the reconstruction period." On the one hand, Dunbar suggests, via the echo of Shakespeare's original, that Black people who lived through Reconstruction had "greatness thrust upon them" as a matter of everyday survival. On the other, he also hints at the ignominies associated with Black life over the same years: the exploitations and violences of white supremacy's reorganization; the opportunism of uplift leadership. Whitman was great, in spite of what was thrust upon him, and what he became in carrying the burden.[26]

His popular appeal through the end of Reconstruction suggests he had tapped into the core cultural-political problems of his moment. Whitman's poems are adventure stories, but in a language too ornate and too idealist to resonate across an increasingly speedy media environment. His heroes' feats of courage take place against the ordinary, historical procedures of slavery and empire; they dramatize the contradictions between ideologies of character, colonialism, racism, and capitalism. Despite his seemingly difficult relationship with changing audiences of the late nineteenth century, he was never so out of touch as his Rodney, the "mental Sampson" who could not enjoy the songs of the enslaved. His daughters, the Whitman Sisters, whom he taught to perform alongside him in church, later became the most popular dance troupe on the Black vaudeville circuit. Through them as through his poems, he played alongside the eternal bass.

Conclusion

Dreams and Nightmares

From the perspective of Black Romanticism and its dream of abolition-democracy, the protests against the removal of Confederate monuments in the summer of 2017 have the quality of a recurring nightmare. A shrinking elite yet again trades on what Du Bois called the "psychological wage" of whiteness and the promise of renewed patriarchy. The vision of abolition-democracy does not, however, evaporate at the sight of torches bought from big box stores.

The main characters of this book have not much appeared in recent conversations around Civil War memory; the conclusion to Frances Harper's "Bury Me in a Free Land" (1864), which appears on her modest gravestone at Eden Cemetery in Collingdale, Pennsylvania, suggests why:

> I ask no monument, proud and high,
> To arrest the gaze of the passers by;
> All that my yearning spirit craves
> Is—*Bury me not in a land of slaves!*

This book began with questions about the intimations of apocalypse among the Black Romantics: did the Civil War really fulfill those predictions, or did they anticipate a longer-term reckoning? Another way of putting the question, now with the spectacular examples of Charlottesville, Ferguson, and Baltimore in mind: can Harper's spirit really rest here? There is, in any case, as she demanded, no monument—no sculptor has ever so much as made a bust.[1]

Memorializing the Bronze muse, who asks no monument, requires careful measurement of the distance between past and present, and between real and ideal, but it also evokes a will to counterintuition, a cultural politics of the hypothetical. The gaps in the extant record of Harper's career elicit wishful thinking; one can hardly read her for long without wanting to know more. So much of her life lived in service and struggle remains shrouded in provocative mystery; it calls forth a curiosity no monument could fulfill: to know how she *sounded*, and just as impossibly, to know what she *wanted*. Horton, and Whitman, and Whitfield, and Simpson, each with their songs of fiercest passion, all have the same effect. To know what they wanted through how they sounded means first accepting that what they wanted was not what they got. They all kept on wanting, and their songs were never silenced even if the sound was lost in the discord between then and now.

Saidiya Hartman has made the most forceful recent case for thinking about the connections between the history of slavery and the present, warning against assumptions about the accessibility of that history. At the outset of her 2007 memoir, *Lose Your Mother: A Journey Along the Atlantic Slave Route*, Hartman makes a critical distinction:

> If slavery persists as an issue in the political life of black America, it is not because of an antiquarian obsession with bygone days or the burden of a too-long memory, but because black lives are still imperiled and devalued by a racial calculus and a political arithmetic that were entrenched centuries ago. This is the afterlife of slavery—skewed life chances, limited access to health and education, premature death, incarceration, and impoverishment.

In this view, what the Black Romantics called the "gloom" of antebellum slavery and racism has not yet dissipated; its shadows have simply taken new forms. Hartman emphasizes the echoes of slavery in the ostensibly masterless context of neoliberalism—how the administration of poverty and the criminalization of Blackness eerily recapitulate the violence of enslavement.[2]

In thinking through Black Romanticism as a prophetic counter to "the afterlife of slavery," a couple of premises follow. Just as the Black Romantics did not exclusively represent the experience of slavery, so recent Black culture need not depict chattel slavery to address the conditions of its aftermath. It might do so while reviving Romantic themes, forms, or techniques, or it might not. It might also, echoing Black Romanticism, still measure the brutal insufficiencies of actually existing liberalism, and make comparisons with more poetic promises of freedom. This conclusion collects a few twentieth- and twenty-first-century incarnations of Black Romanticism, seeking now as before to figure the nightmarish consequences of racist "political arithmetic," to shape the dreamlike possibilities of freedom, and, finally, to wake us all up.

"Then the devil will hand you his instrument to play"

Romanticism did not disappear from African-American culture with the onset of the twentieth century. Instead it moved through the period on what Ralph Ellison called "lower frequencies." The elite cultural nationalism of the Harlem Renaissance owed significant debts to European Romanticism, not least its literary experiments with popular song and what Wordsworth had called the "real language of men." Romantic notions also appeared in less elevated contexts than the little magazines and salons of the New Negro movement. The Black musicians of the Jim Crow South made vital, belated entries into the tradition of Romantic Satanism, which had played such a key role in the iconography of slavery, whispering into the ears of the cruel overseers, calculating masters, frenzied mistresses, alluring Jezebels, and vengeful slaves of the antebellum period. In the rich musical tradition of the Mississippi Delta at the beginning of the twentieth century, this array of Satanic social types coalesced into the myth of a Faustian bargain for musical genius.[3]

In one of the earliest documented versions of this script, white sociologist Newbell Niles Puckett recorded the instructions of a "New Orleans conjurer" in his *Folk Beliefs of the Southern Negro* (1926):

> If you want to make a contact with the devil, first trim your finger nails as closely as you possibly can. Take a black cat bone and a guitar and go to a lonely fork in the roads at midnight. Sit down there and play your best piece, thinking of and wishing for the devil all the while. By and by you will hear music, dim at first but growing louder and louder as the musician approaches nearer. Do not look around; just keep on playing your guitar. The unseen musician will finally sit down by you and play in unison with you. After a time you will feel something tugging at your instrument. Do not try to hold it. Let the devil take it and keep thumping along with your fingers as if you still had the guitar in your hands. Then the devil will hand you his instrument to play and will accompany you on yours. After doing this for a time he will seize your fingers and trim the nails until they bleed, finally taking his guitar back and returning your own. Keep on playing; don't look around. His music will become fainter and fainter as he moves away. When all is quiet you may go home.

Puckett's informant does not stipulate spiritual consequences, nor does he worry much about the ownership of anyone's soul. Instead the bleeding fingernails underscore an emphasis on practice and fleshly sacrifice. Freedom, in the postbellum, meant choosing, again and again, a sense of personhood defined by the contractual obligation to work and pay, over the joys and exposures of vagabondage, or the containments and punishments of criminality. The crossroads myth offered a resolution: a deal for musical talent and technique, the tools of seduction, and all the freedom to wander. The Romantics had found in Satan a representative of the evils of human life, but also of the creativity, productivity, and transformations of a revolutionary period. At the turn of the twentieth century, Black musicians found something similar, a moral outlaw who knew how to navigate a modern world. The crossroads myth especially appealed to Black men, as they were increasingly targeted by lynch law and cut off from the opportunities of industrialization and the emergence of the professions.[4]

Du Bois's early reading of Goethe's *Faust* (1808–32) yielded a very different sense of the fate of Black souls in the twentieth century. In the chapter of *Souls of Black Folk* (1903) entitled "Of the Wings of Atalanta," he quotes Goethe directly, in untranslated German, without naming him, while comparing the white-owned factories of the New South with educational ambitions of his Black students at Atlanta University. He finds his students, surrounded by an increasingly mechanized inequality, nonetheless involved in a kind of idyllic, near-utopian study:

> Not at Oxford or at Leipsic, not at Yale or Columbia, is there an air of higher resolve or more unfettered striving; the determination to realize for men, both black and white, the broadest possibilities of life, to seek the better and the best, to spread with their own hands the Gospel of Sacrifice,—all this is the burden of their talk and dream. Here, amid a wide desert of caste and proscription, amid the heart-hurting slights and jars and vagaries of a deep race-dislike, lies this green oasis, where hot anger cools, and the bitterness of disappointment is sweetened by the springs and breezes of Parnassus; and here men may lie and listen, and learn of a future fuller than the past, and hear the voice of Time: "*Entbehren sollst du, sollst entbehren.*"

The line from Goethe translates roughly as "Forsake you must, you must forsake"; with it, Du Bois underscores the universality of the "Gospel of Sacrifice" and the necessity of living with scarcity to access the good life. He sets an agenda for what would come to be called Black studies: that it must resist the racist and devilish temptations of techno-utopian industrial capitalism.[5]

The line comes from the crucial early scene in Goethe's lyric drama when Mephistopheles convinces Faust to sign away his soul. The devil appears in Faust's study in the guise of a "young nobleman," and advises him to "get yourself / an outfit similar to mine, / so that, released from bondage, you can learn / what life and freedom really are." In response, Faust laments:

> No matter what I wear, I hardly can escape
> the torment of a life confined to earth.
> I am too old to live for pleasure only,
> too young to be without desire.
> What can I hope for from this world?
> You must abstain, refrain, renounce—
> this is the everlasting sound in every ear,
> one that, our whole life long,
> we hear each hour hoarsely singing.

Faust talks himself into falling for temptation, bemoaning the gray drudgery of the ordinary and everyday. The translator could not brook the repetitiveness of Goethe's original, rendering the repeated "*entbehren*" as "abstain, refrain, renounce," but the repetition should echo the "everlasting sound" of the next line. This droning reverberates with what Du Bois's interlocutor Max Weber called "the Protestant ethic and the spirit of capitalism," and sounds far away from both the improvisations of the blues and the Black Romantic songs of fiercest passion.[6]

In his depiction of Black university life, Du Bois recommends a Black asceticism, distinct from the bogus assumptions about possessive individualism and national prosperity that motivated industrialization. His sense of the devil's work is prophetic, embedded in the long history of slavery and postbellum exploitation. Having surveyed the expanses visible from the intellectual heights of Atlanta, Du Bois prescribes a pre-Satanic and preindustrial innocence. He addresses men explicitly, and carefully avoids the questions of gender and romantic love that would be Faust's downfall. Du Bois's Black studies are a more authentically higher learning, inclusive of Egyptian and Persian as well as Greek and Roman antiquities. This perspective gives Du Bois an orientation towards vigilance that recalls a passage from Ephesians (4:26–7): "Be angry, and yet do not sin, do not let the sun go down on your anger, and do not give the devil an opportunity." This passionately masculine rage, against a devil who is always working, would continue to find expression in his work. Du Bois would quote the line from *Faust* again, some five decades later in 1958, in an address to the Pan-African Congress at Accra, Ghana, delivered in absentia by his wife, Shirley Graham Du Bois. His language had grown rougher with time: "You can wait. You can starve a while longer rather than sell your great heritage for a mess of Western capitalistic pottage." Here was yet another crossroads, carved by white-owned modernity—with the violence of sacrifice more pronounced, and seemingly so little of what Billie Holiday sang, "that ole devil called love."[7]

"A drama acted out upon the body"

In the early 1960s, the Civil War centennial and the Civil Rights movement brought slavery and its end back into focus as objects of study, representation, and cultural memory. Robert Hayden's collection of poems, *A Ballad of Remembrance* (1962), marked the turning point among African-American poets, treating the Middle Passage, fugitivity, and Black abolitionism in the jaggedly forbidding rhythms of late modernism. The sonnet "Frederick Douglass" evokes the moment's yearning, its sense of the unfinished business of emancipation, and the sense of return that framed what came to be called the Second Reconstruction:

When it is finally ours, this freedom, this liberty, this beautiful
and terrible thing, needful to man as air,
usable as earth; when it belongs at last to all,
when it is truly instinct, brain matter, diastole, systole,
reflex action; when it is finally won; when it is more
than the gaudy mumbo jumbo of politicians:
this man, this Douglass, this former slave, this Negro
beaten to his knees, exiled, visioning a world
where none is lonely, none hunted, alien,
this man, superb in love and logic, this man
shall be remembered. Oh, not with statues' rhetoric,

not with legends and poems and wreaths of bronze alone,
but with the lives grown out of his life, the lives
fleshing his dream of the beautiful, needful thing.

Hayden insists that actually existing American "freedom," the provisional freedoms of New Deal liberalism and late Jim Crow, was not that freedom sought at the end of slavery. If it were, according to Hayden, it would be felt in the viscera, not trumpeted in the bogus political pageantry and monumental history of postwar patriotism. Douglass stands in for the project of abolition-democracy abandoned, to mark the distance once again between the nation's ideals and the lived experience of its second-class citizens.

Hayden's rhetoric is unmistakably messianic; he proceeds from a certainty about the delayed arrival of a true, embodied freedom: "When it is finally ours ..." In this respect, his orientation is more definitive than Whitfield, for instance, who had asked in the 1850s: "How long, oh gracious God! how long / Shall power lord it over right?" In a century of waiting and forsaking, Hayden and his contemporaries had seen more clearly the burdensome role of Black life in symbolizing the inadequacy of American freedom. In 1964, Ralph Ellison proposed, with referential flourish, that "we view the whole of American life as a drama acted out upon the body of a Negro giant, who, lying trussed up like Gulliver, forms the stage and the scene upon which and within which the action unfolds." In this view, struggles over the form and content of American freedom had long centered symbolically and disproportionately on the fate of Black people. The vaunted and dubious status of slavery as America's "original sin" has everything to do with this "drama." In the course of the Second Reconstruction, African-American identity had become, yet again, both representational and exceptional; the ambivalence of the fugitives, mirroring liberal ideals yet expressing the limitations of liberalism, had returned.[8]

The collective, embodied waiting in Hayden's poetic memorial is the Black body, "trussed up like Gulliver" in Ellison, the "black masses" in Du Bois, walked all over by racist caricature. This symbolic role for Black people continued paradoxically to justify their systemic impoverishment and criminalization through the Civil Rights era. Here were the real obstacles to Hayden's hope for "the lives grown out of [Douglass's] life": white supremacy reorganized in the face of challenges from the Civil Rights movement, and white liberalism clinging to notions of Blackness as abject and infantilized.

"We're living in a sick society"

A historical apocalypse suffused the work of the Black Romantics; their language was filled with floods, storms, and ultimately, bloody violence. The rhetoric of crisis and historical transformation needed retuning for the struggles of the 1960s. In a speech delivered at Olivet Church in 1969, chairman of the Illinois chapter of the Black Panther Party Fred Hampton offered a startling reassurance:

> A lot of people get the word revolution mixed up and they think revolution's a bad word. Revolution is nothing but like having a sore on your body and then you put something on that sore to cure that infection. And I'm telling you that we're living in an infectious society right now. I'm telling you that we're living in a sick society. And anybody that endorses integrating into this sick society before it's cleaned up is a man who's committing a crime against the people.

Hampton redefines revolution in deceptively superficial terms. Reading it through the familiar trope of the body politic, he makes revolution seem attainable, like basic skin care. Like Horton in "Troubled with the Itch, and Rubbing with Sulphur," the remedies are not so simple as they first appear. Following Frantz Fanon, Hampton exacerbates the paradox of deeply rooted epidermalization, a symptom that presents on the surface, but indicates a more total infection. Like a number of his contemporaries, he sought to refract notions of Blackness as pathological back onto racist whites.[9]

Shortly after the above speech, Hampton was assassinated in a raid coordinated by the FBI and the Chicago Police Department. The problems that most concerned him—the overpolicing of Black neighborhoods, the defunding of public schools, and the overreach of corporate capitalism—have only become more acute since his death. Hampton's recourse to the metaphor of the body politic takes on more urgent significance, as what Hartman calls the "life chances" of Black people declined with the legal end of segregation. His rhetoric resonates with efforts by Black feminists of the 1970s and '80s to prioritize the "racial calculus" of unequal outcomes in reproductive health, sexual violence, and domestic labor.

In taking up these concerns, Black feminists reanimated the Romantic sense of culture as the repository of otherwise unrecognized political sentiment. The novelist and activist Toni Cade Bambara made a programmatic claim in a 1982 interview: "As a cultural worker who belongs to an oppressed people my job is to make revolution irresistible." Bambara's usage turns Hampton's notion of revolution as a salve into a kind of minor seduction. She plays with the dynamics of power and desire implied in the word "irresistible." This role for art, in eliciting political urges, sounds like Horton's demand across a century and a half of Black cultural activism: "Come Liberty, thou cheerful sound / Roll through my ravished ears!"[10]

"On the Pleasures of Hating"

The appeal of Romanticism for Black feminists had to do with their political passion, and their resistance to its repackaging as grievance and interest. In her essay "Civil Wars" (1980), June Jordan recalls a generative adolescent encounter with the British Romantic critic William Hazlitt's 1821 essay "On the Pleasure of Hating": "In my teens, I was shocked, awake, by that panegyric to the forbidden emotion. And I was haunted by the devious, the plaintive love so clearly protected by his reverence for the truth of things, especially the hateful truth of things." Jordan's title alludes to the apparently eternal return of the Civil War, even in more intimate, personal conflicts. She reflects on her stormy friendship with the white sociologist Frances Fox Piven, with whom she disagrees vehemently about the primacy of class politics. They replay the postbellum ruptures between the labor organizers, women's rights advocates, and abolitionists. Finding a resource for thinking through the breakdown of activist friendship in a 160-year-old essay, Jordan takes a detour through a certain late Romantic cynicism.[11]

Hazlitt's argument, like Jordan's, moves between personal and historical forms of odium. Passing through a series of variously petty and consequential examples, Hazlitt comes to find in hatred an emotional outlet for the thwarted ideals of revolutionary liberalism:

> Even when the spirit of the age (that is the progress of intellectual refinement, warring with our natural infirmities) no longer allows us to carry our vindictive and headstrong humours into effect, we try to revive them in description, and keep up the old bugbears, the phantoms of our terror and our hate, in imagination.

Hazlitt connects hatred with the fits and starts of progress, with the movement and inertia of history. He finds in it "the very spring of thought and action." Recalling seemingly incidental impulses of hatred leads him to a more sympathetic view of collective, political expressions of rage. By the end, he convicts himself of having sacrificed "real passion": "have I not reason to hate and to despise myself? Indeed I do; and chiefly for not having hated and despised the world enough."[12]

As a young woman, Jordan finds in Hazlitt a way to think through the emotional roots of racial animus. She returns to him as an adult when the conflicts between feminism, Black liberation, labor unions, and neoliberalism seem to make the "pleasure of hating" all the more urgent. The defining event of the essay is the Miami Rebellion of 1980, sometimes referred to as the Miami riots, a moment which reflected the breakdown of civil rights and Black Power structures of community leadership. Hazlitt's argument for hatred also provides a framework for the seeming anarchy of looting and car fires. Jordan is drawn back into dialogue with Piven, seeking context for the riots in her friend's research. In tracing this arc, Jordan arrives at a politics of emotion uncontainable within rote representative politics or sentimental liberalism:

> Neither race nor gender provides the final definitions of jeopardy or refuge. The final risk or final safety lies within each one of us attuned to the messy and intricate and unending challenge of self-determination. I believe the ultimate power of all the people rests upon the individual ability to trust and to respect the authority of the truth of whatever it is that each of us feels, each of us means. On what basis should *what* authority exceed the authority of *this* truth?

Jordan carefully defuses the narratives of victimization that had then begun to make New Left solidarities difficult, pointing to the spatial and temporal impossibility and illogic of prioritizing one or another form of grievance. She wonders what politics could stay with passion, rather than rationalizing experience into political interest. In seeking ground for collaboration and collectivity, in spite of the unevenly distributed effects of racism, sexism, and capitalism, Jordan arrives at a Black feminist account of the "spirit of the age." Its history is present, but ongoing, and its subject collective as well as individual, as true of "each one of us" as we make it and feel it, for ourselves and one another, lifelong.[13]

"An INVASION!"

A contemporary of Jordan's, the conceptual and performance artist Lorraine O'Grady, formulated an art practice combining Jordan's "messy" self-determination and Bambara's "irresistible" revolution. O'Grady's work takes as its point of departure the racism of white cultural institutions. She made her first interventions in the art world in 1980, at age 46, by arriving at New York art world events in character as "Mlle. Bourgeoise Noire."

Lorraine O'Grady, "Untitled (Mme Bourgeoise
Noire Shouts Out Her Poem" (1980–83, 2009),
courtesy Alexander Gray Associates, New York.

Dressed in a gown and cape made of white gloves, with her name
spelled out on a sash like a beauty queen, Mlle. Noire would
provoke partygoers and art patrons by flogging herself with what
she called "the whip-that-made-the-plantations-move," a sailing
rope studded with chrysanthemums. This last detail in particular
drew blood from the canons of taste, distinction, and elevation
built on the history of slavery.

At the opening of a group show called "Persona" at the New
Museum in September 1981, Mlle. Noire read a poem addressed
to Black artists beholden to aging messianisms and deals with
musty devils, calling down the otherwise silent exclusions maintained by cultural institutions:

> WAIT wait in your alternate/alternate spaces
> spitted on fish hooks of hope
> be polite wait to be discovered
> be proud be independent
> tongues cauterized at
> openings no one attends
> stay in your place

> after all, art is
> only for art's sake
> THAT'S ENOUGH don't you know
> sleeping beauty needs
> more than a kiss to awake
> now is the time for an INVASION!

Mlle. Noire elicits a kind of hilarious rage, as if she were the scion of some rich old family, now holding open the back door of the country club for her Black friends; the poem turns this haughty insouciance to cultural politics. O'Grady imagined a Black character who could transgress the gates of ivory towers, shimmy past security, and raise a flag for women of color. In a 1998 interview, O'Grady referred to the performances as "suicidal" for how the character flouted conventional ideas of Blackness and stereotypes of the Black middle class. Mlle. Bourgeoise Noire was also, however, better than a monument to Harper, reincarnating her career-long project of redistributing the fruits of middle-class life to Black people.[14]

At around the time she stopped appearing as Mlle. Bourgeoise Noire, O'Grady was planning a differently public performance for the 1983 African American Day Parade in Harlem: a project entitled "Art Is ..." For this occasion, O'Grady constructed a float in the shape of a gilded frame, so that it would "fram[e] everything it passed as art" on the way down Adam Clayton Powell Boulevard. O'Grady enlisted fifteen actors and dancers to walk with the float and carry empty gold frames, holding them in front of themselves and parade-watchers, making the people over as "art." As a counterpart to Mlle. Bourgeoise Noire's piratical incursion on white art spaces, this work takes the literal frameworks of distinction out of the museum and makes them over as popular; the photographs of the event document the jubilant participation of parade-goers. The piece's commitment to the present cuts into the burdens of the past. "Art Is ..." realizes the idea of the avant-garde as the movement of art into life, not as an expression of elite mastery, but as the staging of a people's self-recognition and a reclamation of the spirit of self-possession in creativity.

"No small bench by the road"

The late 1980s saw yet another explosion of research and cultural production about the history of slavery, prompted by the racially maldistributed effects of neoliberal social policy, the AIDS epidemic, the drug wars, and the deepening urban crisis. The rise of academic Black Studies and other marginal increases in Black people's access to cultural industries provided more opportunities to reopen the archives of the peculiar institution and to restage its history. In an interview about her period-defining novel *Beloved* (1987), Toni Morrison explained that she returned to the history of slavery in literature because of its erasure elsewhere in the landscape of cultural memory:

> There is no place you or I can go, to think about or not think about, to summon the presences of, or recollect the absences of slaves; nothing that reminds us of the ones who made the journey and those who did not make it. There is no suitable memorial or plaque or wreath or wall or park or skyscraper lobby. There's no 300-foot tower. There's no small bench by the road. There's not even a tree scored, an initial that I can visit or you can visit in Charleston or Savannah or New York or Providence or better still on the banks of the Mississippi. And because such a place doesn't exist (that I know of), the book had to. ... I think I was pleading for that wall or that bench or that tower or that tree when I wrote the final words.

Morrison's hopes for her book as a supplementary form of memorialization are both logical and melancholic. How could Black communities ravaged by what Hartman calls "skewed life chances" be expected to rear monuments? Morrison's most ardent readers took up her remark; in 2006, the Toni Morrison Society launched "The Bench by the Road Project," which has since placed twenty memorial benches at important sites in the history of slavery and abolition all over the Atlantic world.[15]

The resonance between Morrison and Harper on the question of memorialization here is not accidental; *Beloved* focuses on the gendered consequences of enslavement that had been Harper's concern. Morrison and her contemporaries had returned to Harper in response to a nightmarish return of the legal doctrine *partus sequitur ventrem*: the misattribution, by a range of politicians and commentators, of the impoverishment and over-policing of Black communities to the breakdown of Black family life in slavery. Morrison's novel contested this premise through a fictionalization of the story of Margaret Garner, a fugitive from slavery who in 1856 killed her own daughter in the middle of her recapture by US Marshals in southern Ohio. Garner's story had shocked Northern liberals, and it was taken as a cardinal example of the brutalization of enslavement.

One of the earliest depictions of Garner's act was Harper's 1857 poem "The Slave Mother: A Tale of Ohio." Speaking in Garner's voice, Harper writes:

> I will save my precious children
>   From their darkly threatened doom,
> I will hew a path to freedom
>   Through the portals of the tomb.

Here, in an intricately wrought and balladic poetic sentence, was consciousness steeling itself, reasoning its way through seething, to an act of violence turned inward. Harper takes Garner as a Byronic hero whose moral darkness tested liberal capacities for redemption; she focuses on Garner's displacement of the dream of freedom to the afterlife. That projection did not originate in Garner of course, but in a world made uninhabitable by slavery. Elsewhere, Harper made clear her sense of motherhood as an imaginative project; she returned repeatedly across her career to the formulation, "Every mother should be a true artist." In Garner, Harper had found a mother at a crossroads, and sought in art to find a way to love her. Morrison's novel expands this project, beginning to imagine how that legacy might look different than it did in the rhetoric of late-twentieth-century politicians, by picking up the story some eight years after the end of the Civil War, as the characters deal with the "rememory" of slavery.[16]

To elaborate Hayden's hope of feeling freedom embodied, Black feminist cultural practice since the '70s has centered on the fleshly traumas of slavery. The visual art of Kara Walker, for instance, calls up that history more ironically than Morrison—her two-dimensional silhouettes of the enslaved and their masters in surreal, hypersexual tableaux play on the flattening effects of the chattel principle. The new millennium has seen yet another renewal of interest in the culture and history of slavery: the election of the first Black president, with the liberal paradox that his ascent did not ameliorate systemic racism, and then the election of an absurd racist provocateur as his successor, have forced another turn back to the nation's history. The range of media in which this confrontation with the past can now take place is much expanded. Major Hollywood movies like Quentin Tarantino's *Django Unchained* (2012) and novels like Colson Whitehead's *Underground Railroad* (2016) have tightened focus on both the ironic and traumatic aspects of the system's legacy. Despite its seemingly residual inconsequence, poetry has been an important part of this resurgence of interest, with poets as various and accomplished as Kevin Young, M. NourbeSe Philip, Dionne Brand, Natasha Tretheway, and Thylias Moss all representing slavery in a rich array of formal experiments, often to great acclaim. This work is rarely antiquarian, and always engaged with the cultural politics of racism in the present. The necessity of abolition as a counterpoint to neoliberalism—the possibility that the people can put a stop to systemic corruption—seems to rise up around us like floodwaters. That it should continue to do so in song, now some two centuries since poetry first played a key role in the abolition movement, is no surprise.

"I used to pray for times like this, to rhyme like this"

Hip-hop has long been the medium of the conspiracy against anti-black social policies of the neoliberal era. Its preoccupation with lurid narratives of Black criminality confirms the perennial but ambivalent appeal of the fugitive romance. In Byronic fashion, the hip-hop emcee embodies and yet disavows, indulges and then

seeks redemption for, the spectral Blackness of racist fantasy. The
drug trade and commodity culture bleed together in hip-hop, with
liberation and capital indistinctly but indissolubly linked. The
genre has thus become the aesthetic of a hounded and yet global
underclass, and lately the soundtrack of a new abolitionism aimed
especially at mass incarceration and police violence.

Meek Mill's "Dreams and Nightmares (Intro)" from the 2012
album *Dreams and Nightmares* narrates the confusions of a man
navigating the ephemeral frontier between international celebrity
and the abject circumstances of Black life in the postindustrial city.
It was not a hit on the album's release, but it has since become an
anthem. Meek Mill became an icon of criminal justice reform as
a result of his repeated incarceration for minor parole violations
related to a 2008 conviction (at age twenty-one) for attempting
to distribute narcotics and possession of an unlicensed firearm.
As media attention focused on developments in his case, "Dreams
and Nightmares (Intro)" became an unqualified hip-hop standard.
Two years after the album's release, Meek Mill's more famous
collaborator and rival Drake tweeted, "Dreams and Nightmares
Intro really one of the best rap moments of our generation." The
2017 NBA Eastern conference champions the Cleveland Cavaliers
(led by LeBron James) listened to the song in the locker room
before and after games, as did the 2018 NFL Super Bowl cham-
pion Philadelphia Eagles (from Meek's hometown).[17]

All this is extraordinarily strange, insofar as the song barely registers as a song at all—it was intended as a mood setter, with Meek
rapping over a soapy piano and synthetic strings, his voice rising
to a shout as the track builds to a crushing welter. Its arrangement
and Meek's notoriously intense delivery communicate a desire for
song more than song itself. The lyrics begin with this premise:

> I used to pray for times like this, to rhyme like this
> So I had to grind like that to shine like this
> In a matter of time I spent on some locked up shit
> In the back of the paddy wagon, cuffs locked on wrists
> See my dreams unfold, nightmares come true
> It was time to marry the game and I said, "Yeah, I do"

These opening lines take off from Romantic premises: the opposition of bondage and self-expression, the sublimation of erotic and spiritual energy into art, the use of the lyric as a way to recall deep feeling. The song is a narrative of a life in art, in terms of European Romanticism, a *biographia literaria* or *künstlerroman*. All the devilish ambivalence and passionate ferocity of Black Romanticism appears here. In this late moment, with the promise of abolition-democracy long past due, hip-hop compensates for, and provides an escape from, a police state.

The song takes off from the fragile impermanence of this escape, the irony of using narratives of criminality to escape the containment of Black life, and the slip between dreams and nightmares. Meek meditates on how far he has come, touting the enjoyment of money, cars, women, and expensive champagne, but also worrying about sliding back into the underclass. These impermanent but pleasurable objectifications emerge and disappear quickly in Meek's rapid-fire delivery. With the acutely double consciousness of Black wealth, his voice becomes increasingly strained, and boasting and complaining blur together: "I'm the type to count a million cash then grind like I'm broke." As the track becomes more intense, and its sonic elements come together, Meek finds himself back in the excruciating, suspenseful context of Philly gang life:

> I'm ridin' around my city with my hand strapped on my toast
> 'Cause these niggas want me dead and I gotta make it back home
> 'Cause my mama need that bill money, my son need some milk

At this moment of pitched terror and internalized threat, Meek is brought back, from the fear of both cops and gangsters, to domestic responsibilities. In the paroxysm of fiercest passion and fugitive ambivalence, the earlier objectification of women falls away and the family drama reappears, motivating and creative. It appears as though Meek might make an entreaty to Black feminism, which in its more capacious moments has ways to love him, like Margaret Garner, in all his destructive and suicidal anxiety. But just as the moment flashes up, it disappears, and the song is, after all, just an introduction.

The album's cover emblematizes the warp between dreams and nightmares in an allegorical image: a police handcuff chained to an expensive gold watch; the luxurious fantasy of the timepiece and the delirium of doing time linked. The devil's bargain of late capital, its material promises and brutal deprivations, is a ruse; the sold soul is obsessed with knowing the time, because it is eternally owned. Life in a state defined by its unfinished revolution means feeling the simultaneity of dreams and nightmares. One hopes the alarm will not only wake us up, but also unlock the handcuffs, and play a good song.

Acknowledgments

This book is dedicated to the memory of Marcellus Blount, who first taught me its subject in 2003. A few months into my study with him about early African diasporic literature, we arrived at a paradox that has guided my orientation since. I saw that I had benefitted from every advantage in my education, and yet I was so drawn to, and so challenged by, the writing of people whose literary art was so hard-won. I cannot recall the source of this insight; Marcellus's subtlety meant that what he taught me often felt like I had thought of it, even though I knew he had led me to it, and that it did not belong to me. In that spirit, what follows is first an accounting of the privileges in my education, and then of the people who held me as I worked through that paradox to write this book.

I must mention the teachers who first pushed me to read and write well as a high school kid in Miami: Freddie Rosenthal, John Davies, Sandy Lewis, and especially Eric Reinholtz. As an undergraduate in the English department of the University of Virginia, I learned so much from Jerome McGann, Jonathan Flatley, Tan Lin, Heather Love, Rita Felski, Michael Levenson, and Eric Lott. In the PhD program in English and Comparative Literature at Columbia University, alongside Marcellus, Bob O'Meally taught me to keep the storehouse of my intellectual life, and to improvise with it. Rachel Adams, Molly Murray, and Ezra Tawil helped along the way and still do. I still hear the voices of Edward Said and Eve Kosofsky Sedgwick from back then; I wish very much I could put this book in their hands as well. I owe enormous debts, personal and intellectual, to Michael Golston. Likewise, my only hope in repaying Jonathan Arac is to give what he gave me to my own students. I have gathered the camaraderie I shared with my peers in graduate school was unusual, so many thanks are due Karen Emmerich, Avishek Ganguly, Bina Gogineni, Rishi Goyal, Hannah Gurman, Andras Kisery, Emily Lordi, Matt Rebhorn, Casey Shoop, Richard So, Stefanie Sobelle, Courtney Thorsson, Penny Vlagopoulos, Eugene Vydrin, and Matt Zarnowiecki.

This book took shape during some long years I spent as an adjunct. At Louisiana State University, the students in my Introduction to African American Literature courses demanded a version of my best that I hope has made it into these pages. My colleagues Dana Berkowitz, Lauren Coates, Michael Cohen, Brannon Costello, Angeletta Gourdine, Jerry Kennedy, John Lowe, and Dan Novak all kindly took me seriously. Rand Dotson's elegant friendship and counsel came in handy again and again. Elsie Michie gave me so much time and taught me so much. During a year at Gettysburg College, I met the estimable Betsy Duquette, and her acuity has oriented me since. At the University of Oregon, I taught an undergraduate class on "Poetries of Slavery" that brought this book into focus, so my thanks to those students as well. Mark Carey, Mai-Lin Cheng, Karen Jackson Ford, Paul Peppis, Helen Southworth, and Mark Whalan made the work feel worth it. The heartfelt exhortations of Joel Elan Black, with whom I shared an office, energized me. To have gotten to think and laugh there with David Bradley is a great gift. Finally, I was lucky to find in Carol Stabile a mentor and fellow traveler of the most admirable commitment.

The Center for Study of Ethnicity and Race at Columbia turned out to be the ideal place to finish this book. To work alongside Teresa Aguayo and Josephine Caputo everyday has been a joy. Frances Negrón-Muntaner inspires me to think, teach, and intervene more creatively. I have benefitted from sustaining moments of collegial kindness from Rachel Adams, Sarah Cole, Denise Cruz, Brent Edwards, Cassie Fennell, Austin Graham, Farah Griffin, Karl Jacoby, Premilla Nadasen, Mae Ngai, Aaron Ritzenberg,

Bruce Robbins, Audra Simpson, Cristobal Silva, Joseph Slaughter, Josef Sorett, Maura Spiegel, Elsa Stamatopoulou, Alan Stewart, and Neferti Tadiar.

Over the years, I've depended enormously on the encouragement and insight of colleagues at other institutions. Any list of these people is inevitably incomplete, but I must mention William Andrews, Alex Black, Chris Castiglia, Noah Comet, Nicole Fleetwood, Daniel Hack, Glenn Hendler, Jared Hickman, Matt Hofer, Virginia Jackson, Deanna Koretsky, Lori Leavell, Carter Mathes, Carla Peterson, Lloyd Pratt, Anthony Reed, Howard Ramsby, Derrick Spires, Claudia Stokes, Priscilla Wald, Susan Wolfson, Edlie Wong, and Teresa Zackodnik.

It has been a dream to get to write this book for Verso, and my enthusiastic thanks to Mark Martin and Jeffrey Klein there for their careful attentions. Earlier drafts of material from the book appear in "Black Byronism," *The Byron Journal*, special issue on "Byron in America," ed. Noah Comet, 45:2, 2017, and in "Black Romanticism and the Lyric in Crisis," *African American Literature in Transition, Vol. 4: 1850–1865*, ed. Teresa Zackodnik, Cambridge University Press (forthcoming).

I must work backward now, and credit some intellectual friendships which have played a significant role in this book. Late in this project's life, I met Manu Chander and Tricia Matthew as a part of the Bigger 6 Collective; they, along with Tina Iemma, read the bulk of the manuscript in ways that both humbled and buoyed me. James Kim's careful attentions and collaborative grace also steadied the last stretch of the composition. My intrepid editor at Verso, Jessie Kindig, found the heart of this book and took a chance on it for which I will be forever grateful. A couple of decisive, agenda-setting conversations with Evie Shockley punctuated the long life of this project. When I have not known what to do next, I have turned repeatedly to Ivy Wilson, whose footsteps I followed closely here. Alexandra Vazquez showed me the way home. Sean Kennedy carried the torch for this work militantly from the moment I explained it to him. The same is true of the faithful Eugene Vydrin, who lent his eye to an early version of the manuscript. The project was born again during dream-work I did in a shotgun house with Jacob Rama Berman; he also read the manuscript. Rishi Goyal's quickening mind is all over these pages, and he kept me going through the worst parts of the journey. Stefanie Sobelle has made it all so much fun somehow, and saved me on a few occasions as well. Above all, this book is the record of my friendship with Courtney Thorsson, who is as much its author as am I. If this book has been a labor of love, that love has been with these people.

Friends outside of academia have kept me gratefully grounded, especially Agnes Berecz, Dan Binkiewicz, Zeus Cortinas, Lina Dorado, Brian Lathrop, Steven Lezama, Sara Elena Moore, Ian Mohler, Bridget Potter, Charles Sano, Peter Thorsson, and Mark and Tony Unger. To share a life in writing with my brother Nathaniel is a rare joy. To my parents, Alan and Michelle, I owe everything; I stand in wonder at their efforts to understand. As George Moses Horton sang in 1829: "But halt my feeble tongue."

Notes

Introduction

1 Frances Ellen Watkins Harper, *A Brighter Coming Day: A Frances Ellen Watkins Harper Reader*, ed. Frances Smith Foster (New York: The Feminist Press of the City University of New York, 1990), 93–4; James Monroe Whitfield, *The Works of James M. Whitfield: America and Other Writings by a Nineteenth-Century African American Poet*, ed. Robert S. Levine and Ivy G. Wilson (Chapel Hill: University of North Carolina Press, 2011), 77.

2 Jules Michelet, *History of the French Revolution*, trans. C. Cocks (London: H.G. Bohn, 1847), 26. Harper's reading is described in William Still, *The Underground Railroad* (Philadelphia: Porter & Coates, 1872), 778.

3 William Blake, *The Complete Poetry and Prose*, ed. David Erdman (New York: Anchor, 1988), 38.

4 Harper, *A Brighter Coming Day*, 93–4.

5 Percy Bysshe Shelley, *Poetry and Prose*, ed. Donald H. Reiman and Sharon B. Powers (New York: Norton, 1977), 508.

6 W.E.B. Du Bois, *Black Reconstruction in America, 1860–1880* (New York: Free Press, 1992), 122, 101, 91.

7 Harriet Martineau, *Retrospect of Western Travel* (New York: Harper and Bros., 1838), 1:251.

8 David Walker, *David Walker's Appeal, in Four Articles, Together With a Preamble, to the Coloured Citizens of the World, but in Particular, and Very Expressly, to Those of the United States of America* (New York: Hill and Wang, 1995), 15; Nathaniel Peabody Rogers, *A Collection from the Miscellaneous Writings of Nathaniel Peabody Rogers* (Boston: Benjamin B. Mussey, 1849), 212.

9 William Wells Brown, "A Lecture Delivered before the Female Anti-Slavery Society of Salem at Lyceum Hall, Nov. 14, 1847," *The*

Works of William Wells Brown (New York: Oxford University Press, 2006), 4.

10 C.L.R. James, *The Black Jacobins: Toussaint L'Ouverture and the San Domingo Revolution* (New York: Vintage, 1989), 86; "Oath of the Cayman Woods," in Doris Y. Kadish and Deborah Jenson, eds., *Poetry of Haitian Independence* (New Haven: Yale University Press, 2015), 226.

11 Joshua McCarter Simpson, *Original Anti-Slavery Songs* (Zanesville, Ohio: printed for the author, 1852), n.p.

12 Joshua McCarter Simpson, *The Emancipation Car* (Miami: Mnemosyne, 1969), 27–33.

13 Ibid., 64–5.

14 Harriet Beecher Stowe, "Sojourner Truth: The Libyan Sybil," *Atlantic*, April 1863, 479.

15 Simpson, *Original Anti-Slavery Songs*, 21.

16 Blake, *The Complete Poetry and Prose*, 27; William Wordsworth and Samuel Taylor Coleridge, *Lyrical Ballads, 1798 and 1802* (New York: Oxford, 2013), 111; Charles Baudelaire, "Fusées XIII," *Oeuvres complétes* (Paris: Gallimard, 1961), I, 662 (author's translation); Comte de Lautréamont, *Maldoror and the Complete Works*, trans. Alexis Lykiard (Cambridge: Exact Change, 1994), 240; Walt Whitman, *Poetry and Prose* (New York: Library of America, 1982), 225.

17 Victoria Earle Matthews, "The Value of Race Literature: An Address," *Massachusetts Review* 27:2, Summer 1986, 173; Harper is quoted in Still, *The Underground Railroad*, 757.

18 Nathaniel Hawthorne, *The House of the Seven Gables* (New York: Modern Library, 2001), 3.

19 G.W.F. Hegel, *Lectures on the Philosophy of World History*, trans. H. B. Nisbet (Cambridge: Cambridge University Press, 1981), 89; Martin R. Delany, *The Condition, Elevation, Emigration, and Destiny of the Colored People of the United States* (Philadelphia: published by the author, 1852), 209; Amiri Baraka, *Home: Social Essays* (New York: Akashic, 2009), 104.

20 Mary Ann Shadd, *A Plea for Emigration, Or, Notes of Canada West: In Its Moral, Social, and Political Aspect: With Suggestions Respecting Mexico, West Indies, and Vancouver's Island, for the Information of Colored Emigrants* (Detroit: G. W. Pattinson, 1852), 44.

21 Hortense J. Spillers, "Cross-Currents, Discontinuities: Black Women's Fiction," in *Conjuring: Black Women, Fiction, and Literary Tradition*, ed. Marjorie Pryse and Hortense J. Spillers (Bloomington: Indiana University Press, 1985), 258.

22 Ralph Ellison, *Invisible Man* (New York: Vintage, 1980), 581.

1. Hereditary Bondsmen, Strike the Blow!

1 Henry Highland Garnet, *A Memorial Discourse* (Philadelphia: J. M. Wilson, 1865), 34; *Minutes of the National Convention of Colored Citizens: Held at Buffalo* (New York: Piercy & Reed, 1843), 13.

2 Garnet, *A Memorial Discourse*, 48; Lord George Gordon Byron, *The Complete Poetical Works*, 7 vols, ed. Jerome J. McGann (New York: Oxford University Press, 1980–1993), III, 157 and II, 69; Garnet, *A Memorial Discourse*, 48–9.

3 Ibid., 48–9.

4 Thomas Carlyle, *Our Heroes, Hero-Worship, and the Heroic in History* (Lincoln: University of Nebraska Press, 1966), 156.

5 Lady Caroline Lamb, quoted in *Lady Morgan's Memoirs: Autobiography, Diaries and Correspondence* (London: Wm. H. Allen & Co., 1862), II, 200.

6 *Byron's Letters and Journals*, ed. Leslie A. Marchand (Cambridge, MA: Harvard University Press, 1973–82), 9: 41.

7 Henry Wadsworth Longfellow, "Defense of Poetry," *North American Review* 34, January 1832, 76; Byron, *The Complete Poetical Works*, II, 93.

8 Byron, *The Complete Poetical Works*, V, 192, 281.

9 Frederick Law Olmsted, *A Journey in the Seaboard Slave States; with Remarks on Their Economy* (London: Sampson, Low, Son, & Co., 1856), 55.

10 Harriet Jacobs, *Incidents in the Life of a Slave Girl*, ed. Jean Fagan Yellin (Cambridge, MA: Harvard University Press, 1987), 38, 37.

11 Byron, *The Complete Poetical Works*, IV, 119.

12 Byron, *The Complete Poetical Works*, III, 380.

13 George Moses Horton, *The Poetical Works of George M. Horton, the Colored Bard of North-Carolina* (Hillsborough: D. Heartt, 1845), 72, 88.

14 George Moses Horton, *Naked Genius* (Raleigh, NC: Wm. B. Smith & Co., 1865), 109, 22.

15 Martin Delany, *The Condition, Elevation, Emigration, and Destiny of the Colored People of the United States* (Philadelphia: published by the author, 1852), 119.

16 George Boyer Vashon writing as Harold, "Revolution in Haiti," *The North Star*, II: 40, September 28, 1849, 3; Vashon to Gerrit Smith, Nov 16, 1850, quoted in Benjamin Quarles, "Letters from Negro Leaders to Gerrit Smith," *Journal of Negro History*, 27:4, October 1942, 444.

17 George Boyer Vashon, "Vincent Ogé," in *Autographs for Freedom*, ed. Julia Griffiths (Auburn, NY: Alden, Beardsley and Co., 1854), 50.

18 Ibid., 54.

19 W.E.B. Du Bois, *The Souls of Black Folk* (London: Oxford University Press, 2007), 102.

20 Frances Ellen Watkins Harper, *A Brighter Coming Day: A Frances Ellen Watkins Harper Reader*, ed. Frances Smith Foster (New York: The Feminist Press of the City University of New York, 1990), 139; Melba Joyce Boyd, *Discarded Legacy: Politics and Poetics in the Life of Frances E. W. Harper, 1825–1911* (Detroit: Wayne State University Press, 1994), 79–113.

21 Harper, *A Brighter Coming Day*, 146; Foster in Harper, *A Brighter Coming Day*, 136.

22 Harper, *A Brighter Coming Day*, 143, 150, 162.

23 Byron, *The Complete Poetical Works*, III, 289 and IV, 36; Pauline Hopkins, "Famous Women of the Negro Race," *The Colored American*, IV: 5, April 1, 1902, 369.

24 Harriet Beecher Stowe, *Lady Byron Vindicated: A History of the Byron Controversy* (Boston: Fields, Osgood, & Co., 1870), 84; James Baldwin, *Notes of a Native Son* (New York: Beacon, 1984), 13.

25 Albery Allson Whitman, *At the Dusk of Dawn: Selected Poetry and Prose of Albery Allson Whitman*, ed. Ivy G. Wilson (Boston: Northeastern University Press, 2009), 308.

26 Charles Waddell Chesnutt, *Stories, Novels, and Essays* (New York: Library of America, 2002), 906–14; Whitman, *At the Dusk of Dawn*, 142, 306.

27 Byron, *The Complete Poetical Works*, V, 71; William Hazlitt, *The Spirit of the Age, or Contemporary Portraits* (London: Henry Colburn, 1825), 164; Anna Julia Cooper, *A Voice From the South*, ed. Mary Helen Washington (New York: Oxford University Press, 1988), 70.

28 Du Bois, *The Souls of Black Folk*, 90.

29 The speech appears in both the March and April 1863 issues of *Douglass' Monthly* (V: v, 801 and V: vi, 826), and then again in the 1881 and 1892 editions of *The Life and Times of Frederick Douglass* (Douglass, *Autobiographies*, 1994, 778–9).

2. The Supernatural Avenger

1 George Moses Horton, *The Poetical Works of George M. Horton, The Colored Bard of North-Carolina* (Hillsborough: D. Heartt, 1845), iv, xi.

2 Collier Cobb, "An American Man of Letters," *The University*

Magazine, 40: 1, October 1909, 6; Caroline Lee Hentz, *Lovell's Folly* (Cincinnati: Hubbard and Edwards, 1833), 259–60.

3 W.E.B. Du Bois, *Black Reconstruction in America, 1860–1880* (New York: Free Press, 1992), 285.

4 J. Saunders Redding, *To Make a Poet Black* (Ithaca: Cornell University Press, 1988), 16, 18; Friedrich Hölderlin, *Poems and Fragments*, trans. Michael Hamburger (Cambridge: Cambridge University Press, 1966), 505.

5 Horton to William Lloyd Garrison, Sept. 3, 1844, Swain Papers, Wilson Library, University of North Carolina, Chapel Hill; Horton, *The Poetical Works*, 1845, xxi.

6 Horton, *The Poetical Works*, xxi.

7 Phillis Wheatley, *Memoir and Poems of Phillis Wheatley, A Native African and a Slave. Also, Poems by a Slave* (Boston: Isaac Knapp, 1838), 23–4.

8 Jonathan Greenleaf Whittier, "The Slave Poet of North Carolina," *National Era*, II: 99, November 23, 1848, 186.

9 Samuel Taylor Coleridge, *The Major Works*, ed. H. J. Jackson (New York: Oxford University Press, 2009), 473.

10 Orlando Patterson, *Slavery and Social Death: A Comparative Study* (Cambridge, MA: Harvard University Press, 1999), 216; George Moses Horton, *Naked Genius* (Raleigh, N.C.: Wm. B. Smith & Co., 1865), 157. The previous citation also appears in a collection of Horton's work entitled *The Black Bard of North Carolina: George Moses Horton and His Poetry*, ed. Joan R. Sherman (Chapel Hill: University of North Carolina Press, 1997), 156. Both citations are provided below when possible.

11 Phillis Wheatley, *The Collected Works,* ed. John C. Shields (New York: Oxford University Press, 1988), 18; Robert Southey, *A Vision of Judgement* (London: Longman, Hurst, Rees, Orme and Brown, 1821), xxi.

12 Charles Baudelaire, *Oeuvres complétes* (Paris: Gallimard, 1961), II, 251, and II, 334, author's translation.

13 Poe, *Essays and Reviews* (New York: Library of America, 1984), 1300.

14 Coleridge, *The Major Works*, 319; W.E.B. Du Bois, *The Souls of Black Folk* (London: Oxford University Press, 2007), 132.

15 James Weldon Johnson, *Writings* (New York: Library of America, 2004), 706; George Moses Horton, *The Hope of Liberty. Containing a Number of Poetical Pieces* (Raleigh: J. Gales and Son, 1829), 11/*The Black Bard*, 79; Horton, *The Hope of Liberty*, 11/*The Black Bard*, 79; Baudelaire, *Oeuvres complétes*, I, 11; Wheatley, *Collected Works*, 18.

16 Horton, *The Hope of Liberty*, 9/*The Black Bard*, 76.

17 Horton, *The Hope of Liberty*, 20/*The Black Bard*, 90; Emily Dickinson, *The Poems of Emily Dickinson*, ed. R.W. Franklin (Cambridge, MA: Belknap Press, 1999), #314.

18 Horton, *The Poetical Works*, 55–6/*The Black Bard*, 116; Fanon, *Black Skin, White Masks,* trans. Charles Lam Markmann (New York: Grove, 1967), 11.

19 Baudelaire, *Oeuvres complétes*, II, 532; Frederick Douglass, *Autobiographies* (New York: Library of America, 1994), 179.

20 Plato, *Plato in Twelve Volumes*, trans. W.R.M. Lamb (Cambridge, MA: Harvard University Press, 1967), 3: 494d.

21 Friedrich Schiller, *On the Aesthetic Education of Man,* trans. Reginald Snell (New Haven: Yale University Press, 1954), letter XIV; Poe, *Essays and Reviews,* 75.

22 Samuel Johnson, *"The Idler" and "The Adventurer": The Yale Edition of the Works of Samuel Johnson,* Vol. 2 (New Haven: Yale University Press, 1963), 457; Paul Laurence Dunbar, *Collected Poetry*, ed. Joanne M. Braxton (Charlottesville: University of Virginia Press, 1993), 71.

23 Langston Hughes, *Laughing to Keep From Crying* (New York: Henry Holt, 1952), n.p.

24 Horton, *The Hope of Liberty*, 15/*The Black Bard*, 86.

25 Kemp P. Battle, *History of the University of North Carolina from its Beginning to the Death of President Swain, 1789–1868, Vol. 1* (Raleigh: Edwards and Broughton, 1907), 194; Horton, *The Poetical Works*, xvi–xvii; Battle, *History*, 603–4 and 585; Horton, *The Poetical Works*, 55/*The Black Bard*, 112.

26 Battle, 690; Horton, 1248.

27 Horton, "An Address to the Collegiates of the University of N.C.: The Stream of Liberty and Science," ca. 1859, North Carolina Collection, Wilson Library, University of North Carolina, Chapel Hill, 4, 2. Transcription by Constance Chia, 2016.

28 Baudelaire, *Oeuvres complétes*, 1, 286.

29 Horton quoted in Reginald H. Pitts, " 'Let Us Desert this Friendless Place': George Moses Horton in Philadelphia—1866," *The Journal of Negro History,* 80: 4, Autumn 1995, 149.

30 Ralph Waldo Emerson, *Early Lectures*, ed. Stephen E. Whicher and Robert E. Spiller (Cambridge, MA: Harvard University Press, 1959–72) 5; Frances Ellen Watkins Harper, *A Brighter Coming Day: A Frances Ellen Watkins Harper Reader*, ed. Frances Smith Foster (New York: The Feminist Press of the City University of New York, 1990), 218–9.

31 Horton quoted in Pitts, "'Let Us Desert,'" 151.

32 Alexander Crummell, *The Future of Africa: Being Addresses, Sermons, Etc., Etc., Delivered in the Republic of Liberia* (New York: Charles Scribner, 1862), 148.

33 Delany collected in Wilson Moses, ed., *Liberian Dreams: Back-to-Africa Narratives from the 1850s* (University Park: Pennsylvania State University Press, 1998), 86.

34 Lydia Maria Child, *The Freedmen's Book* (Boston: Ticknor and Fields, 1865), 113; Sarah Webster Fabio, "Tripping with Black Writing," in *The Black Aesthetic,* ed. Addison Gayle, Jr., (Garden City, NY: Doubleday and Co., 1971), 183.

3. The Seething Brain

1 Thomas Carlyle, *The French Revolution: A History* (New York: Modern Library, 2002), 101.

2 Joshua McCarter Simpson, *The Emancipation Car* (Miami: Mnemosyne, 1969), iv.

3 J. Saunders Redding, *To Make a Poet Black* (Ithaca: Cornell University Press, 1988), 40.

4 For variations on "the seething brain," see James Monroe Whitfield, *The Works of James M. Whitfield: America and Other Writings by a Nineteenth-Century African American Poet*, ed. Robert S. Levine and Ivy G. Wilson (Chapel Hill: University of North Carolina Press, 2011), 70, 71, 77, 91, 182–3; Ralph Waldo Emerson, *Essays and Lectures* (New York: Library of America, 1983), 199–200.

5 Hortense J. Spillers, *Black, White, and in Color: Essays on American Literature and Culture* (Chicago: University of Chicago Press, 2003), 206.

6 Edward Jarvis, *Insanity among the Coloured Population of the Free States,* (Philadelphia: T. K. & P. G. Collins, 1844), 12.

7 Samuel Cartwright, "Diseases and Peculiarities of the Negro Race," *DeBow's Review,* 11: 1, July 1851, 66.

8 Emerson, *Essays and Lectures*, 450; Langston Hughes, "The Negro Artist and the Racial Mountain," *Nation,* 122, June 23, 1926, 694.

9 Rev. E. P. Rogers, *The Repeal of the Missouri Compromise Considered* (Newark: A. Stephen Holbrook, 1854), 6.

10 William Wells Brown, *The Black Man: His Antecedents, His Genius, and His Achievements* (New York: Thomas Hamilton; Boston: R. F. Wallcut, 1863), 272, 274.

11 Audre Lorde, *Sister Outsider: Essays and Speeches* (Berkeley, CA: Crossing Press, 2007), 127; James Monroe Whitfield, *The Works of James M. Whitfield: America and Other Writings by a*

Nineteenth-Century African American Poet, ed. Robert S. Levine and Ivy G. Wilson (Chapel Hill: University of North Carolina Press, 2011), 70; Frederick Douglass, *Autobiographies* (New York: Library of America, 1994), 23.

12   Daphne A. Brooks, *Bodies in Dissent: Spectacular Performances of Race and Freedom, 1850–1910* (Durham: Duke University Press, 2006), 3; Whitfield, *America and Other Writings*, 74.

13   Martin R. Delany, *The Condition, Elevation, Emigration, and Destiny of the Colored People of the United States* (Philadelphia: published by the author, 1852), 132.

14   Whitfield, *America and Other Writings*, 39, 77; John Stuart Mill, "Thoughts on Poetry and Its Varieties," *The Crayon*, 7: 4, April 1860, 95; Delany, *Blake, or The Huts of America*, ed. Floyd. J. Miller (Boston: Beacon, 1970), 285–6.

15   Whitfield, *America and Other Writings*, 78.

16   George Boyer Vashon as G.B.V., "The Progress of the Mind in Self-Investigation," *Frederick Douglass' Paper*, VIII: 20, May 4, 1855, n.p.

17   George Boyer Vashon, "Vincent Ogé," in *Autographs for Freedom*, ed. Julia Griffiths (Auburn, NY: Alden, Beardsley and Co., 1854), 52; John Ruskin, *The Genius of John Ruskin: Selections from His Writings*, ed. John D. Rosenberg (Charlottesville: University of Virginia Press, 1998), 61–72; Vashon, "The Progress of Mind."

18   Vashon, "Vincent Ogé,", 59–60; Wordsworth, *The Major Works* (New York: Oxford University Press, 1984), 282.

19   "George B. Vashon," *Frederick Douglass' Paper*, VII: 38, Sept. 8, 1854, 3; James Theodore Holly, *Black Separatism and the Caribbean, 1860*, ed. Howard Holman Bell (Ann Arbor: University of Michigan Press, 1970), 39, 63.

20   George Boyer Vashon, "A Life-Day," in Daniel A. Payne, *The Semi-Centenary and the Retrospection of the African Methodist Episcopal Church* (Baltimore: Sherwood, 1866), 173–4.

21   Simpson, *The Emancipation Car*, iv; Walt Whitman, *Poetry and Prose*, (New York: Library of America, 1982), 302; Whitfield, *America and Other Writings*, 41, 44.

22   For "A Parody," see *The Liberator*, VIII: 30, July 27, 1838, 120, and *The Colored American*, II: 23, July 28, 1838, 92; Whitfield, *America and Other Writings*, 41.

23   Simpson, *The Emancipation Car*, 17, v.

24   Ibid., 18.

25   William Blake, *The Complete Poetry and Prose*. ed. David Erdman (New York: Anchor, 1988), 233; Simpson, *The Emancipation Car*, 139, 141.

26 James Madison Bell, *The Poetical Works* (Lansing, MI: Wynkoop Hallenbeck Crawford, Co. 1901), 59, 69, 60.

27 Frances Ellen Watkins Harper, *A Brighter Coming Day: A Frances Ellen Watkins Harper Reader*, ed. Frances Smith Foster (New York: The Feminist Press of the City University of New York, 1990), 177–8; Karl Marx, *The 18th Brumaire of Louis Bonaparte*, (New York: International, 1968), 15.

28 Bell, *The Poetical Works*, 36, 43.

29 Ibid., 107; W.E.B. Du Bois, *Black Reconstruction in America, 1860–1880* (New York: Free Press, 1992), 237–324.

4. Uprising of Women

1 Grace Greenwood, "Lectures in Philadelphia—A Letter from Grace Greenwood," *New York Independent*, March 15, 1866, n.p.

2 Frederick Douglass, *Autobiographies* (New York: Library of America, 1994), 103. Douglass's quotation from Coleridge is slightly altered from *A Dissertation on the Science of Method; or, The Laws and Regulative Principles of Education* (1818).

3 Frances Ellen Watkins Harper, *A Brighter Coming Day: A Frances Ellen Watkins Harper Reader*, ed. Frances Smith Foster (New York: The Feminist Press of the City University of New York, 1990), 45.

4 Karl Marx, *Capital, Vol. 1* (New York: International, 1992), 46, 76; G.W.F. Hegel, *Lectures on the Philosophy of World History*, trans. H. B. Nisbet (Cambridge: Cambridge University Press, 1981), 173–89.

5 Francis Ellen Watkins Harper as Frances Ellen Watkins, "The Free Labor Movement," *Frederick Douglass' Paper*, VIII: 28, June 29, 1855, n.p.; Marx, *Capital*, 76–87. Harper, *A Brighter Coming Day*, 81.

6 Harper, *A Brighter Coming Day*, 1990, 81.

7 Gotthold Ephraim Lessing, *Laocoön: An Essay on the Limits of Poetry and Painting*, ed. Edward Allen McCormick (Baltimore: Johns Hopkins University Press, 1984), 38; Thomas Carlyle, *Sartor Resartus* (New York: Oxford University Press, 1999), 207.

8 James W. C. Pennington, *The Fugitive Blacksmith; or, Events in the History of James W. C. Pennington, Pastor of a Presbyterian Church, New York, Formerly a Slave in the State of Maryland, United States* (London: Gilpin, 1849), iv–viii.

9 Harper, *A Brighter Coming Day*, 114–16.

10 William Still, *The Underground Railroad* (Philadelphia: Porter and Coates, 1872), 757.

11 Mary Wollstonecraft, *A Vindication of the Rights of Woman and A Vindication of the Rights of Man,* (New York: Oxford University Press, 2008), 91.

12 Barbara Christian, *Black Women Novelists: The Development of the Tradition, 1892–1976* (Westport, CT: Greenwood, 1980), 32; Deborah McDowell, *"The Changing Same": Black Women's Literature, Criticism, and Theory* (Bloomington: Indiana University Press, 1995), 40; Darlene Clark Hine, "Rape and the Inner Lives of Black Women in the Middle West," *Signs,* 14: 4, Special Issue: Common Grounds and Crossroads: Race, Ethnicity, and Class in Women's Lives (Summer 1989), 920; Pauline Hopkins, "Famous Women of the Negro Race," *The Colored American,* IV: 5, April 1, 1902, 369.

13 Harper, *A Brighter Coming Day,* 218; Harper quoted in Frederick Douglass, *Speeches, Debates and Interviews (The Frederick Douglass Papers Series I),* ed. John Blassingame (New Haven: Yale University Press, 1979–1992), IV, 220 (this material is also included in Susan B. Anthony, Elizabeth Cady Stanton, and Matilda Joslyn Gage's *History of Woman Suffrage* [1881]); Frances Ellen Watkins Harper, *Minnie's Sacrifice, Sowing and Reaping, Trial and Triumph,* ed. Frances Smith Foster (New York: Beacon, 1994), 78.

14 Edgar Allan Poe, *Essays and Reviews* (New York: Library of America, 1984), 38, 33, 19.

15 Harper, *A Brighter Coming Day,* 182–3; Anna Julia Cooper, *A Voice from the South,* ed. Mary Helen Washington (New York: Oxford University Press, 1988), 31.

16 Fannie Barrier Williams, "The Intellectual Progress of the Colored Women of the United States Since the Emancipation Proclamation," in *The World's Congress of Representative Women,* ed. May Wright Sewall (Chicago and New York: Rand McNally and Co., 1894), 696; Algernon Charles Swinburne, *The Swinburne Letters,* ed. Cecil Y. Lang, (New Haven: Yale University Press, 1960), 3: 12.

17 Harper, *A Brighter Coming Day,* 225.

18 Ibid., 225–6; Percy Bysshe Shelley, *Poetry and Prose,* ed. Donald H. Reiman and Sharon B. Powers (New York: Norton, 1977), 103.

19 Frances Smith Foster, "Gender, Genre, and Vulgar Secularism: The Case of Frances Ellen Watkins Harper and the AME Press," in *Recovered Writers/Recovered Texts,* ed. Dolan Hubbard (Knoxville: University of Tennessee Press, 1997), 56; Harper, *A Brighter Coming Day,* 286.

20 Frances Ellen Watkins Harper, "Woman's Political Future," in *World's Congress of Representative Women,* 434.

21 Harper, *A Brighter Coming Day,* 281; Evelyn Brooks Higginbotham,

"African-American Women's History and the Metalanguage of Race," *Signs,* 17: 2, Winter 1992, 272.

22 Victor Hugo, "Victor Hugo on Women's Rights," *New York Times,* April 18, 1875, 10; W.E.B. Du Bois, *The Souls of Black Folk* (London: Oxford University Press, 2007), 1.

23 Louise Michel, *The Red Virgin: Memoirs of Louise Michel,* trans. Bullitt Lowry and Elizabeth Ellington Gunter (Tuscaloosa: University of Alabama Press, 1981), 68.

24 Daudet and Gautier quoted in Kristin Ross, *The Emergence of Social Space: Rimbaud and the Paris Commune* (New York: Verso, 2008), 149.

25 Harper, *A Brighter Coming Day,* 49; Still, *The Underground Railroad,* 778.

26 Frances Ellen Watkins Harper, *Iola Leroy, or Shadows Uplifted* (Mineola, NY: Dover, 2010), 48.

27 Coleridge, *The Major Works,* ed. H. J. Jackson (New York: Oxford University Press, 2009), 28; Shelley, *Poetry and Prose,* 481.

28 Harper, *Iola Leroy,* 187, 45, 156.

29 Harper, *A Brighter Coming Day,* 231–2.

30 Ibid., 232, 217.

5. Freedom Is an Empty Name

1 See W.E.B. Du Bois, *Black Reconstruction in America, 1860–1880* (New York: Free Press, 1992), 197–8; The exact language of Stevens's speech quoted here is from "An Address Delivered to the Citizens of Lancaster, Sept. 6, 1865," *New York Times,* Sept. 10, 1865, 2.

2 Greeley quoted in Eric Foner, *Free Soil, Free Labor, Free Men: The Ideology of the Republican Party Before the Civil War* (New York: Oxford University Press, 1995), 27; Vernon Louis Parrington, *Main Currents in American Thought, Vol. 3: The Beginnings of Critical Realism in America* (Norman: University of Oklahoma Press, 1987), 23.

3 Houston A. Baker, Jr., *Long Black Song: Essays in Black American Culture* (Charlottesville: University of Virginia Press, 1972), 2; Melvin Dixon, *Ride Out the Wilderness: Geography and Identity in Afro-American Literature* (Urbana: University of Illinois Press, 1987), 3.

4 Mark Twain, *Mississippi Writings* (New York: Library of America, 1982), 500–1.

5 William Sanders Scarborough, *The Autobiography of William*

Sanders Scarborough: An American Journey from Slavery to Scholarship, ed. Michele Valerie Ronnick (Detroit: Wayne State University Press, 2004), 66, 65.

6 James D. Corrothers, *In Spite of the Handicap: An Autobiography* (New York: George H. Doran Co., 1916), 63–5.

7 Albery Allson Whitman, *Not a Man, and Yet a Man* (Springfield, Ohio: Republic Printing Co., 1877), 7, 9. This citation also appears in a more readily available collection of Whitman's work, *At the Dusk of Dawn: Selected Poetry and Prose of Albery Allson Whitman*, ed. Ivy G. Wilson (Boston: Northeastern University Press, 2009), 305, 304. Citations from both are included below wherever possible.

8 Whitman, *Not a Man*, 101/*At the Dusk of Dawn*, 83; Black Hawk, *Life of Black Hawk, or Mà-ka-tai-me-she-kià-kiàk, Dictated by Himself*, ed. J. Gerald Kennedy (New York: Penguin 2008), 87.

9 Whitman, *Not a Man*, 45, 81/*At the Dusk of Dawn*, 52, 73; Walter Scott, *The Lady of the Lake: A Poem in Six Cantos* (New York: T. Y. Crowell, 1888), 43.

10 Whitman, *Not a Man*, 122/*At the Dusk of Dawn*, 95.

11 Whitman, *Not a Man*, 36/*At the Dusk of Dawn*, 46–7; John Keats, *Selected Letters* (New York: Oxford University Press, 2002), 41.

12 Whitman, *Not a Man*, 158, 180/*At the Dusk of Dawn*, 116, 127.

13 Whitman, *Not a Man*, 200/*At the Dusk of Dawn*, 136.

14 Whitman, *Not a Man*, 211–2/*At the Dusk of Dawn*, 142–3.

15 Whitman, *At the Dusk of Dawn*, 308, 304; Booker T. Washington, *Up from Slavery* (New York: Modern Library, 1999), 144.

16 Du Bois, *Black Reconstruction*, 580–636; Edmund Wilson, *Patriotic Gore: Studies in the Literature of the American Civil War* (New York: W. W. Norton, 1994), 613; Albery Allson Whitman, *The Rape of Florida* (St. Louis: Nixon-Jones Printing Co., 1884), 4–5/*At the Dusk of Dawn*, 307.

17 Whitman, *The Rape of Florida*, 12, 19/*At the Dusk of Dawn*, 98, 99; Joshua Reed Giddings, *The Exiles of Florida: or, The Crimes Committed by Our Government Against the Maroons, Who Fled From South Carolina and Other Slave States, Seeking Protection Under Spanish Laws*, (Columbus: Follett, Foster, and Co., 1858), 98–9.

18 Whitman, *The Rape of Florida*, 19/*At the Dusk of Dawn*, 149–50.

19 Whitman, *The Rape of Florida*, 27/*At the Dusk of Dawn*, 154.

20 Whitman, *The Rape of Florida*, 25/*At the Dusk of Dawn*, 153–4.

21 William J. Simmons, *Men of Mark: Eminent, Progressive, Rising* (Cleveland: Geo. M. Rewell & Co., 1887), 1122; Bishop Daniel Alexander Payne, *Recollections of Seventy Years* (Nashville: AME Sunday School Union, 1888), 238; Frederick Douglass, *Speeches,*

Debates and Interviews (The Frederick Douglass Papers Series I), ed. John Blassingame (New Haven: Yale University Press, 1979–92), 4: 515.

22 Whitman, *At the Dusk of Dawn*, 295–7.

23 For "the nadir" see Rayford Logan, *The Negro in American Life and Thought: The Nadir, 1877–1901* (New York: The Dial Press, 1954); for "the golden age" see Wilson J. Moses, *The Golden Age of Black Nationalism, 1850–1925* (New York: Oxford University Press, 1978).

24 Albery Allson Whitman, *An Idyl of the South: An Epic Poem in Two Parts* (New York: Metaphysical Publishing Company, 1901), 123–4.

25 Whitman, *An Idyl of the South*, 126.

26 Paul Laurence Dunbar, *Collected Poetry*, ed. Joanne M. Braxton (Charlottesville: University of Virginia Press, 1993), 189.

Conclusion

1 W.E.B. Du Bois, *Black Reconstruction in America, 1860–1880* (New York: Free Press, 1992), 700; Frances Ellen Watkins Harper, *A Brighter Coming Day: A Frances Ellen Watkins Harper Reader*, ed. Frances Smith Foster (New York: The Feminist Press of the City University of New York, 1990), 178.

2 Saidiya Hartman, *Lose Your Mother: A Journey Along the Atlantic Slave Route* (New York: Farrar, Straus, Giroux, 2007), 6.

3 William Wordsworth and Samuel Taylor Coleridge, *Lyrical Ballads, 1798 and 1802* (New York: Oxford University Press, 2013), 95; Ralph Ellison, *Invisible Man* (New York: Vintage, 1980), 581.

4 Newbell Niles Puckett, *Folk Beliefs of the Southern Negro* (Chapel Hill: University of North Carolina Press, 1926), 554.

5 W.E.B. Du Bois, *The Souls of Black Folk* (London: Oxford University Press, 2007), 59.

6 Johann Wolfgang von Goethe, *Faust I & II*, trans. Stuart Atkins (Princeton: Princeton University Press, 1984), 40–1; see Max Weber, *The Protestant Ethic and the Spirit of Capitalism* (New York: Scribner, 1958), 180.

7 *The Oxford W.E.B. Du Bois Reader*, ed. Eric J. Sundquist (New York: Oxford University Press, 1996), 666; Billie Holiday, "Lover Man (Oh, Where Can You Be?)"/"That Ole Devil Called Love," Decca, 23391, 1945.

8 James Monroe Whitfield, *The Works of James M. Whitfield: America and Other Writings by a Nineteenth-Century African American Poet*, ed. Robert S. Levine and Ivy G. Wilson (Chapel Hill: University

of North Carolina Press, 2011), 56; Ralph Ellison, *Collected Essays* (New York: Modern Library, 1995), 85.

9 Fred Hampton, *You've Got to Make a Commitment!* (Chicago: People's Information Center, 1969), 7.

10 Toni Cade Bambara and Thabiti Lewis, *Conversations with Toni Cade Bambara* (Jackson: University Press of Mississippi, 2012), 35; George Moses Horton, *The Black Bard of North Carolina: George Moses Horton and His Poetry*, ed. Joan R. Sherman (Chapel Hill: University of North Carolina Press, 1997), 75.

11 June Jordan, *Civil Wars: Observations from the Front Lines of America* (New York: Touchstone, 1995), 179.

12 William Hazlitt, *The Fight and Other Writings* (London: Penguin, 2000), 436–7, 445–6.

13 Jordan, *Civil Wars*, 1995, 187.

14 Lorraine O'Grady, "Mlle Bourgeoise Noire: Performance 1980–83," artist's website, lorraineogrady.com.

15 Toni Morrison and Robert Richardson, "A Bench by the Road: *Beloved*," *The World*, January–February 1989, 4–5, 37–41.

16 Harper, *A Brighter Coming Day*, 85, 110; Toni Morrison, *Beloved* (New York: Alfred A. Knopf, 2006), 47.

17 Drake (@drake), "Dreams and Nightmares Intro really one of the best rap moments of our generation ...," Twitter, 1:27 AM, April 30, 2014.

Bibliographic Essay

Though most of the main characters of this book have not been the subjects of substantial scholarly inquiry, two of its wider areas of concern, Romanticism and slavery, have produced vast bodies of research, spanning disciplines and language traditions on both sides of the Atlantic. In what follows, I list the research that focuses on the Black Romantics, as well as some of the important academic debates and areas of inquiry that have guided my perspective. In general, my gratitude for the work of earlier scholars on these subjects far outweighs my disagreements with their methods or conclusions, and I often have learned more from their work than I can say in the space allotted.

This book engages in what is sometimes called literary "recovery," but it would be wrong to suggest that it "discovers" the poets who are its focus. Their names have appeared in indexes and surveys of African-American literature since the beginning of the twentieth century. Arthur A. Schomburg's *A Bibliographic Checklist of American Negro Poetry* (1916) lists all the main characters here, as does Robert Thomas Kerlin's *Negro Poets and Their Poems* (1923), Vernon Loggins's *The Negro Author in America* (1931), Sterling Brown et al.'s anthology *The Negro Caravan* (1941), and Dorothy B. Porter's *North American Negro Poets: A Bibliographic Checklist of Their Writings, 1760–1944* (1945). After the rise of Black Studies in the academy, this kind of work continued. William H. Robinson Jr.'s anthology *Early Black American Poets* (1969), Joan R. Sherman's annotated bibliography *Invisible*

Poets: Afro-Americans of the Nineteenth Century (1974), and Blyden Jackson and Louis D. Rubin Jr.'s *Black Poetry in America: Two Essays in Historical Interpretation* (1974) all provide crucial groundwork. Sherman's editorial work was especially important, for instance her indispensable *African American Poetry of the Nineteenth Century: An Anthology* (1992). More recent editorial efforts are listed below in sections devoted to the individual chapters, again with gratitude.

African-Americanist literary historians have long mentioned the poets covered here on the way to focusing on other figures in other historical periods. Benjamin Brawley established the conventional chronology of early African-American poetry in a programmatic essay entitled "Three Negro Poets: Horton, Mrs. Harper, and Whitman" in *The Journal of Negro History* (2:4, Oct. 1917). There he notes the defects of lyric writing in "the long period between Phillis Wheatley and Paul Dunbar" (384). Brawley wrote this essay as preparation for *The Negro in Literature and Art in the United States* (1918), later revised and republished as *The Negro Genius: A New Appraisal of the Achievement of the American Negro in Literature and the Fine Arts* (1937). Later synoptic assessments of African-American poetry that reformulate Brawley's dismissal of the poets "between Wheatley and Dunbar" include James Weldon Johnson's preface to *The Book of American Negro Poetry* (1922), William Stanley Braithwaite's essay on "The Negro in American Literature" from Alain Locke's 1925 *New Negro* anthology, and J. Saunders Redding's literary history, *To Make a Poet Black* (1939).

Critics often give short shrift to Horton, Harper, Whitman, and their contemporaries because their work is too Romantic or too political. Two important publications from the Black Arts era signal the prospect of reversing this evaluation: Stephen Henderson's *Understanding the New Black Poetry: Black Speech and Black Music as Poetic References* (1975) and Eugene Redmond's *Drumvoices: The Mission of Afro-American Poetry, a Critical History* (1976). Redmond writes: "Little said by the so-called 'Armageddon' writers of the 1960's and 1970's can be any more 'revolutionary' than Walker, Whitfield, and Albery

Whitman" (85). In the 1980s, however, Henry Louis Gates Jr. and Houston Baker followed the "between Wheatley and Dunbar" periodization, and largely ignored the nineteenth-century poets. Gates's notion of Black authors "signifyin(g)" on Euro-American literature is nonetheless applicable to Black Romanticism, as is Baker's narrative of Black aesthetics moving from "mastery of form" to "deformation of mastery."

A number of critics have hinted at the role of Romanticism in early African-American literature, including William L. Andrews in "The 1850s: The First Afro-American Literary Renaissance" in *Literary Romanticism in America* (1981), Dwight A. McBride in *Impossible Witnesses: Truth, Abolitionism, and Slave Testimony* (2002), Ifeoma Nwankwo in *Black Cosmopolitanism: Racial Consciousness and Transnational Identity in the Nineteenth-Century Americas* (2005), and Chris Castiglia in *Interior States: Institutional Consciousness and the Inner Life of Democracy in the Antebellum United States* (2008). On race, slavery, and abolition in British Romanticism, see Moira Ferguson's *Subject to Others: British Women Writers and Colonial Slavery, 1670–1834* (1992), Howard L. Malchow's *Gothic Images of Race in Nineteenth-Century Britain* (1996), Peter J. Kitson's " 'Bales of Living Anguish': Representations of Race and the Slave in Romantic Writing," *ELH* (67.2, 2000), Helen Thomas's *Romanticism and Slave Narratives: Transatlantic Testimonies* (2004), Debbie Lee's *Slavery and the Romantic Imagination* (2004), and a special issue of *European Romantic Review* edited by Manu Chander and Tricia Matthew (29:4, 2018). The editorial work of Paul Youngquist on this question has been decisive; see *Race, Romanticism, and the Atlantic* (2013), and a special issue of *Romantic Circles* he edited with Frances Botkin, "Circulations: Romanticism and the Black Atlantic" (October 2011). For Black culture and British Victorianism, see Jennifer DeVere Brody's *Impossible Purities: Blackness, Femininity, and Victorian Culture* (1998), Elisa Tamarkin's "Black Anglophilia; or, The Sociability of Antislavery" in *American Literary History* (Fall 2002), Vanessa Dickerson's *Dark Victorians* (2008), and Daniel Hack's *Reaping Something New: African American Transformations of Victorian Literature* (2016).

Two anthologies of Anglophone verse about slavery have been crucially useful: James Basker's *Amazing Grace: An Anthology of Poems About Slavery, 1660–1810* (2002) and Marcus Wood's *The Poetry of Slavery: An Anglo-American Anthology, 1764–1865* (2003). See also Debbie Lee and Peter Kitson's multivolume collection *Slavery, Abolition and Emancipation: Writings in the British Romantic Period* (1999).

For "romantic racialism" and other notions of race which became key targets of Black Romantic critique, see Winthrop D. Jordan's *White Over Black: American Attitudes Toward the Negro, 1550–1812* (1968) and George Fredrickson's *The Black Image in the White Mind: The Debate on Afro-American Character and Destiny, 1817–1914* (1987); for its role in American literature, see Toni Morrison's *Playing in the Dark: Whiteness and the Literary Imagination* (1993), Dana Nelson's *The Word in Black and White: Reading "Race" in American Literature, 1638–1867* (1992), Colin (Joan) Dayan's "Romance and Race" in *The Columbia History of the American Novel* (1991), Teresa Goddu's *Gothic America: Narrative, History, and Nation* (1997); for "romantic racialism" in early African-American literature, see Gene Andrew Jarrett's *Deans and Truants: Race and Realism in African American Literature* (2007); for its role in period popular culture, see Eric Lott's *Love and Theft: Blackface Minstrelsy and the American Working Class* (1993), and for its role in activist literature, see Kari J. Winter's *Subjects of Slavery, Agents of Change: Women and Power in Gothic Novels and Slave Narratives, 1790–1865* (1992).

Scholarship on nineteenth-century African-American print culture has expanded substantially in recent decades in ways that have substantially inflected the story I tell here. See Todd Vogel's anthology *The Black Press: New Literary and Historical Essays* (2001), Elizabeth McHenry's *Forgotten Readers: Recovering the Lost History of African American Literary Societies* (2002), Robert Fanuzzi's *Abolition's Public Sphere* (2003), Frances Smith Foster's "A Narrative of the Interesting Origins and (Somewhat) Surprising Development of African-American Print Culture" in *American Literary History* (17.4, 2005) and "Genealogies of Our Concerns, Early (African) American Print Culture, and Transcending Tough

Times" in *American Literary History* (22.2, 2010), Jordan Alexander Stein and Lara Langer Cohen's anthology *Early African American Print Culture* (2012), and Eric Gardner's *Black Print Unbound: "The Christian Recorder," African American Literature, and Periodical Culture* (2015).

My sense of the public life of poetry in the nineteenth century has benefited from performance studies; see Joseph Roach's *Cities of the Dead: Circum-Atlantic Performance* (1996), Daphne Brooks's *Bodies in Dissent: Spectacular Performances of Race and Freedom, 1850–1910* (2006), Alex W. Black's "Abolitionism's Resonant Bodies: The Realization of African American Performance," *American Quarterly* (63:3, 2011), and Douglas A. Jones's "Slavery's Performance-Texts," *The Cambridge Companion to Slavery in American Literature* (2016). For the beginnings of African-American musical traditions, see Dena J. Epstein's *Sinful Tunes and Spirituals: Black Folk Music to the Civil War* (1977), Jon Cruz's *Culture on the Margins: The Black Spiritual and the Rise of American Cultural Interpretation* (1999), Ronald M. Radano's *Lying up a Nation: Race and Black Music* (2004), and Katrina Dyonne Thompson's *Ring Shout, Wheel About: The Racial Politics of Music and Dance in North American Slavery* (2014). For studies of American poetry which parse the different significances of "the lyric," see Virginia Jackson's *Dickinson's Misery: A Theory of Lyric Reading* (2005), Ivy Wilson's *Specters of Democracy: Blackness and the Aesthetics of Politics in the Antebellum U.S.* (2011), Faith Barrett's *To Fight Aloud Is Very Brave: American Poetry and the Civil War* (2012), Max Cavitch's "Slavery and its Metrics" in *The Cambridge Companion to Nineteenth-Century American Poetry* (2011), and Michael C. Cohen's *The Social Lives of Poems in Nineteenth-Century America* (2015).

For the free communities of the North, see Leon F. Litwack's *North of Slavery: The Negro in the Free States, 1790–1860* (1961), Benjamin Quarles's *Black Abolitionists* (1969), Leonard P. Curry's *The Free Black in Urban America, 1800–1850: The Shadow of the Dream* (1981), James Oliver Horton and Lois E. Horton's *In Hope of Liberty: Culture, Community and Protest among Northern Free Blacks, 1700–1860* (1998), Leslie Alexander's *African or American?: Black Identity and Political Activism in New York City, 1784–1861* (2008), Erica Dunbar's *A Fragile Freedom: African American Women and Emancipation in the Antebellum City* (2008), Erica Ball's *To Live an Antislavery Life: Personal Politics and the Antebellum Black Middle Class* (2012), Kellie Carter Jackson's *Force & Freedom: Black Abolitionists and the Politics of Violence* (2019), and Derrick Spires's *The Practice of Citizenship: Black Politics and Print Culture in the Early United States* (2019). For interracial collaboration in the abolition movement, see John Stauffer's *The Black Hearts of Men: Radical Abolitionists and the Transformation of Race* (2002) and Manisha Sinha's *The Slave's Cause: A History of Abolition* (2016). For Black women's contributions, see Shirley J. Yee's *Black Women Abolitionists: A Study in Activism, 1828–1860* (1992) and P. Gabrielle Foreman's *Activist Sentiments: Reading Black Women in the Nineteenth Century* (2009).

Many of the figures of this book participated in different forms of nineteenth-century Black nationalism. See Floyd J. Miller's *The Search for a Black Nationality: Black Emigration and Colonization, 1787–1863* (1975) and Wilson J. Moses, *The Golden Age of Black Nationalism, 1850–1925* (1978). For Liberian colonization in early Black political theorizing, see Claude Clegg's *The Price of Liberty: African Americans and the Making of Liberia* (2009) and David Kazanjian's *The Brink of Freedom: Improvising Life in the Nineteenth-Century Atlantic World* (2016). For the Haitian Revolution in US political discourse, see Matthew J. Clavin's *Toussaint Louverture and the American Civil War: The Promise and Peril of a Second Haitian Revolution* (2010) and Elizabeth Maddox Dillon and Michael Drexler's anthology *The Haitian Revolution and the Early United States: Histories, Textualities, Geographies* (2016). For Haiti in transatlantic literature, see Marlene L. Daut's *Tropics of Haiti: Race and the Literary History of the Haitian Revolution in the Atlantic World, 1789–1865* (2015). For the Bois Caïman oath, see Doris Y. Kadish and Deborah Jenson's anthology *Poetry of Haitian Independence* (2015), Caroline E. Fick's *The Making of Haiti: The Saint Domingue Revolution from Below* (1990) and David Patrick Geggus's *Haitian Revolutionary Studies* (2002). For abolition in the Anglophone Caribbean and its impacts on slavery in the US, see Edward Rugemer's *The Problem of Emancipation: The Caribbean Roots of the American Civil War* (2008). For studies of emancipation in the Caribbean useful for understanding the postbellum US, see Rebecca J. Scott's *Degrees of Freedom: Louisiana and Cuba After Slavery* (2008) and Natasha Lightfoot's *Troubling Freedom: Antigua and the Aftermath of British Emancipation* (2015).

African-American intellectual history tested M. H. Abrams's theory of Romanticism as the "secularization of inherited theological ideas" (*Natural Supernaturalism: Tradition and Revolution in Romantic Literature*, 1973, 12). Unfortunately, I was unable to find room to cover Bishop Daniel A. Payne's 1850 collection *The Pleasures and Other Miscellaneous Poems*. For the cultural politics of African-American religion more generally, see Albert J. Raboteau's *Slave Religion: The "Invisible Institution" in the Antebellum South* (1978), Theophus H. Smith's *Conjuring Culture: Biblical Formations of Black America* (1995), and Eddie S. Glaude Jr.'s *Exodus!: Religion, Race, and Nation in Early Nineteenth-Century Black America* (2000). For secularization and debates about Atlantic slavery, see Jared Hickman's *Black Prometheus: Race and Radicalism in the Age of Atlantic Slavery* (2017). For slavery and Christianity, see David Brion Davis's *The Problem of Slavery in Western Culture* (1966, 29–121) and Jennifer A. Glancy's *Slavery in Early Christianity* (2002). For prophecy in European Romanticism, see Ian Balfour, *The Rhetoric of Romantic Prophecy* (2002). For Milton in African-American literature, see Reginald A. Wilburn's *Preaching the Gospel of Black Revolt: Appropriating Milton in Early African American Literature* (2014).

Theoretical accounts of African-American literary tradition have long engaged Romantic theories of aesthetics. See, for example, the readings of Hegel in Houston Baker's *Blues, Ideology, and Afro-American Literature: A Vernacular Theory* (1984), James A. Snead's "On Repetition in Black Culture" in *Black American Literature Forum* (15:4, Winter 1981), Henry Louis Gates Jr.'s *Figures in Black: Words, Signs, and the "Racial" Self* (1987), Paul Gilroy's *The Black Atlantic: Modernity and Double Consciousness*

(1993), and Fred Moten's *In the Break: The Aesthetics of the Black Radical Tradition* (2003). Saidiya Hartman's *Scenes of Subjection: Terror, Slavery, and Self-Making in Nineteenth-Century America* (1997) and Marcus Wood's *Slavery, Empathy, and Pornography* (2002) both work through theories of the sublime. Cedric J. Robinson's *Black Marxism: The Making of the Black Radical Tradition* (1983), Robert Gooding-Williams's *In the Shadow of Du Bois: Afro-Modern Political Thought in America* (2009), and Nahum Chandler's *X: The Problem of the Negro as a Problem for Thought* (2013) all address the role of Romanticism in Du Bois's thinking.

For the relations between abolitionism, liberalism, and capitalism, see David Brion Davis's *The Problem of Slavery in the Age of Revolution, 1770–1823* (1975), Robin Blackburn's *The Overthrow of Colonial Slavery, 1776–1848* (1988), Thomas Bender's anthology *The Anti-Slavery Debate: Capitalism and Abolitionism as a Problem in Historical Interpretation* (1992), and Christopher Leslie Brown's *Moral Capital: Foundations of British Abolitionism* (2006). For Romanticism and liberalism, see Michael Löwy and Robert Sayre's *Romanticism Against the Tide of Modernity* (2001). For slavery and philosophy of history, see Ian Baucom's *Specters of the Atlantic: Finance Capital, Slavery, and the Philosophy of History* (2005), David Scott's *Conscripts of Modernity: The Tragedy of Colonial Enlightenment* (2004), and Susan Buck-Morss's *Hegel, Haiti, and Universal History* (2009). For time in nineteenth-century American literature, see Lloyd Pratt's *Archives of American Time: Literature and Modernity in the Nineteenth Century* (2009), Cody Marrs's *Nineteenth-Century American Literature and the Long Civil War* (2015), and Jeffrey Insko's *History, Abolition, and the Ever-Present Now in Antebellum American Writing* (2018).

The conception of the Civil War as a revolution has long historiographic precedent besides Du Bois. In 1927, Charles and Mary Beard referred to the Civil War as the "Second American Revolution" in *The Rise of American Civilization*, because of its redistribution of wealth (1927, 54). Barrington Moore declared the Civil War the "last capitalist revolution" because of its benefit to Northern, urban industrialism (*Social Origins of Dictatorship and Democracy: Lord and Peasant in the Making of the Modern World*, 1966, 152). Eric Foner's *Reconstruction: America's Unfinished Revolution, 1863–1877* (1988), James McPherson's *Abraham Lincoln and the Second American Revolution* (1990), Steven Hahn's *A Nation Under our Feet: Black Political Struggles in the Rural South from Slavery to the Great Migration* (2005), and David Roediger's *Seizing Freedom: Slave Emancipation and Liberty for All* (2014) all follow Du Bois in taking recourse to the concept of revolution, as do cultural critics like Michael Paul Rogin in *Subversive Genealogy: The Politics and Art of Herman Melville* (1985), Eric Sundquist in *To Wake the Nations: Race in the Making of American Literature* (1993), Eric Lott in "The Eighteenth Brumaire of Abraham Lincoln: Revolutionary Rhetoric and the Emergence of the Bourgeois State" in *Clio* (22, Winter 1993), and Larry J. Reynolds in *European Revolutions and the American Literary Renaissance* (1988) and *Righteous Violence: Revolution, Slavery, and the American Literary Renaissance* (2011).

On the value of "failed" cultural and political projects across the African diaspora, see Robin D. G. Kelley's *Freedom Dreams: The Black Radical Imagination* (2002). I have also benefited from Michel Rolph-Trouillot's *Silencing the Past: Power and the Production of History* (1995), on the ways the Haitian Revolution became "unthinkable" for Enlightenment political philosophy. For "the spirit of the age" in the German philosophical tradition, see Karl Lowith's *From Hegel to Nietzsche: The Revolution in Nineteenth-Century Thought* (1991). For its resonance in English poetry, see M. H. Abrams's "English Romanticism: The Spirit of the Age," in *The Correspondent Breeze: Essays in English Romanticism* (1986), and James Chandler's *England in 1819: The Politics of Literary Culture and the Case of Romantic Historicism* (1998). For the concept of the spirit in African-American literature and culture, see Harryette Mullen's "African Signs and Spirit Writing," *Callaloo* (19:3, 1996) and Josef Sorett's *Spirit in the Dark: A Religious History of Racial Aesthetics* (2016). For nineteenth-century African-American theories of history, see Wilson J. Moses'

Afrotopia: The Roots of African American Popular History (1998), John Ernest's *Liberation Historiography: African American Writers and the Challenge of History, 1794–1861* (2004) and Stephen G. Hall's *A Faithful Account of the Race: African American Historical Writing in Nineteenth-Century America* (2009).

The notion of the "fugitive romance" makes for a geopolitical counter to Harold Bloom's definition of Romanticism as "the internalization of quest-romance" in his *Romanticism and Consciousness: Essays in Criticism* (1970). For fugitivity as a theoretical paradigm in African-American literature and culture, see Nathaniel Mackey's "Other: From Noun to Verb" in *Representations* (39, 1992), Fred Moten (2003), and Neil Roberts's *Freedom as Marronage* (2015). My account also relies on Kristin Ross's discussion of "centrifugal poetics" in *The Emergence of Social Space: Rimbaud and the Paris Commune* (1988), Nadia Ellis's sense of diaspora as framed by longing in *Territories of the Soul: Queered Belonging in the Black Diaspora* (2015), and María Rosa Menocal's reading of the romance tradition as reshaped by New World colonialism in *Shards of Love: Exile and the Origins of the Lyric* (1994).

Chapter 1. Hereditary Bondsmen, Strike the Blow!

Literary critics have debated the significance of the Byron quotation for decades. Above-named texts by Eric Sundquist (1993), John Stauffer (2002), and Jared Hickman (2017) all engage the citation of Byron by Black abolitionists, as do Robert S. Levine in *Martin Delany, Frederick Douglass, and the Politics of Representative Identity* (1997), Rowan Ricardo Phillips in *when blackness rhymes with blackness* (2010), and Deanna Koretsky in "Boundaries Between Things Misnamed: Social Death and Radical (Non-)existence in Frederick Douglass and Lord Byron" in *European Romantic Review* (29.4, 2018). For Byron in America, see the contents of a recent special issue of *Byron Journal* (45:1, 2017) entitled "Byron in America," edited by Noah Comet.

For discussions of originality and imitation in early African-American literature relevant to Black Byronism, see John Sekora's

"Black Message/White Envelope: Genre, Authenticity, and Authority in the Antebellum Slave Narrative," *Callaloo* (32, Summer 1987), John Ernest's *Resistance and Reformation in Nineteenth-Century African-American Literature: Brown, Wilson, Jacobs, Delany, Douglass, and Harper* (1995), Rafia Zafar's *We Wear the Mask: African Americans Write American Literature, 1760–1870* (1997), and Geoffrey Sanborn's *Plagiarama!: William Wells Brown and the Aesthetic of Attractions* (2016); for a similar set of questions in British Romanticism, see Tilar Mazzeo's *Plagiarism and Literary Property in the Romantic Period* (2006); and in a transatlantic (but especially US) frame, see Meredith L. McGill's *American Literature and the Culture of Reprinting, 1834–1858* (2007). For repetition in nineteenth-century American poetry, see Eliza Richards's *Gender and the Poetics of Reception in Poe's Circle* (2004) and Claudia Stokes's "The Poetics of Unoriginality: The Case of Lucretia Davidson" in *Legacy* (32:1, 2015).

For work on the fugitive slave narratives, see John W. Blassingame's "Using the Testimony of Ex-Slaves: Approaches and Problems" in *The Journal of Southern History* (41:4, Nov. 1975), James Olney's " 'I Was Born': Slave Narratives, Their Status as Autobiography and as Literature" in *Callaloo* (20, Winter 1984), Mary Helen Washington's *Invented Lives: Narratives of Black Women, 1860–1960* (1987), William L. Andrews's *To Tell a Free Story: The First Century of Afro-American Autobiography, 1760–1865* (1988), Robert Stepto's *From Behind the Veil: A Study of Afro-American Narrative* (1991), Charles T. Davis and Henry Louis Gates Jr.'s anthology *The Slave's Narrative* (1991); and Frances Smith Foster's *Written by Herself: Literary Production by African American Women, 1746–1892* (1993).

Black feminist scholarship has long emphasized the sexual exploitation of enslaved women. See Jacqueline Jones's *Labor of Love, Labor of Sorrow: Black Women, Work and the Family, From Slavery to the Present* (1985), Deborah Gray White's *Ar'n't I a Woman?: Female Slaves in the Plantation South* (1999), Nell Irvin Painter's "Soul Murder and Slavery: Toward a Fully Loaded Cost Accounting" in *Southern History Across the Color Line* (2002), Jennifer L. Morgan's *Laboring Women: Gender and*

Reproduction in New World Slavery (2004) and *"Partus sequitur ventrem*: Law, Race, and Reproduction in Colonial Slavery" in *Small Axe* (22:1, March 2018), Frances Smith Foster's anthology *Love and Marriage in Early African America* (2007), Treva B. Lindsey and Jessica Marie Johnson's "Searching for Climax: Black Erotic Lives in Slavery and Freedom" in *Meridians* (12:2, 2014), Daina Ramey Berry's *The Price for Their Pound of Flesh: The Value of the Enslaved, From Womb to Grave, in the Building of a Nation* (2017), Tera W. Hunter's *Bound in Wedlock: Slave and Free Black Marriage in the Nineteenth Century* (2017), Diedre Cooper Owens's *Medical Bondage: Race, Gender, and the Origins of American Gynecology* (2017), and Sasha Turner's *Contested Bodies: Pregnancy, Childrearing, and Slavery in Jamaica* (2017).

For Black masculinity, see Robert Reid-Pharr's "Violent Ambiguity: Martin Delany, Bourgeois Sadomasochism, and the Production of Black National Masculinity" in Marcellus Blount and George P. Cunningham's anthology *Representing Black Men* (1986), Maggie Montesinos Sale's *The Slumbering Volcano: American Slave Ship Revolts and the Production of Rebellious Masculinity* (1997), John Saillant's "The Black Body Erotic and the Republican Body Politic, 1790–1820" in *Sentimental Men: Masculinity and the Politics of Affect in American Culture* (1999), and Maurice Wallace's *Constructing the Black Masculine: Identity and Ideality in African American Men's Literature and Culture, 1775–1995* (2002). For the "bad man" as a figure of Black culture, see John W. Roberts's *From Trickster to Badman: The Black Folk Hero in Slavery and Freedom* (1990). For the race man and racial uplift in the late nineteenth and twentieth centuries, see Kevin K. Gaines's *Uplifting the Race: Black Leadership, Politics, and Culture in the Twentieth Century* (1996), Hazel V. Carby's *Race Men* (1998), and Marlon Ross's *Manning the Race: Reforming Black Men in the Jim Crow Era* (2004). For the race man and the bad man, see Wilson J. Moses' *Black Messiahs and Uncle Toms: Social and Literary Manipulations of a Religious Myth* (1993) and Fred Moten's "Uplift and Criminality," *Next to the Color Line: Gender, Sexuality, and W.E.B. Du Bois* (2006).

For Byron and gender, see Lewis Crompton's *Byron and Greek Love: Homophobia in 19ᵗʰ Century England* (1985), Caroline Franklin's *Byron's Heroines* (1992), Marlon Ross's *The Contours of Masculine Desire: Romanticism and the Rise of Women's Poetry* (1990), Anne Mellor's *Romanticism and Gender* (1993), Andrew Elfenbein's *Romantic Genius: The Prehistory of a Homosexual Role* (1999), and Susan Wolfson's *Borderlines: The Shiftings of Gender in British Romanticism* (2006). For Byron and chattel slavery, see Mark Canuel's "Race, Writing, and *Don Juan*" in *Studies in Romanticism* (54, Fall 2015). For Byron and the Americas, see Rebecca Cole Heinowitz's *Spanish America and British Romanticism, 1777–1826: Rewriting Conquest* (2010). For Stowe on Byron, see Caroline Franklin's "Stowe and the Byronic Heroine" in *Transatlantic Stowe: Harriet Beecher Stowe and European Culture* (2006). For Byron's use of the epic, see Nicholas Halmi's "The Very Model of a Modern Epic Poem" in *European Romantic Review* (21:5, 2010). For the epic in American poetry, see Christopher N. Phillips's *Epic in American Culture: Settlement to Reconstruction* (2012). For the epic in African-American poetry, see Raymond R. Patterson's "African American Epic Poetry: The Long Foreshadowing" in *The Furious Flowering of African American Poetry* (1999) and John Levi Barnard's *Empire of Ruin: Black Classicism and American Imperial Culture* (2014).

Chapter 2. The Supernatural Avenger

Some important work has emerged about Horton in recent years. For a discussion of his late visit to Philadelphia, see Reginald H. Pitts, " 'Let us Desert this Friendless Place': George Moses Horton in Philadelphia—1866" in *The Journal of Negro History* (80:4, 1995), who shows that Horton intervened on Black cultural life in Philadelphia before departing for Liberia. For a detailed discussion of the publication of his first book, see Leon Jackson's *The Business of Letters: Authorial Economies in Antebellum America* (2007). Faith Barrett has done some important work on Horton, both in her 2012 book and in "*Naked Genius*: The Civil

War Poems of George Moses Horton" in *The Literary Cultures of the Civil War* (2016). An undergraduate at the University of North Carolina, Constance Chia, did a complete transcription of Horton's 1859 "Address: The Stream of Liberty and Science" in 2016, and book historian Jonathan Senchyne discovered an essay by Horton from the mid-1850s entitled "Individual Influence," *PMLA* (132.5, 2017). This work expands on earlier comments on Horton by literary historians from Brawley to Redmond, as well as an important essay by Sondra O'Neale, "Roots of Our Literary Culture: George Moses Horton and Biblical Protest" in *Obsidian* (7, 1981), and Joan R. Sherman's collection *The Black Bard of North Carolina: George Moses Horton and His Poetry* (2000).

The idea of "genius" as a mechanism for Black liberation has been long debated; for the role of this idea in poetry and literary criticism, see Keith D. Leonard's *Fettered Genius: The African American Bardic Poet from Slavery to Civil Rights* (2006). On Wheatley and Romanticism, see the above-named work by Helen Thomas (2004) and John Shields's *Phillis Wheatley and the Romantics* (2010). For the Romantic figure of "the poet" in colonial contexts, see Manu Chander's *Brown Romantics: Poetry and Nationalism in the Global Nineteenth Century* (2017).

My perspective on Horton is framed by readings of Baudelaire by Theodor Adorno and Walter Benjamin. For nineteenth-century French literature, Blackness, and slavery, see Christopher L. Miller's *Blank Darkness: Africanist Discourse in French* (1985). A more fulsome account of the early role of Francophone poetry in the early history of African-American literature would need to address the Creole poets of New Orleans, especially those represented in the 1845 anthology *Les Cenelles*, for which see Lloyd Pratt's *The Strangers Book: The Human of African American Literature* (2016). On "social death," see revisions of Patterson in Sharon Holland's *Raising the Dead: Readings of Death and (Black) Subjectivity* (2000), Karla F. Holloway's *Passed On: African American Mourning Stories* (2002), and Vincent Brown's "Social Death and Political Life in Some Recent Histories of Slavery" in *The American Historical Review* (114:5, 2009). On death and liberal personhood in the nineteenth-century US, see

Russ Castronovo's *Necro Citizenship: Death, Eroticism, and the Public Sphere in the Nineteenth-Century United States* (2001), Dana Luciano's *Arranging Grief: Sacred Time and the Body in Nineteenth-Century America* (2007), and Drew Gilpin Faust's *This Republic of Suffering: Death and the American Civil War* (2009).

Chapter 3. The Seething Brain

The poets discussed in this chapter have been the object of scattered scholarly investigation over the years. On Vashon, see Paul N. D. Thornell's "The Absent Ones and the Providers: A Biography of the Vashons" in the *Jounral of Negro History* (83:4, 1998), Catherine M. Hanchett's two-part essay "George Boyer Vashon, 1824–1878: Black Educator, Poet, Fighter for Equal Rights" in *The Western Pennsylvania Historical Magazine* (68:3–4, 1985), and a collaboratively authored piece by Eric Gardner, Aldon Lynn Nielson, Keith D. Leonard, Evie Shockley, and Tara Bynum, "George Boyer Vashon's 'In the Cars': A Poem and Four Responses" in *American Periodicals: A Journal of History & Criticism*, (25:2, 2015). For Simpson, see Vicki Lynn Eaklor's "The Songs of the Emancipation Car: Variations on an Abolitionist Theme" in *Bulletin of the Missouri Historical Society* (36, January 1980). For Whitfield, see Joan Sherman's "James Monroe Whitfield, Poet and Emigrationist: A Voice of Protest and Despair" in *The Journal of Negro History* (57:2, 1972), Edward Whitley's *American Bards: Walt Whitman and Other Unlikely Candidates for National Poet* (2010), and Robert S. Levine and Ivy G. Wilson's excellent edition of Whitfield's collected works listed below.

For white writers of the period on phrenology, see David Reynolds's *Beneath the American Renaissance: The Subversive Imagination in the Age of Emerson and Melville* (1989). For racial science in nineteenth-century America with emphases on African-American writers, see Bruce Dain's *A Hideous Monster of the Mind: American Race Theory in the Early Republic* (2003) and

Britt Rusert's *Fugitive Science: Empiricism and Freedom in Early African American Culture* (2017). For the brain in English verse, see Alan Richardson, *British Romanticism and the Science of the Mind* (2001). For psychological interiority in African-American poetry, see Elizabeth Alexander, *The Black Interior* (2004). For a philosophical discussion of the census of 1840, see Calvin Warren's *Ontological Terror: Blackness, Nihilism, and Emancipation* (2017). For the relationship between African-American poetry and music, see Lauri Ramey's *Slave Songs and the Birth of African American Poetry* (2008) and Meta DuEwa Jones's *The Muse Is Music: Jazz Poetry From the Harlem Renaissance to Spoken Word* (2013).

For Vincent Ogé, see John D. Garrigus, " 'Thy coming fame, Ogé! Is sure': New Evidence on Ogé's 1790 Revolt and the Beginnings of the Haitian Revolution" in *Assumed Identities: The Meaning of Race in the Atlantic World* (2010). For Soulouque, see Laurent DuBois's *Avengers of the New World: The Story of the Haitian Revolution* (2005) and Colin (Joan) Dayan's *Haiti, History, and the Gods* (1998). For African Americans and Haiti in the mid-nineteenth century, see Howard Holman Bell's anthology *Black Separatism and the Caribbean, 1860* (1970) and Chris Dixon's *African America and Haiti: Emigration and Black Nationalism in the Nineteenth Century* (2000). For the importance of Delany's choice, in his novel *Blake, or the Huts of America* (1859–61) to ventriloquize Whitfield's poem through the Afro-Cuban poet Plácido, see Jerome McGann's introduction to his 2017 edition of the novel. A more properly transnational version of this book would spend more time on the radical poetries of Plácido and his contemporary Juan Francisco Manzano, both of whose work was known in the antebellum US.

On African Americans and war, see George Washington Williams's *A History of the Negro Troops in the War of Rebellion, 1861–1865* (1887) and Joseph Thomas Wilson, *The Black Phalanx: African American Soldiers in the War of Independence, the War of 1812, and the Civil War* (1890). For Black enlistment and debates about slavery and citizenship, see Chandra Manning's *What This Cruel War Was Over: Soldiers, Slavery, and the Civil*

War (2007) and Jennifer C. James's *A Freedom Bought With Blood: African American War Literature From the Civil War to World War II* (2007).

Chapter 4. The Uprising of Women

Harper has received the most scholarly attention of any figure in the book, especially her late novel *Iola Leroy* (1892), which figures prominently in a number of classic works of black feminist literary theory and cultural history. See Barbara Christian's *Black Women Novelists: The Development of a Tradition, 1892–1976* (1980) and " 'Somebody Forgot to Tell Somebody Something': African-American Women's Historical Novels" (1990, collected in *New Black Feminist Criticism, 1985–2000* [2007]), Hazel Carby's *Reconstructing Womanhood: The Emergence of the Afro-American Woman Novelist* (1989), Claudia Tate's *Domestic Allegories of Political Desire: The Black Heroine's Text at the Turn of the Century* (1992), and Deborah E. McDowell's *"The Changing Same": Black Women's Literature, Criticism, and Theory* (1995). Harper's legacy has also benefited from the editorial work of Frances Smith Foster, Maryemma Graham, and Koritha Mitchell, whose editions are all listed in the "Works Cited" section below.

For Harper's work before *Iola Leroy*, see Patricia Liggins Hill, "Frances W. Harper's Aunt Chloe Poems from *Sketches of Southern Life*: Antithesis to the Plantation Literary Tradition" in *Mississippi Quarterly* (Fall 1981) and " 'Let Me Make the Songs for the People': A Study of Frances Watkins Harper's Poetry" in *Black American Literature Forum* (15:2, Summer 1981), Melba Joyce Boyd's *Discarded Legacy: Politics and Poetics in the Life of Frances E. W. Harper, 1825–1911* (1994), Frances Smith Foster's "Gender, Genre, and Vulgar Secularism: The Case of Frances Ellen Watkins Harper and the AME Press," *Recovered Writers/ Recovered Texts: Race, Class, and Gender in Black Women's Literature* (1997), Mary Loeffelholz's *From School to Salon: Reading Nineteenth-Century American Women's Poetry* (2004), Alice Rutkowski's "Leaving the Good Mother: Frances E. W. Harper, Lydia

Maria Child, and the Literary Politics of Reconstruction," *Legacy* (25:1, 2008), Meredith L. McGill's "Frances Ellen Watkins Harper and the Circuits of Abolitionist Poetry," *Early African American Print Culture* (2012), Tricia Lootens's *The Political Poetess: Victorian Femininity, Race, and the Legacy of Separate Spheres* (2016), and Eric Gardner's "African American Literary Reconstructions and the 'Propaganda of History'" in *American Literary History* (30:3, 2018).

For the Free Produce movement, see Lawrence Glickman's "'Buy for the Sake of the Slave': Abolitionism and Origins of American Consumer Activism" in *American Quarterly* (56:4, December 2004) and Carol Faulkner's "The Root of Evil: Free Produce and Radical Anti-Slavery, 1820–1860" in *Journal of the Early Republic* (27:3, 2007). Free Produce borrowed from British abolitionism; see Charlotte Sussman's *Consuming Anxieties: Consumer Protest, Gender, and British Slavery, 1713–1833* (2000) and forthcoming work from Patricia Matthew. For slavery and capitalism, see Walter Johnson's *Soul by Soul: Life Inside the Antebellum Slave Market* (1999), "The Pedestal and the Veil: Re-thinking the Capitalism/ Slavery Question" in *Journal of the Early Republic* (24:2, 2004), and *River of Dark Dreams: Slavery and Empire in the Cotton Kingdom* (2013), Edward E. Baptist's *The Half Has Never Been Told: Slavery and the Making of American Capitalism* (2014), Sven Beckert's *Empire of Cotton: A Global History* (2015), and Sven Beckert and Seth Rockman's anthology *Slavery's Capitalism: A New History of American Economic Development* (2016).

Harper's thinking on objectification presages Fred Moten's notion of "the resistance of the object" (2003, 1–24) as a point of departure for Black radical aesthetics. She also anticipates Stephanie Smallwood's notion of the Middle Passage as turning captives into commodities, for which see *Saltwater Slavery: A Middle Passage From Africa to American Diaspora* (2008). For people as property, see also Stephen Best's *The Fugitive's Properties: Law and the Poetics of Possession* (2004). For commodity capitalism as "hauntological" see Jacques Derrida's *Specters of Marx: The State of Debt, the Work of Mourning, and the New International*, trans. Peggy Kamuf (1994), and for metaphor in

Marx, see Hayden White's *Metahistory: The Historical Imagination in Nineteenth-Century Europe* (1973). For women and the rise of commodity fetishism, see Ann Douglas's *The Feminization of American Culture* (1998), Andreas Huyssens's *After the Great Divide: Modernism, Mass Culture, and Postmodernism* (1986, 4–64), Rita Felski's *The Gender of Modernity* (1995, 61–90), and Jeff Nunokawa's *The Afterlife of Property: Domestic Security and the Victorian Novel* (2003).

For the collaboration between abolition and feminism, see Karen Sánchez-Eppler's *Touching Liberty: Abolition, Feminism, and the Politics of the Body* (1993), Jean Fagan Yellin and John C. Van Horne's anthology *The Abolitionist Sisterhood: Women's Political Culture in Antebellum America* (1994), Christine Stansell's "Missed Connections: Abolition Feminism in the Nineteenth Century" in *Elizabeth Cady Stanton, Feminist as Thinker* (2007). For the implications of slavery in the domestic sphere, see Xiomara Santamarina's *Belabored Professions: Narratives of African American Working Womanhood* (2005) and Thavolia Glymph's *Out of the House of Bondage: The Transformation of the Plantation Household* (2008). For the domestic sphere as a site of both imperial ideology and political radicalism, see Lora Romero's *Home Fronts: Domesticity and Its Critics in the Antebellum United States* (1997), Laura Wexler's *Tender Violence: Domestic Visions in an Age of U.S. Imperialism* (2000), and Amy Kaplan's *The Anarchy of Empire in the Making of U.S. Culture* (2002).

For postbellum Black women's activism, see Deborah Gray White's *Too Heavy a Load: Black Women in Defense of Themselves, 1894–1994* (1999, 21–141), Paula Giddings's *When and Where I Enter: The Impact of Black Women on Race and Sex in America* (1984, 17–135), Carla L. Peterson's *"Doers of the Word": African-American Women Speakers and Writers in the North* (1998), Martha Jones's *"All Bound Up Together": The Woman Question in African American Public Culture, 1830–1900* (2007), Mia Bay, Farah J. Griffin, Martha S. Jones, and Barbara D. Savage's anthology *Toward an Intellectual History of Black Women* (2015), and Brittney Cooper's *Beyond Respectability: The Intellectual Thought of Race Women* (2017). For Black community work and political formations in the postbellum, see Eric Foner's "Black Reconstruction Leaders at the Grass Roots" in *Black Leaders of the Nineteenth Century* (1991), Elsa Barkley Brown's "Negotiating and Transforming the Public Sphere: African American Political Life in the Transition from Slavery to Freedom" in *Public Culture* (7:1 1994), and Tera W. Hunter's *To 'Joy My Freedom: Southern Black Women's Lives and Labors after the Civil War* (1998).

For the Commune and radical aesthetics, see Kristin Ross's *The Emergence of Social Space: Rimbaud and the Paris Commune* (1988) and *Communal Luxury: The Political Imaginary of the Paris Commune* (2015). For parallels between the Reconstruction and the Commune, see Philip Katz's *From Appomattox to Montmartre: Americans and the Paris Commune* (2009) and Heather Cox Richardson's *The Death of Reconstruction: Race, Labor, and Politics in the Post–Civil War North, 1865–1901* (2004, 83–121).

Chapter 5. Freedom Is an Empty Name

Albery Allson Whitman has also been the subject of some focused research, starting yet again with Joan Sherman, in a useful essay entitled "Albery Allson Whitman: Poet of Beauty and Manliness" in *CLA Journal* (15:2, 1971). Some crucial early commentary on Whitman appears in Dickson Bruce Jr.'s *Black Writing From the Nadir: The Evolution of a Literary Tradition, 1877–1915* (1989). See also James R. Hays's thorough dissertation "Albery Allson Whitman (1851–1901), Epic Poet of African American and Native American Self-Determination" (Florida State University, 2000). Whitman's daughters, the Whitman sisters, became a famous vaudeville act, and Nadine George-Graves covers their training in the church by their father in *The Royalty of Negro Vaudeville: The Whitman Sisters and the Negotiation of Race, Gender and Class in African American Theater, 1900–1940* (2000). Whitman's work is also collected in a volume edited by Ivy G. Wilson listed below.

Scholars have begun to pay attention to the role of space and geography in African-American culture and history in ways that inform this chapter. Quintard Taylor's *In Search of the Racial Frontier: African Americans in the American West, 1528–1990* (1999) is definitive. See also Margaret Washington's "African American History and the Frontier Thesis" in *Journal of the Early Republic* (13:2, 1993), Michael Johnson's *Black Masculinity and the Frontier Myth in American Literature* (2002), Katherine McKittrick's *Demonic Grounds: Black Women and the Cartographies of Struggle* (2006), Eric Gardner's *Unexpected Places: Relocating Nineteenth-Century African American Literature* (2009), Thadious M. Davis's *Southscapes: Geographies of Race, Region, and Literature* (2011), Martha Schoolman's *Abolitionist Geographies* (2014), and Judith Madera's *Black Atlas: Geography and Flow in Nineteenth-Century African American Literature* (2015). For postbellum Kansas, see Nell Irvin Painter's *Exodusters: Black Migration to Kansas After Reconstruction* (1986).

For Afro-Indigenous cultural exchange, see Tiya Miles and Sharon Holland's anthology *Crossing Water, Crossing Worlds: The African Diaspora in Indian Country* (2006), Jonathan Brennan's *When Brer Rabbit Meets Coyote: African-Native American Literature* (2003), and Tiffany Lethabo King's *The Black Shoals: Offshore Formations of Black and Native Studies* (2019). For the collaboration between abolitionists and advocates against Indian Removal, see Alisse Portnoy's *Their Right to Speak: Women's Activism in the Indian and Slave Debates* (2005) and Mary Hershberger's "Mobilizing Women, Anticipating Abolition: The Struggle Against Indian Removal in the 1830s" in *Journal of American History* (86:1, 1999). For the enlistment of recently freed men in colonizing the postbellum West, see Elizabeth D. Leonard's *Men of Color to Arms!: Black Soldiers, Indian Wars, and the Quest for Equality* (2010). My argument about Whitman has benefited from work in Indigenous studies, including Jodi A. Byrd's *The Transit of Empire: Indigenous Critiques of Colonialism* (2011) and Audra Simpson's *Mohawk Interruptus: Political Life Across the Borders of Settler States* (2014). The scholarship on the Sauk and Black Hawk's autobiography is extensive, see especially Arnold Krupat's *For Those Who Came After: A Study of Native American Autobiography* (1985) and Cheryl Walker's

Indian Nation: Native American Literature and Nineteenth-Century Nationalisms (1997). On the Seminoles, see Andrew K. Frank's "Red, Black, and Seminole: Community Convergence on the Florida Borderlands, 1780–1840," in *Borderland Narratives: Negotiation and Accommodation in North America's Contested Spaces, 1500–1850* (2017). For white appropriations of Native culture, see Philip J. Deloria's *Playing Indian* (1999) and Shari Huhndorf's *Going Native: Indians in the American Cultural Imagination* (2001). For visions of indigeneity in British Romanticism, see Tim Fulford's *Romantic Indians: Native Americans, British Literature, and Transatlantic Culture 1756–1830* (2006).

For the period implications of sexual violence, see Diane Miller Sommerville's *Rape and Race in the Nineteenth-Century South* (2004) and Crystal Feimster's *Southern Horrors: The Politics of Rape and Lynching* (2009). For the cultural consequences of racial hybridity, see Tavia Nyong'o's *The Amalgamation Waltz: Race, Performance, and the Ruses of Memory* (2009). Whitman does not appear in Barbara McCaskill and Caroline Gebhard's useful anthology *Post-Bellum, Pre-Harlem: African American Literature and Culture, 1877–1919* (2006) or in Yogita Goyal's nonetheless relevant *Romance, Diaspora, and Black Atlantic Literature* (2010), but he does show up in James Edward Smethurst's *The African American Roots of Modernism: From Reconstruction to the Harlem Renaissance* (2011). For periodical culture and the memorialization of the war, see David W. Blight's *Race and Reunion: The Civil War in American Memory* (2002).

For discussions of the *Life of Black Hawk, or Mà-ka-tai-me-she-kià-kiàk* (1833), see Arnold Krupat's *For Those Who Come After: A Study of Native American Autobiography* (1985) and Cheryl Walker's *Indian Nation: Native American Literature and Nineteenth-Century Nationalisms* (1997). For Florida and fugitives from slavery, see Larry Eugene Rivers's *Rebels and Runaways: Slave Resistance in Nineteenth-Century Florida* (2013) and Matthew J. Clavin's *Aiming for Pensacola: Fugitive Slaves on the Atlantic and Southern Frontiers* (2015). For the planter class in Florida, see Edward Baptist's *Creating an Old South: Middle Florida's Plantation Frontier Before the Civil War* (2002). For Florida and literary history, see Anne E. Rowe's *The Idea of Florida in the American Literary Imagination* (1986) and Michele Navakas's *Liquid Landscape: Geography and Settlement at the Edge of Early America*. For marronage on the borders of the US, see Sylviane A. Diouf's *Slavery's Exiles: The Story of the American Maroons* (2014). Kate McIntyre's dissertation on the poetics of plantation ecologies has considerably inflected my own thinking, in this chapter especially.

Conclusion

The scholarly literature on the cultural memory of slavery is substantial; in addition to Hartman's memoir, I have relied especially on Ashraf H. A. Rushdy's *Neo-slave Narratives: Studies in the Social Logic of a Literary Form* (1999), Arlene R. Keizer's *Black Subjects: Identity Formation in the Contemporary Narrative of Slavery* (2004), and Salamishah Tillet's *Sites of Slavery: Citizenship and Racial Democracy in the Post–Civil Rights Imagination* (2012). For slavery in recent Black visual art, see Kimberly Juanita Brown's *The Repeating Body: Slavery's Visual Resonance in the Contemporary* (2015). For the blues and the Devil, see Jon Michael Spencer's *Blues and Evil* (1993) and Adam Gussow's *Beyond the Crossroads: The Devil and the Blues Tradition* (2017). For Du Bois and feminism, see Farah Jasmine Griffin's "Black Feminists and Du Bois: Respectability, Protection, and Beyond," *Annals of the American Academy of Political and Social Science* (568, March 2000).

Index